Agent of Empire

Agent of Empire

*William Walker and the Imperial Self
in American Literature*

BRADY HARRISON

The University of Georgia Press
Athens and London

© 2004 by the University of Georgia Press
Athens, Georgia 30602
All rights reserved

Set in Janson by G&S Typesetters
Printed and bound by Maple-Vail
The paper in this book meets the guidelines for
permanence and durability of the Committee on
Production Guidelines for Book Longevity of the
Council on Library Resources.

Printed in the United States of America

08 07 06 05 04   C   5 4 3 2 1

Library of Congress Cataloging-in-Publication Data

Harrison, Brady, 1963–
Agent of empire : William Walker and the imperial
self in American literature / Brady Harrison.
p.   cm.
Includes bibliographical references and index.
ISBN 0-8203-2544-9 (alk. paper)
1. American literature—History and criticism.
2. Imperialism in literature.   3. Walker, William,
1824–1860—In literature.   4. Walker, William,
1824–1860—In motion pictures.   5. Nicaragua—
History—Filibuster War, 1855–1860—Literature
and the war.   6. Biographical fiction, American—
History and criticism.   7. Americans—Nicaragua—
History—19th century.   8. Politics and literature—
United States.   9. Literature and history—United
States.   10. Nicaragua—In literature.   I. Title.
PS169.I45H37   2004
810.9′351—dc22   2003023788

British Library Cataloging-in-Publication Data available

For Jean & Larry

CONTENTS

Acknowledgments / ix

INTRODUCTION. The Life, Death, and Literary Resurfacings of William Walker, Filibuster / 1

ONE. "Tossing Creation like a Bauble": Walker and Emerson / 27

TWO. "What Is Good for *Them*": Harte and the Mercenary Romance / 52

THREE. The Spectacular Empire: Davis and Roosevelt / 80

FOUR. Soldiers of Misfortune: Davis and O. Henry / 118

FIVE. "The Female of the Species": Teilhet and Cardenal / 144

SIX. Walker, with a Vengeance: Cox and Didion / 171

CONCLUSION. William Walker, Redux? / 191

Notes / 199

Index / 231

ACKNOWLEDGMENTS

This book is very much a collaborative effort, and I wish to thank the many readers, colleagues, and friends who have shared their insights, ideas, critiques, and, especially, time. Whatever virtues are found in this book must in great measure be attributed to the hard work of the generous people here named; whatever faults remain can be traced to the name on the dust jacket. My thanks—and admiration—go first to my mentors: Michael Bérubé, Robert Dale Parker, and Cary Nelson. Some centuries ago, they helped me begin my investigations of the literatures and cultures of United States imperialism. I wish also to thank my friends and coconspirators from those days: Stacy Alaimo, Barry Faulk, Mary Hocks, and Lauren Onkey.

I also owe a great deal to my colleagues at the University of Montana–Missoula: Bill Bevis, Bruce Bigley, Albert Borgmann, Gerry Brenner, Casey Charles, John Glendening, John Hunt, Katie Kane, Chris Knight, David Moore, Jocelyn Siler, Pam Voekel, Lois Welch, and Phil West. This book could not have been written without their support and advice. My thanks, as well, to the generous research and travel opportunities provided by Dean James Flightner and Dean Tom Storch; they allowed me both the time and resources to follow some of William Walker's trails—both in the world and on paper.

A number of librarians and libraries have also dedicated their time, energy, knowledge, and resources to this project. My gratitude in particular to Sue Samson and the staff at the Mansfield Library at the University of Montana–Missoula, to Guillermo Nánez Falcón and the staff at Tulane University's Latin American Library, to William B. Eigelsbach and the Special Collections Library at the University of Tennessee, and to Pamela D. Arceneaux at the Kemper and Leila Williams Foundation's Historic New Orleans Collection.

An early version of chapter 1 appeared in *American Studies* 40, no. 3 (fall 1999), 77–97, and is reprinted by permission of the Mid-American Studies Association. I wish to thank David M. Katzman, Norman R. Yetman,

William Graebner, and the anonymous readers for their feedback and commentary. A very early draft of chapter 5 was published in the *Journal of Men's Studies* 4, no. 4 (May 1996) under the title "Mercenary Romances: Masculinity, William Walker, and U.S. Imperialism" (copyright © 1996 Men's Studies Press); my thanks to James A. Doyle and the readers at *JMS* for their diligent and thoughtful comments.

Finally, and perhaps most importantly, my thanks to my closest readers and associates. My deepest gratitude to Derek Krissoff and the readers at the University of Georgia Press for their good will and always thoughtful and challenging responses to my work. The book is immeasurably smarter and stronger due to their careful and detailed readings. This book would also not have been possible without the contributions, insights, and humor of four exceptional persons: cheers, as always, to my Buffalo Jump Brothers, Rick Canning and Steve Davenport; more than cheers to Jill Bergman and Emma Harrison, agents of a better nature.

INTRODUCTION

The Life, Death, and Literary Resurfacings of William Walker, Filibuster

I N THE CAPITAL of Costa Rica, Richard Harding Davis explains to readers of his travelogue *Three Gringos in Venezuela and Central America* (1896),

> there is a statue of the Republic in the form of a young woman standing with her foot on the neck of General Walker, the American filibuster.[1] We had planned to go to the capital for the express purpose of tearing that statue down some night, or blowing it up; so it is perhaps just as well for us that we could not get there; but it would have been a very good thing for Costa Rica if Walker, or any other man of force, had put his foot on the neck of every republic in Central America and turned it to some account.[2]

In this remarkable passage, Davis, one of the great fin de siècle champions of American power, not only rehearses an imperialist commonplace that had been circulating in United States political culture since at least the 1840s—the corrupt and incompetent Central American needs an American to run the show—but also reveals a measure of unimperial faintheartedness. Already well known as a reporter, as Charles Dana Gibson's model for the escort to the famous Gibson girl, and as an all-around dashing young man, Davis admits to being a little less daring than one of his freebooting heroes: where William Walker had the nerve to invade foreign countries with armies of less than sixty men, Davis and his fellow gringos could not muster the courage to bomb a statue and risk spending time in a Costa Rican prison. Still, the pals were on vacation; Davis would grab a gun from a fallen soldier and prove his mettle under fire during the Rough Riders' famous victory at Las Guásimas in 1898.

If the passage shows Davis to be both an apologist for Walker and an advocate of American imperialism, it also suggests that the statue's bravado, read against the United States' ever-increasing power in the hemisphere in the latter half of the nineteenth century, would be abundantly repaid. You may have puffed and swaggered when the combined forces of Central America defeated Walker in 1857, Davis tells them, but your days of political and economic autonomy are numbered. And as an agent of the imperium, Davis was fulfilling his duty; as Christopher P. Wilson and Charles H. Brown remind us, the job of the globe-trotting reporter of the 1890s was not only to tell his stateside readers what to think but also to tell the politicians and elites in other nations—should they be listening—what to expect.[3] Even so, Davis perhaps need not have warned the isthmians that the Americans would be back. While the journalist may have brushed aside the foot on the throat as so much useless Latin machismo, the hyperbolic gesture suggests that the statue's commissioners could see the future as clearly as Davis. They knew that the Americans would return and with more than an army of mercenaries and failed forty-niners. Hyperbole, in this case, betrays dread; the statue stands not only as a figure of triumph but also as a figure of impending doom.

The passage also contains some psychological complexities and ironies that Davis doubtlessly would not have acknowledged, at least not in print. He enjoyed the company of men and wrote extensively about war and warriors. His romances, particularly *Soldiers of Fortune* (1897), celebrated American hypermasculinity and martial derring-do, and he championed the mercenary as an ideal of manhood in his collection *Real Soldiers of Fortune* (1906). He much admired Theodore Roosevelt at times, and touted swashbucklers such as Philo Norton McGiffin and the young Winston Churchill as the sort of men any real man would wish to number among his friends. If Davis prized men of action, he had less luck with women: he possessed a deep veneration for his mother, novelist Rebecca Harding Davis, but divorced his first wife, lived unhappily with his second, and ventured abroad about as often as he could. At some level, he likely would not have wanted to see a woman towering over one of his heroes, a visceral representation of American masculine defeat. As Davis suggests in his romances, women should be spectators to masculine deeds, not figures of conquest.[4]

The moment may also contain a series of deeper repressions on Davis's part: some commentators (novelist Robert Houston, for example, and historian Laurence Greene) have suggested that Walker may have been, to use a term from our era, queer, and if Davis ever considered this possibility, he certainly would have pushed aside any such suggestion.⁵ How could one of his paladins be less than a full, terribly masculine man? At least one of Walker's chroniclers takes this current a step further: Darwin Teilhet, an American writer of romances, hints that Walker may have been a woman disguised as a man. A cross-dressing agent of empire? A woman astride a woman? What image of American imperialism and ideal manhood would that be? If we can assume that Davis would have had nothing to do with such scandalous suggestions, we do know that he entertained rather grandiose notions about the freebooter: had Walker not died by firing squad on a beach in Honduras in 1860, he might have found his greatest forum in the Civil War and its aftermath. As a brilliant general for the South, Davis imagines in "William Walker, the King of the Filibusters" (1906), the Tennessean might have changed the course of history, landing in the White House instead of Ulysses S. Grant.⁶ Davis had his Walker fantasies, but not the ones held by later writers.

However unfortunate matters might appear for Walker crushed beneath Costa Rica's shoe, we must count him an exemplum of the American imperial self. In his short life—he fell at thirty-six—he graduated from medical school and then from law school, quit the law to work as a journalist and to dally with politics, then in short order gave that up to turn to filibustery. Like Theodore Roosevelt, a turn-of-the-century compeer, he lived an accelerated life and aimed his considerable energies at creating an American empire beyond the nation's continental boundaries. Smart, fearless, and ruthless, the freebooter circumvented American neutrality laws, made enemies of such important men as Franklin Pierce, William L. Marcy, and Cornelius Vanderbilt, among many others, and yet somehow managed to master Nicaragua. Imperial in thought and deed, he stood, if briefly, a five-foot-five colossus astride the isthmus. Whatever else he was, he was a remarkable force.

For Davis, Walker was an object of considerable fascination, and in this regard the journalist was (and is) by no means alone. However obscure or known Walker may be in U.S. history and among American studies scholars, he has one other crucial claim to fame (beyond conquering Nicaragua) that makes him the primary subject of this study: the petite freebooter has inspired poets, romancers, novelists, and filmmakers from the 1870s to the present to tell and retell his story as a means to explore the always-evolving—yet strangely inveterate?—history of American imperialism. They tell and retell his story as a means to sound the ever-shifting desires, fantasies, arguments, and ideologies underwriting both private and public imperial ventures. If his body was dumped in an unmarked grave, we at least have enough of a literary corpus to exhume, dissect, and argue over.

To date, I have uncovered over a dozen retellings of Walker's story. The first list includes works that feature Walker as an important character (either under his own name or an invented one) or that identifiably take up the substance and history of his exploits and recast them into a story about mercenaries, adventurers, scoundrels, shady entrepreneurs, or the lovelorn. These are tales demonstrably "about" the freebooter, and we can begin with Walker's book, the first major recounting of his adventures:

1860 William Walker, a memoir, *The War in Nicaragua*[7]
1871 Joaquin Miller, a narrative poem, "With Walker in Nicaragua"
1875 Bret Harte, a short story, "Peter Schroeder"
1887 Bret Harte, a romance, *The Crusade of the Excelsior*
1897 Richard Harding Davis, a romance, *Soldiers of Fortune*
1902 Richard Harding Davis, a romance, *Captain Macklin*
1904 O. Henry, a novel, *Cabbages and Kings*
1906 Joaquin Miller, a narrative poem, "Walker in Nicaragua"
1922 Edgar Young, a short story, "William Walker, Filibuster"[8]
1926 Arthur D. Howden Smith, a novel, *A Manifest Destiny*
1932 Merritt Parmelee Allen, a "history" for boys, *William Walker, Filibuster*
1950 Ernesto Cardenal, poems, "Con Walker en Nicaragua"[9]
1955 Darwin Teilhet, a romance, *The Lion's Skin*
1964 Fritz Leiber, a Hugo Award–winning science fiction novel, *The Wanderer*
1977 Joan Didion, a novel, *A Book of Common Prayer*
1984 Robert Houston, a novel, *The Nation Thief*
1987 Alex Cox, a film, *Walker*
1996 Albert J. Guerard, a novel, *The Hotel in the Jungle*

To the list of tales in which Walker figures as the central character (or as one of the central characters), we can add a second list of works that do not present Walker as a character but nevertheless recount adventures that closely recall the freebooter or evoke the Tennessean as a historical touchstone:

1950   Gore Vidal, a novel, *Dark Green, Bright Red*
1981   Robert Stone, a novel, *A Flag for Sunrise*
1985   Cormac McCarthy, a novel, *Blood Meridian*

If we were to add a third list of works that strikingly resemble—in plot, characters, and settings—perhaps the two most important early rewrites of the filibuster's exploits, Harte's *The Crusade of the Excelsior* and Davis's *Soldiers of Fortune*, the catalog of Walkeresque tales would grow exponentially. One could easily ask what American novel or film set in Central America does not feature some lost or exiled soul caught up in a coup, revolution, massacre, invasion, or episode of gunboat diplomacy? If we do not have the space here to do this question justice, we can still say with confidence—based on the works I have listed—that Walker's story serves as the raw material for a number of literary explorations of American imperialism and the American imperial self.

This body of mercenary adventure tales constitutes one of the most important, if understudied, narrative paradigms in the literatures of American imperialism, and we must grant Walker his place in American literary history. He always knew he would have a place in U.S. history—he told his men, as they were doing their best to burn Granada, Nicaragua, to the ground, that they had "written a page of American history which it is impossible to forget or erase."[10] And in the October 18, 1856, edition of *El Nicaragüense*, the newspaper Walker founded in Nicaragua, he or one of his agents claimed that "there was a mighty purpose to be achieved, and [Walker] longed to be foremost in its accomplishment": "The result is now a page of history. It is also a most suggestive theme for the novelist."[11] He was right. For many famous, near-famous, forgotten, or little-known writers and filmmakers, Walker's exploits resonate with U.S. economic, military, and political forays into Mexico, Central America, the Caribbean basin, the Philippines, Southeast Asia, and other places in the world: these artists retell his tale to plumb not only the history and culture of the 1850s but, more importantly, of their own times. A curious, and vicious, conquistador, Walker dwells restlessly in American letters; he keeps resurfacing, the imperial self as the ghost that cannot quite be forgotten.

A Portrait of the Imperial Self as a Young Man

Before turning to a more detailed consideration of why Walker continues to resurface in American literature, a word or two about his early days and exploits. Born in Nashville, Tennessee, on May 8, 1824, he was raised in a strict Calvinist home by his father, James Walker, a Scotsman who had inherited property and a dry-goods store from an uncle, and his mother, Mary Norvell, the daughter of a wealthy, slave-owning Kentucky family. After his marriage to Mary, James "founded a commercial insurance company and became its president; and as one of Nashville's rising men, lost no time in building a substantial brick house in Nashville's best district." James's firm prospered, and William was the first of four children (followed by two brothers, Norvell and James, and a sister, Alice). As a boy, William formed an especially close bond with his mother—particularly after she became, in the parlance of the day, "an invalid"—and a family friend remarked that she "used often to go to see his mother and always found him entertaining her in some way."[12] In fact, William appears to have been closer to his mother than to his father, and accounts suggest that he often rebelled against his father's authority. When James, for example, attempted to persuade his son to study for the ministry, William refused. A delicate, almost feminine child—in an oft-cited letter, Jane H. Thomas, a friend of the family, characterized the boy as "very intelligent and as refined in his feelings as a girl"—he nevertheless displayed flashes of resolve.[13]

The young Walker possessed not only a sturdy will but a formidable intellect as well. As a teenager, he showed considerable intellectual promise and even greater restlessness: he graduated at age fourteen summa cum laude from the University of Nashville (then more a preparatory school than what we think of as a university) and received his medical degree from the University of Pennsylvania in 1843 when he was only nineteen; at twenty-one, he returned from Europe after receiving additional medical training in Paris, Heidelberg, London, and Edinburgh, but instead of going into practice, he studied to be a lawyer and was admitted to the Louisiana bar at twenty-three. From there, he turned to journalism, and edited the *New Orleans Crescent* (1848–49). Soon after leaving Louisiana, he went to work as an editor for the *San Francisco Herald* (1850–51). Still restless, he abandoned yet another career and turned to freebooting.

Some commentators—especially James J. Roche and Albert Z. Carr—

argue that the death of Walker's betrothed, Helen Galt Martin, in 1849, set him on the path from journalism to adventurism. As Roche puts it in *By-Ways of War: The Story of the Filibusters* (1901), Walker gave himself over to dreams of empire after Martin died of the plague:

> Just before the date fixed for their marriage the breath of pestilence poisoned the Gulf breezes, and the dreaded yellow fever became epidemic in the coast cities [including New Orleans where Martin lived]. Among the first to fall victim to the scourge was Miss Helen Martin, and her death changed the entire life-current, if not the heart of William Walker. From the ashes of a buried love ambition rose supreme.

In purplish prose, Roche ascribes a tormented, romantic genesis to Walker's imperial ambitions, and Carr makes much the same assertion. With Ellen gone, "He felt an evangelical mission in which the highest ideals of the America of his time were fused—the spreading of democracy—the enhancement of the national power—the uplifting of downtrodden peoples—the prevention of fratricidal war."[14] As Roche and Carr would have it, Walker sublimated his feelings and sorrow for Martin into a chivalric and idealized desire to do some good in the world, and if such an assertion seems too easy (and seems to ignore the violence of Walker's invasions), we can at least say that Walker had little to hold him in the States and that he was due, after his brief time in San Francisco, for another abrupt career move. His first imperial venture, however, did not go well.

In October 1853 Walker led forty-five men into Mexico with the idea of conquering Lower California and Sonora; after capturing La Paz and Ensenada—and without setting foot in Sonora—he declared the creation of the "Republic of Sonora" and named himself president. This rather odd *coup de plume*—to borrow Brown's phrase—not only provoked Mexican authorities but earned Walker some derisive press at home. An editorialist for the *Alta California*, a newspaper in San Francisco, wrote that "Santa Anna must feel obliged to the new president that he has not annexed any more of his territory than Sonora. It would have been just as cheap and easy to have annexed the whole of Mexico at once, and would have saved the trouble of making future proclamations."[15] After pronouncing himself president of a republic that did not exist in a territory he did not control, Walker remained in Mexico for a few months more, but his supporters in the United States could not raise additional forces or resources. Mexican bandits and regular forces hounded his tiny army, and in May 1854 the Tennessean and his nearly bootless remnant were chased back across the American border at San Diego. His first filibustering venture ended in failure. Once back in the States, however, he enjoyed considerable notoriety—there were speeches and editorials in his honor—and he began to consider his options.

From Mexico, the would-be Napoleon set his sights on Nicaragua. In 1854 Walker became interested in a "colonization scheme" proposed by Francisco Castellón, the leader of the Democrats of León. The Democrats, one of the two dominant, long-feuding factions in Nicaraguan politics, had lost the 1853 presidential election to Fruto Chamorro, leader of the Legitimists of Granada. The Democrats charged the Legitimists with fraud and immediately began to plan a coup from their stronghold in León, the most populous and prosperous city in Nicaragua. Castellón wanted "the renowned Walker" to raise an army of Americans to aid their cause; in turn, the Americans were promised Nicaraguan citizenship and land. The "colonization" scheme offered Walker a means to circumvent American neutrality laws, and with fifty-eight men—whom he dubbed "The Immortals"—he landed at Realejo on the Pacific coast of Nicaragua in June 1855.[16] Walker promptly ignored Castellón's military authority and eventually captured Granada, a city on the northern edge of Lake Nicaragua and seat of the Legitimist government. Through a series of negotiations, deceptions, secret financial deals, and executions, he called a presidential election and became the *de facto* dictator of Nicaragua in July 1856. He immediately set into motion a number of decrees opening the way for the American colonization of Nicaragua. In May 1857 the combined forces of Central America (along with mercenaries funded by Walker's arch-American enemy, Cornelius Vanderbilt) forced the filibusters from the isthmus. In 1860, attempting yet another filibuster invasion in Central America, Walker was eventually captured and executed on a beach in Honduras on September 12, 1860.[17]

One other "fact" about Walker continually receives attention in works that explore his life and adventures: he was, like Napoleon, a physically small man. He stood barely five feet, five inches tall, and weighed approximately one hundred and twenty pounds. Nearly all of his chroniclers remark upon his size, and—to move from facts to impressions—almost all report that he possessed a strangely mechanical manner. T. Robinson Warren, an American adventurer who met Walker in Guaymas, Mexico, records his impression of the freebooter in *Dust and Foam* (1859): "His appearance was that of anything else than a military chieftain. Below the medium height, and very slim, I should hardly imagine him to weigh over a hundred pounds. His hair was light and towy, while his almost white eyebrows and lashes concealed a seemingly pupilless, grey, cold eye and his face was a mass of yellow freckles, the whole expression very heavy." Eduardo Galeano, in *Faces and Masks* (1987), the second part of the *Memory of Fire* trilogy, builds upon such early records as Warren's and offers one of the most concise descriptions of Walker as a deadly automaton: "The son of Tennessee shoots from the hip and buries without epitaph. He has eyes of cinders. He neither laughs nor drinks. He eats as a duty. No woman has been seen with him since his deaf and dumb fiancée died; and God is his only friend worthy of trust. He calls himself the Predestined. He dresses in black. He hates anyone touching him."[18] Galeano represents Walker as a miserable, cold, and murderous man, and many commentators describe the freebooter in similar terms. He seems to have been without affect or emotion or pleasure; he seems, too, to have been calculating, resolute, eloquent, and vicious to ally and foe alike. His stature and manner have doubtless contributed to his popularity among writers and filmmakers; he seems as odd as his achievements.

If the facts of Walker's size and campaigns can be largely agreed upon, what he was up to cannot be. Everyone has a theory about who funded Walker, for whom he worked (if he worked for anyone), what political reorganization of the New World his filibustering sought to achieve, and what his greatest ambitions were, but we cannot finally settle these matters. Darwin Teilhet, for example, suggests in his romance *The Lion's Skin* (1955) that Walker's Nicaraguan campaign was part of a southern states "secessionist conspiracy": as one character remarks, "What were Walker and his California secesh friends after if not to establish a slave empire in the Caribbean to bulwark the eventual establishment of a separate Southern Confederacy?" Davis, a keen apologist for Walker, offers a similar theory in "William Walker, the King of the Filibusters" (1906), but ties it less firmly to the idea of a southern conspiracy: "Throughout [Walker's] brief career one must remember that the spring of all his acts was this dream of an empire where slavery would be recognized." Rather than linking himself to the

South, Davis suggests, Walker set out to found his own empire. Brown, a fine historian on filibustering, avoids speculating on motives and concentrates more on goals: "Walker's grand design was to reunite the five Central American states into a confederacy, but this was a project that would have to wait for the future."[19] In fiction, essays, and history books, dozens of writers and scholars have attempted to understand Walker's invasions, but we ultimately cannot know what he hoped to achieve in Central America. He exists for us now as a complicated series of textual representations and traces.

Fellow Freebooters

Although Walker stands here as an exemplum of mid-nineteenth-century imperial desires and ambitions, he was by no means the only freebooter at work in the era of Manifest Destiny. He was one of many, and while he may have been the most successful, others were likewise celebrated or reviled in their day. Many raised expeditionary forces—or at least attempted to raise expeditionary forces—and launched invasions against Mexico, Cuba, and Nicaragua. Like Walker, they dreamed of their own pocket empires. And, like Walker, many of them met sudden and untimely ends; the freebooters were often captured and executed, sometimes in particularly gruesome ways. A number of the freebooters, once again like Walker, have also been the subject of poems and romances, and, with some diligent research, one might be able to study works about them as a means to explore the imperial self in American literature. We will stay with Walker and his many resurfacings, but we can at least make note of some of his fellow swashbucklers.

In 1804, for example, Aaron Burr, along with James Wilkinson, began to plan an invasion of Mexico with the idea of perhaps establishing—no one knows his true plans—a new nation between the United States and its southern neighbor. Once an American political luminary, Burr fell quickly and precipitously into freebooting. After failing—due in no small measure to the campaigns Alexander Hamilton waged against him—to win the Republican nomination for president in 1800 and then to win renomination as Jefferson's vice president in 1804, and then failing—once more due to Hamilton's efforts—in his endeavor in 1804 to capture the governorship of New York, Burr challenged his detractor to a duel. After Hamilton discharged his pistol into the air, Burr mortally wounded his opponent. His career in ruins following Hamilton's death, Burr sought to rehabilitate his fortunes through filibustering, and he raised a force of about one hundred men. Nevertheless, and despite a number of shadowy intrigues aimed at conquering some or all of Mexico, he failed to launch an invasion force. After enduring a public trial for treason in 1807—for plotting, the Jefferson administration charged, to seize U.S.-held territories as part of his freebooting scheme—Burr lived out his life as a lawyer in relative obscurity in New York. Remarkably, with a few twists and turns, his plan looks very much like Walker's invasion of Nicaragua some fifty years later. Both adrift in their professional lives, they raised similar complements of men and set forth with ambitions to become emperors.

One of the most infamous figures in U.S. history, Burr has been the subject of a number of literary treatments. In *Burr* (1973), for example, Gore Vidal offers one of the most popular versions of his life, and in the opening pages of the novel, he sums up the politician's remarkable ambitions and failures:

> In 1804 Colonel Burr—then vice-president of the United States—shot and killed General Alexander Hamilton in a duel. Three years after this lamentable affair, Colonel Burr was arrested by order of President Thomas Jefferson and charged with treason for having wanted to break up the United States. A court presided over by Chief Justice John Marshall found Colonel Burr innocent of treason but guilty of the misdemeanor of proposing an invasion of Spanish territory in order to make himself emperor of Mexico.

Just as Walker was tried and acquitted for contravening the neutrality laws following his unsuccessful invasion of Mexico in 1853–54, Burr was tried and acquitted in his effort to become the "emperor of Mexico." Although Burr's plans for Mexico remain shadowy, Vidal, as a novelist, has the latitude to speculate, and he attempts to sound the would-be freebooter's desires: "When I left Washington in the spring of 1805, everyone from Jefferson to the Creoles at New Orleans not only expected but wanted a war with Spain that would give the United States the Floridas, fix the western border of the United States, and open for me Texas and Mexico."[20] Although I do not have the space here, a reading of the retellings of Burr's careers would allow us not only to see the failed politician as one of Walker's progenitors but also to see Walker's adventures within the longer and greater story of American westward and southward expansion.

Other freebooters of Walker's era include a number who led missions against Mexico, Cuba, and Central America. In 1851, for example, Narciso López—a Venezuelan who had fought with the Spanish against Simón Bolívar and who had later married into a Cuban family—raised a small army, with the financial and tactical support of Americans such as John L. O'Sullivan, and attempted to invade Cuba. He was captured and publicly executed by garrote on September 1, 1851. His American ally, William L. Crittenden, a member of a well-known Southern family and nephew of the U.S. attorney general, had been captured and executed by firing squad sixteen days earlier.[21] In an act of defiance that received a great deal of play in U.S. newspapers, Crittenden had refused to kneel with his back to his executioners and instead stood, without blindfold, and faced them; the press dubbed him an American hero for his fortitude. Between 1851 and 1853, to take another example, José Carvajal, a San Antonio adventurer, tried on several occasions to invade northern Mexico and establish what he hoped to call the Republic of the Sierra Madre. He later gave up his filibustering ambitions and joined rebel forces struggling for power in Mexico. In 1855 John A. Quitman, a hero of the Mexican-American War, unsuccessfully attempted to invade Cuba. In 1857 Henry A. Crabb, a boyhood friend of Walker, led his own mission against Mexico only to be captured and executed in Caborca, Sonora, on April 6, 1857. His head was cut off and preserved in a jar of alcohol.[22] Like Walker, many of the freebooters met abrupt ends at the hands of those they sought to conquer, and the moral of the filibustering story seems clear: stay home or die young. Or, to look forward to the end of the nineteenth century: raise a sufficient force and have the backing of the U.S. government.[23]

Walker's Literary Resurfacings

We can, without too much difficulty, account for why writers and filmmakers from the 1860s to the present have told and retold Walker's story. For some, the freebooter's adventures serve as a means to explore the expansionist desires and actions of the era of Manifest Destiny. Through

Walker run many of the major currents of his day—Jacksonianism, expansionism, Young Americanism, annexationism, idealism, evolutionism, Puritanism rewritten as American exceptionalism, and more—and writers have turned to his adventures as a means to plumb the furious, often competing energies of the mid-nineteenth century. In a single historical figure, they have access to many of the contradictory impulses in American culture; his story weaves together utopian sensibilities and land-lust, beneficence and rapacity, romanticism and industrialization, progressive politics and militarism. For writers with a historical sensibility—for those who want to dive deeply into the maelstrom of American expansionist desires following the annexation of Texas in 1845, the formal acquisition of the southern half of Oregon in 1846, the Mexican cession of 1848, and the Gadsden Purchase in 1853—there could hardly be a more appealing or compelling figure. Few writers, however, retell Walker's exploits simply as a means to reflect on the 1840s and 1850s.

Walker's adventures serve as a means for poets, romancers, and filmmakers to sound the expansionist desires and actions of Manifest Destiny *and* the foreign policy and adventures (or misadventures) of their own eras and the intervening years. By bringing Walker forward, writers take possession of a ready-made story of imperial desire, conquest, and disaster and, in the process, bring forward the history of the imperium: rewriting his tale not only allows them to counterpoint the imperial ambitions and interventions of their own moment with the ambitions and interventions of the era in which U.S. energies began to turn from continental expansionism to overseas adventurism, but it also allows them, if they wish, to contextualize their moment within the broader sweep of Western imperial history. They can compare their time to Walker's (as Cox, for example, does at the end of his film *Walker*, when U.S. marine helicopters, a symbol of the Vietnam era, land to rescue Walker and the Immortals) or situate their moment within the much longer history of European and U.S. imperialism (as Robert Stone does in *A Flag for Sunrise* when he links Walker to the often bloody Spanish conquest of the New World, to American failure in Vietnam, and, most importantly for his purposes, to U.S. interference in Central America following the liberation of Saigon). Writers return again and again to Walker's story as a means to explore the imperial past and the impact of Manifest Destiny on the growth and development of the republic; even more importantly, they rewrite his exploits as a means to explore the imperial desires, ambitions, interventions, victories, defeats, and debacles of their own eras.

Writers also take up the freebooter's tale for very writerly reasons: it has plenty of color and action. Walker's career involved battles on land, lake, and sea, and he executed not only a number of shady business deals but a number of his political rivals as well. He engaged in political intrigues, "nationalized" Cornelius Vanderbilt's commercial assets in Nicaragua (including the boats of his Accessory Transit Company), and employed a motley army of European mercenaries, American Indian killers, failed forty-niners, and drunks he more or less impressed from the docks in San Francisco. Moreover, he invaded both Mexico and Central America with armies of less than a hundred and managed, at least for a time, to prevail militarily and politically. Better still for some writers, his story offers all this adventure *and* a few kinks; some writers foreground the themes that Davis seemingly would not admit to under any circumstances: homosexuality, transgendering, and murderous automatonism.[24] The soldier of fortune's story offers a great deal of raw material for the writer to work with, and for this reason it has survived as one of the primary literary vehicles for the exploration of U.S. imperialism.

If writers return to Walker as a means to explore the events of their eras, they also take up the freebooter's life and adventures as a means to explore the American imperial self. Although I offer a more detailed description of what I mean by the "American imperial self" later, we can at least say at this point that Walker, as nation-conquering filibuster, can be put into the company of such American conquistadors and would-be conquistadors as Aaron Burr, John A. Quitman, John L. O'Sullivan, Theodore Roosevelt, Samuel Zemurray, Lee Christmas, Minor Keith, and others. Indeed, and as we shall also see later in more detail, Walker believed himself to be predestined for (freebooting) greatness. In his journalism and memoir, *The War in Nicaragua* (1860), he sets out how an American agent of empire should think and act, and he thereby builds a composite portrait of what he imagines as the imperial self, the American colossus who raises a force and imposes his will upon other nations. If Walker was not the first writer to describe the qualities and beliefs of the American imperial self—John Smith began to describe such a being as early as 1608 in *A True Relation . . . of Virginia*—he nevertheless provides a description and set of actions against which writers can weigh the actions and pronouncements of their contemporary leaders and imperial agents. Once more, Walker provides a counterpoint to later figures: Davis, for example, compares Walker to Theodore Roosevelt; Cox compares him to Oliver North and John Rambo, two icons of the Reagan era. In his or her turn, the writer or filmmaker interrogates—or celebrates or condemns or muses upon—the beliefs, actions, and attributes of what they take to be the most recent incarnation of the American imperial self.

If we can make a case for why Walker continues to resurface in the overlapping realms of literary and popular culture, we can also account for when he shows up: historical events seem to call him to mind. In general, he tends to resurface as U.S. foreign policy and interventionism heat up or meet with disaster. Davis, for example, reached back to Walker's adventures in the years leading up to the Spanish-American War in order to celebrate American masculinity and the United States' impending imperial ascendancy. Focusing on the freebooter's daring and victories, the journalist and novelist based his best-known and best-selling romance, *Soldiers of Fortune* (1897), on Walker's exploits and championed him as an exemplum of the American imperial self. The Tennessean, he suggests, knew what had to be done and had the will to do it. Remarkably, only a few years later and in response, in part, to U.S. atrocities in the Philippines, to Roosevelt's antimonopoly legislation, and to his own desires for a masculine world completely apart from women, Davis once more based a romance—*Captain Macklin* (1902)—on Walker, but this time focused on the filibuster's brutality and failure. Imperial desires, corporate avarice, and brutality abroad worked, at least for Davis, to bring Walker to mind as vehicle for exploring both U.S. triumphs and defeats.

To take another example, Walker also resurfaces with a vengeance in the wake of the Vietnam War: once more, history seems to call the freebooter to mind. When casting about for a narrative upon which to base an exploration of American savagery and defeat in the late 1970s and early 1980s, writers and directors as politically and stylistically diverse as Robert Stone, Joan Didion, Alex Cox, Cormac McCarthy, and others all directly or indirectly evoke Walker. We can say why without too much difficulty: Walker's story can easily be rewritten into the American story in Vietnam. Supremely confident in his abilities and in his right to enforce his will upon others, Walker raised—at least at first—a small army of irregulars, and, as soon as he could, he pushed aside the local authorities. Once entrenched, he began to recruit more and more men to maintain his power and became involved in a protracted, losing struggle with enemies both "at home" and "abroad." Ultimately, and despite retaliatory acts of considerable viciousness, he could not prevail militarily; a brown-skinned, physically smaller, and technologically inferior foe destroyed his vision of a tropical American empire. Overconfidence, a faith in one's superiority in all regards, truculence, defeat: Walker becomes the perfect emblem for the American misadventure in Vietnam. To summarize, poets, novelists, and filmmakers have most often rewritten his narrative as a means to weigh imperial ventures and imperial selves at moments of national ascendancy or defeat (or, as we shall see in our consideration of Walker's Cold War reappearances, at moments of widespread anxiety over American power and challenges to its global authority).

The American Imperial Self

In American studies, the phrase "imperial self" belongs most famously to Quentin Anderson, and my task here is to argue for my own definition and description. Since Anderson holds the patent—and many critics have followed in his wake—we must begin with his masterful, if impressionistic study of the inward empires of Ralph Waldo Emerson, Walt Whitman, and Henry James. In particular, since Walker seems to have drawn inspiration from Emerson (as we shall see in detail in chapter 1), and since numerous scholars since Anderson have explored the bard's writings in terms of American power and the American self, we will here concentrate on Anderson's reading of the transcendentalist. The early, radical Emerson, he claims, argued for the primacy of the individual, for an intensely personal, intensely idiosyncratic vision and voice; the more particular and unique the vision, the closer one came to transcendence: "The more clearly distinctive the voice of the celebrant, the more unmistakably does he attest the divine in him." The imperial self looks inward, seeks to establish the empire of one: "The road to transcendence lay through self-absorption, one had to take possession of the imperium of one's own consciousness." Like Whitman and James, Anderson claims, the early Emerson rejected notions of the social as the proper fate and forum of the individual; in contrast, say, to

Nathaniel Hawthorne and Henry Adams, who were "quite sure that our fate was wholly bound up with the fate of the polity,"[25] the transcendentalist sought the imperial self apart from society, apart from accepted beliefs and practices.[26]

Emerson's imperial self, Anderson contends, was not interested in looking outward, not interested in acting in the world. The imperial self had no desire to make others see matters his way, to enforce his vision with feats of arms or language: "The social hope was firmly subordinated in Emerson, for whom heroic action was just one more of the conditioned human states that he tried to reduce to the unconditioned abstractness of the self which creates its world instead of acting in it."[27] Anderson offers a ferocious, antinomian Emerson, an Emerson fueled by an extraordinary emotional and intellectual intensity, an Emerson standing hard against lived experience and the tragic losses of his brother, wife, and son to tuberculosis. Although Anderson's Emerson is not my Emerson, we cannot but admire Anderson's bard; one feels the intensity of vision and will.

In contrast to Anderson, Myra Jehlen does not limit herself to the early Emerson, and she offers in *American Incarnation* (1986) a more worldly philosopher, one more along of the lines of the imperial self one finds in men like Walker and Roosevelt. For Jehlen, the self looks inward in order to claim the world as his own, as an image of himself: "Emersonian Transcendentalism is the philosophy of the American incarnation, and its fulfillment in an unlimited individualism whereby the self transcends its mortal limits by taking total possession of an actual world." The American self does not, however, merely possess the world in a passive manner; the self must act in the world:

> Emerson's great idea was that the power to act—not just to think, but to act—lay not in the individualist's hands but in his mind and soul, so that he would look out most effectively precisely by looking in. For Emerson was not less concerned with action than [Benjamin] Franklin. Not unlike the indefatigable Poor Richard, "The true scholar grudges every opportunity of action past by, as a loss of power."[28]

Jehlen's Emerson looks inward in order to look outward, and while this moves us closer to my conception of the American imperial self, in her reading the philosopher-poet of *American Incarnation* remains too exalted, too much concerned with the replacement of God with the self.

The imperial self that interests us here—Walker and men like him—does not have much time to worry about metaphysics, and while he shares with Jehlen's Emerson an absolute conviction in the right of the American to take possession of the earth, he does so in a somewhat less resplendent manner. Where "Franklin took 'America' to be an exceptional entity that was at once, and necessarily, nation and continent," Emerson went a step further. In "an intensification of consciousness so powerful that the material universe dissolves into the observer's universal knowledge,"[29] he envisioned the fusion of the self with the nation and continent. As we will see in more detail in the next chapter, Walker, like many of the agents of Manifest Destiny, also identified the self with the nation and the continent, but in a more conventional, less intense way: he believed that the United States was predestined to conquer the continent and beyond; he believed that Americans had the right to reshape the hemisphere and the world in their own image.

If the imperial self of this study lacks the majesty of Anderson's and Jehlen's Emersons, he nevertheless possesses an intensity of vision. While he must first look inward, must first establish an intense personal vision of an inward empire, he does so only in preparation for looking outward, for imagining an empire. In the context of American expansionism, the imperial self feels an appropriately Emersonian inflowing sensation of power, but understands his epiphany—a sudden gust of omnipotence—as the authorization to run wild and set a few fires in Mexico or Central America or Cuba. The imperial self does not dive deeply into the self only to emerge in the oceanic divine; rather, he plunges wildly into his Napoleonic fantasies, into his monstrous sense of self (though he would not see himself as deformed or awful in any measure), and imagines a rush across a frontier, a pirate raid on another country. Look inward, but then look outward; the inward and outward empires, in the literatures and cultures of U.S. imperialism, are part or particle of an intertwining impulse to impose one's will and desires upon others. The imperial self lives very much in the world; he carries a gun, and knows he has the right to do so.

Wai-chee Dimock, in *Empire for Liberty* (1989), her analysis of Melville and the "poetics of individualism," also describes an imperial self somewhat like the one I have in mind; even as Melville pursues the inward empire, he stands as an artist thoroughly enmeshed in the political and literary currents and rhetorics of his day. Dimock's Melville (like Anderson's Emerson) sees the lone artist as an imperial self, as—and here she quotes one of Melville's letters to Hawthorne—a "man who, like Russia or the British Empire, declares himself a sovereign nature (in himself) amid the powers of heaven, hell, and earth." Melville imagines the artist as the self who calls into being magnificent, idiosyncratic works of art, who produces "imperial folios." However much he might wish to see authorship as "almost exclusively an exercise in freedom, an attempt to proclaim the self's sovereignty over and against the world's," Melville was, as Dimock abundantly shows, a man of his day.[30] His thinking and language stand, in part, as a product of the 1840s and 1850s.

Dimock sets Melville's claim to sovereignty in relation to U.S. expansionism and Jacksonian democracy:

> Melville's authorial enterprise can be seen, in this regard, as a miniature version of the national enterprise. It can be seen, more specifically, as a miniature version of Manifest Destiny—understood here not as a specific set of events, but as an informing logic of freedom and dominion, a logic that underwrites not only what Michael Rogin calls the "internal imperialism" of an expansionist nation but also what (following John L. O'Sullivan) we might call the "great experiment of liberty" of the literary self.

Melville shares rhetorical strategies and imperial desires with his countrymen, and Dimock sees the imperial self as both idiosyncratic *and* representative, as inward- *and* outward-looking: "Unlike the ones Quentin Anderson describes... these imperial selves are 'imperial' not only in consciousness but also in conduct: indeed, their very mode of existence seems to have something in common with the Russian and British empires."[31] *Imperial not only in consciousness but in conduct*; this is the imperial self of my study. The discourses and currents of Manifest Destiny streamed throughout the United States, and while Melville was writing *Pierre* (1852) and *The Confidence-Man* (1857), Walker was raising armies to invade Sonora and Nicaragua. Imperial folios, imperial fervors. The inward and outward empires.[32]

In Walker's case—as in the case of Roosevelt, Reagan, North, and others—we can also identify elements of the performative in the American imperial self. As Judith Butler and other theorists of the decentered, polyvalent, and provisional self have argued, neither gender nor the self can be taken as fixed or fixable entities. As Butler, following Derrida, Foucault, Irigaray, Kristeva, and others, argues in *Gender Trouble* (1990), "There is no gender identity behind expressions of gender; that identity is performatively constituted by the very 'expressions' that are said to be its results."[33] If gender has no stable identity, the poststructuralists and postmodernists argue that neither does anything else; we live in a world of performance, spectacle, theatricality; there is no essential "I" but a not-quite-self in constant, unstable flux. In Walker, we can see this performative sense of self. The Tennessean, for varying amounts of time, was a doctor, a lawyer, a would-be politician, a journalist, a freebooter, a dictator, and he grew from a sensitive child that adored his mother into a man without affect. In some measure, these rapidly shifting roles require elements of performance, however consciously or unconsciously assumed, and public display. In some measure, however intensely he developed his inward and outward empires, the imperial self can never be a full, replete, and perfect self, can never be the transcendent being he claims—as we shall see in the next chapter—to be. The freebooter *played* his parts as necessary, following the course of his visions, ambitions, and desires.[34] And, as we shall see in later chapters, the performance of masculinity becomes an increasingly important component of the American imperial self.

If the performative American imperial self arises, in part, from a lack of essence, from the American tradition of identifying the self with the nation and the continent, and from an intensely developed inward-into-outward vision, we must also address the other factors and forces—historical, literary, personal, and otherwise—that help call into being and shape the imperial self, particularly in Walker's case. Each of these will be borne out in more detail in later chapters. For one, the history of American racism fosters the imperial self. Walker, like many of his expansionist peers, was thoroughly racist, and the imperial self bears the history of the two most profound expressions of Anglo-American racism: slavery and the Indian Wars. Walker's mother's family owned slaves, and although he wrote abolitionist columns as a journalist, once in power in Nicaragua, he attempted to reintroduce slavery to the isthmus. And, as his remarks on "savages" in *The War in Nicaragua* reveal, he was well steeped in what Melville dubbed, in *The Confidence-Man*, "The Metaphysics of Indian-Hating."[35] Like many in the

1850s, he also demonstrates considerable disdain for "Catholic nations" and "hybrid races."

The imperial self is also a product of continental expansion. Walker, like many of the freebooters, turned his attention to Mexico and Central America following the formal settling of the United States' continental borders in the 1840s and early 1850s. If much work remained in the rationalizing of the American West into the political and economic order of the East, the obvious question to Walker and others was, where next? The filibusters were merely taking the next "logical" steps in U.S. expansionism, and Walker's writings and adventures abundantly participate in the rhetorics and discourses of Manifest Destiny and "regeneration." If a product, in part, of American history, the American imperial self also stands as a partial product of Western history: Walker had lots of tyrants and conquistadors to model himself after.

The imperial self is also a product, in part, of literary romances. Literature does its part in shaping consciousness, and we can see this clearly in Walker. As a boy, he read romances and perhaps absorbed—as some commentators have suggested—some of his ideals from adventure tales. We know, for example, that he read Walter Scott (and perhaps Thomas Malory) to his ailing mother and, as a southern boy of his time, class, and educational background, he probably read other tales on his own. As Albert Z. Carr speculates, Walker

> must have evoked and been carried away by the mood of chivalry, in which any damsel in distress had a claim on a true knight, in which no honorable chevalier permitted a woman to be wronged if he could help her, in which one willingly gave up one's life for a friend, in which the feat of derring-do had the greater fame if the odds against one seemed hopeless. These were attitudes that stayed with him all his life.[36]

At some level, whether conscious or not, the freebooter may have seen himself as Locksley or Sir Wilfred of Ivanhoe; in some unquantifiable measure, he may have seen himself as engaged in a crusade to liberate lands from the heathens; he may have seen himself as Sir Kenneth battling Saladin or Conrade of Montferrat. While such assertions might seem far-fetched, we can point to other possible examples: Theodore Roosevelt, as we shall see, also read and admired romances; John Kennedy often quoted John Buchan;

Ronald Reagan favored Tom Clancy's massive technoromances.[37] As one of the most enduring literary forms, the romance exerts a subtle, if unmeasurable pressure on perception and self-image, and Walker, as much as any American imperial self, acted out his fantasy of conquest.

Finally, we can also argue that the imperial self is in part a product of personal experiences and not-so-idiosyncratic desires. In some measure, we can understand Walker's filibustering as a sublimation of sexual energy; as I noted earlier, he turned to freebooting following the death of this betrothed, and, as many commentators observe, he seems not to have been interested in women (though he shows, as we shall see, some interest in men). He seems to have poured his libido into a desire for power, and as we have seen many of his contemporaries comment upon his lack of affect and personal warmth; he fashioned himself into a militaristic automaton.[38] Moreover, Walker hardly stands alone in history in wanting to conquer foreign lands. He was subject to the same desires for land, wealth, and power as other adventurers. Like Alexander or Napoleon or Roosevelt, Walker believed in himself, and believed in his vision of how the world—or at least a small corner of it—should be. He could only walk forward, no matter the obstacles, and he would or could not turn away from his ambitions. He tried for an imperium in Mexico, then in Nicaragua, and finally in Honduras, and he never gave up. He set his entire energy—until it ultimately deformed and destroyed him—upon conquest and his own manifest destiny. He wanted to be great; he wanted to be an undeterrable imperial self.

Forms of the Imperial Self

Three forms of the imperial self interest us in this study. We are concerned, for one, in the imperial self as an agent of empire in the world. Walker serves as our exemplum, but later chapters will also include discussions of Theodore Roosevelt, Joseph McCarthy, Oliver North, Ronald Reagan, and others; these figures become important here as rewriters of the Walker narrative explore the imperial selves of their own eras. Cox, as we have already noted, very clearly has North and Reagan in mind in *Walker*, and we will have occasion to refer to a number of other real-life adventurers, soldiers, reporters, politicians, diplomats, and entrepreneurs who have done the work of the American imperium and who, in the many rewrites of the freebooter's adventures, cross (literary) paths with Walker. Of all the real-world agents of empire that serve as inspiration for the writers we will be reading here, Roosevelt stands second only to Walker: no discussion of the American imperial self would be complete without a serious consideration of the Rough Rider and his writings on manliness and the imperial self; and, as the literary trail will show (and as we shall see), the story of William Walker intertwines with the story of Theodore Roosevelt. In American literary history, Davis forever joins the two.

The work of Anderson, Jehlen, and Dimock points us toward the second form of the imperial self that interests us: the writer as imperial self. As we have seen, some of the most important studies of the American imperial self have focused on literary colossi such as Emerson and Whitman, and although my anatomy also includes writers who stand, if at all, on the remote slopes of the canon, this study continues in that tradition: just as no consideration of the imperial self in American literature would be complete without an analysis of Roosevelt's adventures and writing, no assessment would be complete without at least some attention given to Emerson, Whitman, and other giants, who devoted their considerable energies, at some point in their careers, toward matters of empire and who, either literally or figuratively, crossed paths with Walker. Of all the rewriters of Walker's exploits that I consider here, one stands above the rest as an in-the-world imperial self: Richard Harding Davis. Not only did he write two Walker romances (and one biographical sketch), he also did his part—in both his fiction and nonfiction—to push the United States toward war against Spain. In many ways, he can be considered *the* literary agent for the American overseas empire.

Third, I am interested in two types of literary representations of the American imperial self. On the one hand—and as a means not only to illuminate Walker's particular embodiment of the American imperial self but also as a means to chart the evolution of American conceptualizations of the imperial self—we will concentrate on the imperial self as he exists on the page as an ideal, as a notion; this is the self as Emerson imagines him in "The Young American" (1844) or as Roosevelt reimagines him in "The Strenuous Life" (1899) and other essays. In Emerson, the self has no precise real-world counterpart, but rather represents a hope for how young Americans ought to be in the world; in Roosevelt, the ruggedly idealized self arises from the men (and women) he has known and admired and serves as a call to young Americans to do their part at all levels of the national and imperial enterprise. The imperial self lives on the page as a precept, a paragon, a possibility.

On the other hand—and most importantly—we will concentrate on representations of Walker as the imperial self in American fiction, film, and poetry. This imperial self races across the screen and through the pages of romances, stories, and narrative poems. He appears as "William Walker," or he has a solid, even earthy-sounding name, a name that suggests he means business, that he will triumph: James Hurlstone, Robert Clay, Peter Ormerod, Frank Goodwin.[39] Young, confident, energetic, he swings a sword, fires a pistol, wins the girl, and stands over fallen foes as the glamorous representation of American masculine power, grace, wit, intelligence, and derring-do. He dresses and speaks well, and like his real-world counterparts, upon whom he is in part based, he orchestrates military affairs, runs mines, governs plantations, cozies up with local tyrants, oligarchies, or security officers. He manages huge industrial enterprises, as in Davis's *Soldiers of Fortune*, and finds himself in control of a Latin American republic. He stands a colossus in the Americas. Or, if he is a bit more modest—and if he exemplifies Harte's notions of a genteel, beneficent imperialism—he might not run an army but rather a mine *and* a school for displaced Indian children. A philanthropist, he does good deeds, commands a sizeable fortune, *and* gets along with the locals. Or he might—as an ironic representation of the imperial self in O. Henry's satire on Davis's filibustering fictions, *Cabbages and Kings*—be "a banana king, a rubber prince, a sarsaparilla, indigo, mahogany baron" all in one.[40] In O. Henry's mild world, the heroes triumph easily, while semiheroic wastrels get caught up in bogus filibustering schemes and end up (once they escape the chain gang) mocking their imperial ambitions and ideals. In later tales, the imperial self falls from Emersonian heights and becomes a murderous psychopath. The Walker that concerns us here is the only Walker we have: the one that appears on paper.

What follows is a study of the literary resurfacings of William Walker, but we will not consider every retelling. Some of the rewrites plod painfully along and do not add much to the corpus in terms of literary innovation or historical insight. Some works are better left with the dust quietly accumulating. Others, such as Robert Houston's *The Nation Thief*, perhaps deserve more attention than they receive here, but the full-frontal assault of contemporary works such as Cox's *Walker* or the thorough rehistoricizing of Didion's *A Book of Common Prayer* prevail. At certain times, as I have suggested in this introduction, Walker enjoys minirenaissances, and for the most part we will concentrate on those moments of intense revival. I am not here so much interested in a complete reading of the Walker corpus as I am in the close, historical examination of those works that most rigorously laud, interrogate, decry, or sound their contemporary eras. For that reason, we will make occasional jumps of several decades and focus on those eras in which writers turn to Walker as a means to explore the triumphs or disasters of empire. Most importantly, although this is not a text-by-text account of the Walker narrative, this study nevertheless charts the sometimes deliberate, sometimes haphazard evolution of the paradigm as a means to explore the American empire and the American imperial self.

From here, then, we turn to chapter 1 and a direct consideration of Emerson, Walker, and the American imperial self of the 1840s and 1850s. This is the era of Manifest Destiny, Young Americans, filibusters, imperial eloquence, and organic metaphors of "regeneration"; visions of empire circulate in the culture, burn their way through newspaper articles, essays, public addresses, poems, and policy statements. Politicians and private citizens alike entertain dreams of an American ascendancy in the hemisphere and beyond, and the agents of empire are as likely to raise private armies to invade foreign lands as they are to argue in favor of direct U.S. intervention. At midcentury, West Pointers and freebooters contend for the vanguard position. With the continental United States continually more secure, the furious energies of the nineteenth century began to turn abroad; from along the Mexican border and the shores of the Pacific, the agents of empire began to look beyond Texas, Arizona, and California. They began to look at Cuba, the Caribbean basin, and Central America. While Emerson imagines a gentle imperial self in "The Young American" address (1844), Walker fashions himself into a vicious expression of U.S. imperialism and describes his imperial self in his memoir, *The War in Nicaragua*.

From our reading of Emerson and Walker, we turn in chapter 2 to the early journalistic representations of Walker as they influenced the first full-length romance about the freebooter, Bret Harte's *The Crusade of the Excelsior*. Here we have the founding of the subgenre that most interests us in this study: the mercenary romance. In chapter 3, we continue our exploration of the genre as Davis—who knew and admired Harte's work—revises the elements into his slick best-seller, *Soldiers of Fortune*. Deeply concerned with the connections between American masculinity and American imperialism, Davis leads naturally to a study of the adventures and writings of his sometime friend, Theodore Roosevelt. Both writers offer models of a hypermasculine imperial self. Chapter 4, however, sees Davis backing away from his unconditional celebration of American imperial derring-do. In *Captain Macklin*, we have the first truly pessimistic and dark example of the mercenary romance. The chapter concludes with a reading of O. Henry's satire of Davis, *Cabbages and Kings*.

Chapter 5 takes a fifty-year leap to the next moment of Walker's conspicuous resurfacing: the Cold War. If the Tennessean surfaces with considerable energy in the years preceding the Spanish-American War, he enjoys some downtime before retaking the stage at a time of great imperial anxiety. Once more, the two most interesting rewrites—Teilhet's *The Lion's Skin* and Cardenal's *With Walker in Nicaragua*—offer complex readings of gender, sexuality, and American imperialism. Finally, chapter 6 makes the relatively more modest jump from the 1950s to the Vietnam era, perhaps Walker's era of greatest return. Focusing in particular on Cox and Didion, the final chapter explores the rewriting of the Walker narrative into a narrative of Vietnam. The study concludes with a question—Why, in spite of his many resurfacings, doesn't anyone remember Walker?—and speculations on the imperial self at the turn of the twenty-first century.

CHAPTER ONE

"Tossing Creation like a Bauble": Walker and Emerson

In "The Deciding Machine, Piece by Piece," Eduardo Galeano traces the connections between the United Fruit Company and U.S. administrators involved in the 1954 Guatemalan coup. Upset with President Jacobo Arbenz Guzmán's agrarian reform policies, United Fruit conspired with the White House and the Central Intelligence Agency to topple Arbenz's democratically elected government. This conspiracy, as Galeano delineates, was aided by an oligarchic structure among the American political and economic elite. John Foster Dulles, Galeano tells us, worked as a United Fruit lawyer before becoming Dwight Eisenhower's secretary of state; Allen Dulles, John's brother and director of the CIA, had also done legal work for United Fruit, and together the brothers ran "Operation Guatemala." John Moors Cabot, the secretary of state for Inter-American Affairs, also worked on the *golpe* along with the Dulles brothers and his own brother, Thomas Cabot, the president of United Fruit; Henry Cabot Lodge, the U.S. representative to the United Nations, owned United Fruit stock and received money from the company for speeches made in the Senate. Galeano's list goes on, and the catalog of the coup's planners reads like the invitation list to an extended family reunion. At the very highest levels, the journalist-historian tells us, a small yet powerful club, at least in 1954, ran the American empire.[1]

If this was true in the 1950s, a similar, if less sinister, case can be made regarding some of the key literary, political, and military agents for and against the empire in the 1850s. A number of the players, if not so familially connected, knew one another, worked together, or drew inspiration from one another's works. If we begin with John L. O'Sullivan, the journalist who, in 1845, coined the phrase "Manifest Destiny," we can rapidly trace out a number of intertangled connections.² In the late 1840s O'Sullivan not only attempted to persuade James Polk to purchase Cuba from Spain but also raised money, arms, and men for Narciso López's freebooting missions against the island in the early 1850s. A would-be filibuster, O'Sullivan joined annexationists such as Stephen A. Douglas, George Sanders, Edwin de Leon, and others in forming a loosely organized, pro-expansionist movement that borrowed its name, in part, from Emerson's 1844 address "The Young American."³ Although Emerson opposed the annexation of Texas and the war with Mexico, and although he doubtlessly also opposed the Young Americans' desires for Cuba, the philosopher did, in 1855, send a letter of praise to a little-known young poet who had just published his first collection of poems, *Leaves of Grass* (1855);⁴ Walt Whitman, the literary record shows, had already published his first stories in O'Sullivan's *United States Magazine and Democratic Review* and had served for a time in 1846 as the editor of the *Brooklyn Eagle*. While at the *Eagle*, the poet-journalist wrote bellicose editorials calling for U.S. intervention in Mexico, and after working in the North, he journeyed south and served as the founding editor for another newspaper, the *New Orleans Crescent*. At the paper for just three months (March–May 1848), Whitman fell out with its owners yet perhaps made the acquaintance of another would-be annexationist who joined the *Crescent* in the summer of 1848: William Walker. And if Walker never met Emerson or saw him speak, he may have read the philosopher's work, and if he did not join O'Sullivan for visits to Polk's White House, he was the more successful filibuster, and he certainly drew the hostile attention of Franklin Pierce and his administration. Filibusters, philosophers, journalists, poets, politicians, agents of empire, imperial selves—everyone seems to have crossed paths, discourses, and *Weltanschauungen* with everyone else; to understand the filibuster's adventures and writings, we need to see them as fully as we can in their historical, cultural, and intellectual milieus.

Of all these intersections, the ones between Emerson and Walker interest us most in this chapter. Walker seems to have drawn inspiration from the bard's essays. In his journalism and memoir, he reveals the intensity of his pursuit of the inward and outward empires, and like Emerson, he experienced a revelation, a sudden inflowing of power. Unlike Emerson, however, he was not content with mere transcendence and the mind on fire; like other filibusters, he wanted to set his fires elsewhere. The connection between the freebooter and the philosopher also interests us in another way: in Walker, we have a feral counterpart to the imperial self the philosopher conjures in *Nature* (1836) and "The Young American" (1844). In these two seminal meditations on the United States' growing power and responsibilities, Emerson imagines a beneficent and mild imperial self, a self dedicated to idealism and altruism. But where Emerson foresaw acts of kindness and generosity, Walker set out with a military force to "regenerate" the "degenerate" races of Central America. Even as the Tennessean developed, in part, his conception of the greater-than-self from the philosopher's writings, one could hardly imagine two more antithetical visions: in the philosopher and the filibuster we have a perfect pair in which to consider the American imperial self in the mid–nineteenth century. In Emerson, we have one of the most important theorists of the imperial self; in Walker, we have the literal, cold-blooded converse to the Emersonian ideal.

To tell the story of the filibuster and the midcentury imperial self, however, we must consider more than just Walker and Emerson. We must also see the freebooter and the philosopher in the context of the Tennessean's expansionist rivals. The Young Americans and their movement interest us in at least two ways. First, the focus on the outward empire on the part of Douglas, O'Sullivan, and others nicely highlights the relatively more sophisticated meditations of Emerson and Walker; if Walker does not dive nearly so deeply into the implications and possible meanings of the "imperial self" as the bard, he takes a considerably more intellectual approach to the inward and outward empires than his compeers. The bringing together of Emerson, Walker, and O'Sullivan also draws our attention to a key aspect of the imperial self: his or her voice, his or her ability to persuade others, to use language to reshape the world. Second, then, the intersections between these figures gives us access to a subject that is of interest throughout this study: imperial eloquence.

Finally, this chapter explores the deformation of the imperial self by the logic of imperialism. In a series of key passages in *The War in Nicaragua*, one of the first major treatments of the freebooter's adventures and the first sustained textualization of Walker as the American imperial self, the filibuster delineates the "requisite" logic or engine of a colonial venture; a series of interlocking steps must be taken in order to conquer and control a foreign country. His blueprint reveals the ethically and ideologically warping momentum of imperialism: in Walker's case at least, it overruns its agent, transforming him from a moderate abolitionist and believer in political and cultural "regeneration" into an advocate of slavery and a destroyer of Granada, Nicaragua. For all its implied autonomy and majesty, the imperial self becomes, like Melville's Ahab, subject to an overriding mission that strips control away from the self; the imperial self becomes a less-than-self, a self no longer in self-control.

The Philosopher and the Freebooter (and Other Young Americans)

Despite Quentin Anderson's claims that Emerson rejected the social as the proper forum for the individual in favor of "the imperium of one's own consciousness," we know that Emerson also addressed his considerable intellect and energy at American imperial currents. No matter how reluctantly he sometimes took up political issues, he was nevertheless enmeshed in the debates surrounding U.S. nation- and empire-building. In an open letter to President Martin Van Buren (April 23, 1838), for example, he protested the U.S. government's forced removal of the Cherokees from Georgia and parts of Tennessee and North Carolina. With uncharacteristic fervor, he decried the relocation to Indian Territory and demanded that Van Buren end it: "Such a dereliction of all faith and virtue, such a denial of justice, and such deafness to screams for mercy were never heard of in times of peace and in the dealing of a nation with its own allies and wards, since the earth was made."[5] Just as he condemned the treatment of the Cherokees, he also attacked slavery in an address delivered on August 4, 1844. In "On Emancipation in the British West Indies," he finds in the "black man" an "indispensable element of a new and coming civilization": "So now, the arrival in the world of such men as Toussaint [L'Ouverture] and the Haytian heroes, or of the leaders of their race in Barbadoes [sic] and Jamaica outweighs in good omen all the English and American humanity."[6] Contrary to Anderson's claims, Emerson not only pursued his idiosyncratic inward vision but also looked outward and attempted to intervene in the sometimes violent, interlocking processes of nation and empire.

As Myra Jehlen contends, the later, less radical Emerson *does* concern himself with the external world. In his "Ode" (1846) to W. H. Channing, a trenchant statement against the United States' 1846 invasion of Mexico, the bard weighs energy against ethics: "Things are in the saddle, / And ride mankind." We possess incredible powers; we live in a maelstrom of forces, of history, of teeming need and desire; we stand enmeshed in swirling, abundant life and nature; we dwell in a great and mysterious universe; yet despite the chaos we must know how to act, how to conduct ourselves, how not to visit catastrophic harm on others. He hopes in his early writings that Nature will lead us to ever deeper virtues, but here he acknowledges the storms around us; he saw the American imperial self unleashed in Texas and Mexico, and he could foresee the agents of the nation roaring over the world. He sees "little men" who prevaricate—"Virtue palters; Right is hence; / Freedom praised, but hid"—who set out to conquer and destroy: "The over-god / Who marries Right to Might, / Who peoples, unpeoples, / He who exterminates / Races by stronger races, / Black by white faces. . . ."[7] He is critical of the imperial self who deploys artful rhetoric in the service of military goals, who conquers and colonizes, who displaces dark faces with light ones.[8]

Emerson may have decried the imperium, but he nevertheless inspired its agents: on February 7, 1844, in a lecture read in Boston before the Mercantile Library Association, the philosopher unwittingly helped call into being the "Young America" movement. The Young Americans believed in the United States as a youthful and energetic nation poised to take its place on the world stage, believed in it as the nation of the future. Active in both politics and the press, they not only worked to influence national debates and public policy regarding overseas expansionism but also favored the spread of American power through private as much as public interventions. These young and politically and militarily aggressive men—Sanders and O'Sullivan, for example, lobbied for the repeal of the neutrality laws in order to permit filibusters to move against Cuba and Central America—saw themselves as models of the willing and able young Americans Emerson describes in his address, and in lines that must have thrilled these would-be agents of empire, the philosopher suggests that where "official government" fails to act, America must rely upon "the increasing disposition of private adventurers to assume its fallen functions."[9] Although we could hardly call "The Young American" a filibuster manifesto, we can imagine the delight the expansionists must have experienced when they realized they could claim Emerson as an intellectual progenitor to their movement. Although Walker was not directly allied with the Young American movement, he was part of the greater collection of expansionists and freebooters.

As exempla of Young American discourse, we can look at the writings and speeches of O'Sullivan and Douglas. In "The Great Nation of Futurity," for example, an editorial from the November 1839 issue of the *United States Magazine and Democratic Review*, O'Sullivan offers many of the same themes he would later articulate in support of the movement:

> Our national birth was the beginning of a new history, the formation and progress of an untried political system, which separates us from the past and connects us with the future only; and so far as regards the entire development of the natural rights of man, in moral, political, and national life, we may confidently assume that our country is destined to be *the great nation* of futurity.[10]

Sounding like the Emerson of "The American Scholar" (1837) and "Self-Reliance" (1841), the expansionist sees the United States as fresh, unencumbered, and ready to assume its place in the world and in history. The United States will soon enough lead the leaders. The same themes of youth, vigor, and leadership can be seen in Douglas's March 10, 1853, speech in the Senate, in which he condemned the Clayton-Bulwer Treaty (1850) and challenged John M. Clayton (by then back in the Senate)[11] to "let us look the future in the face, and let us prepare to meet that which cannot be avoided": "You may make as many treaties as you please to fetter the limits of this giant Republic, and she will burst them all from her, and her course will be onward to a limit which I will not venture to prescribe." Like O'Sullivan, Douglas saw the United States as the nation of the future and foresaw its continued expansion into Mexico, Central America, and beyond. Nothing, the Young Americans imagined, could contain American energies. Unlike Emerson and Walker, however, the Young Americans did not sound—at least in print—matters of the inward empire; they were too busy looking outward.[12]

If Douglas, O'Sullivan, and their annexationist cohort did not worry too much about theorizing the American imperial self—"have gun, will travel" probably says a great deal—Emerson went deeper than many of his contemporaries into an exploration of what it would mean to be imperial, to be able, as he puts in *Nature*, to toss creation like a bauble. For the philosopher, there have been only a few truly imperial selves, only a few who have possessed a truly imperial mind, and in *Nature*, he names his colossus par excellence: William Shakespeare. The poet, he writes, possessed "the power of subordinating nature for the purposes of expression, beyond all poets. His imperial muse tosses the creation like a bauble from hand to hand, and uses it to embody any caprice of thought that is uppermost in his mind. The remotest spaces of nature are visited, and the farthest sundered things are brought together, by a subtle spiritual connection." In particular, Emerson focuses on *The Tempest* (1611), and just as Prospero can raise a storm, the philosopher tells us, the poet dominates nature and reshapes it into peerless language. The poet realizes any idea, makes unexpected, truth-telling connections, visits the edges of creation, and calls into being entire worlds. While Emerson's poet may not be a Napoleon, moving men and machines about the earth, he nevertheless stands sovereign over outward and inward empires; a giant, he reigns over creation, makes it subject to his will, recreates it, changes our understanding of it, dominates us just as surely as Bonaparte or Alexander. If, in these remarkable lines, we can see Emerson's notion of the poet as an imperial self, as one who "unfixes the land and the sea, makes them revolve around the axis of his primary thought, and disposes them anew," we can also discover the philosopher's nascent sense of an American imperial self, a self poised, as he will phrase it in "The Young American," to "lead the leaders" of the world.[13]

Eric Cheyfitz, in *The Poetics of Imperialism* (1997), argues that where Emerson praises Shakespeare, he just as importantly celebrates America: the nation will be great, and it will be guided by citizens who can also make the world revolve around their primary axes. Like the poet, Americans will visit the remotest spaces of the New World (and beyond) and will bring together the farthest sundered nations and peoples. The American imperial self will take control of the land, will enjoy dominion over the seas. Cheyfitz suggests that *Nature*—written three decades after Meriwether Lewis and William Clark's expedition (1803–6) and a decade before the annexation of Texas (1845) and the acquisition of the Oregon territory (1846)—is about the United States becoming imperial, about the imperial Nature of the New World calling into being the American imperial self. In Emerson's first masterpiece, his eloquent statement of the regenerative and meliorist power of Nature, Prospero becomes a Yankee looking toward the Pacific.

If the energy of Emerson's *Nature* looks to the West and the future, it also looks to the Atlantic and the past. It not only forecasts the emergence of an American imperium but also recalls the founding moment of the Anglo-American nation: *The Tempest* anticipates an "American" imperial self; the play, in part, is about the creation of a British colony in the New World. Cheyfitz "synchronizes" *Nature* with Shakespeare's late masterpiece, he tells us, in order to interpret "the play within the context of the Jamestown colony, what Richard Beale Davis calls precisely 'Britain's first major experiment in Empire,' an experiment that, as we know, would eventuate in the formation of the United States."[14] Shakespeare had *A True Declaration of the Estate of the Colonie in Virginia* (1610) before him as he wrote *The Tempest*, and Cheyfitz links Emerson's emergent American imperial self with England's first colonial venture in the New World. *Nature* simultaneously reaches back to the creation of the Europeanized New World and looks forward to an ever-expanding, ever greater nation; it documents the moment when the old imperial self becomes the new imperial self who, in turn, will become the greatest imperial self in history. Despite Emerson's famous calls for New World persons and ideas—"There are new lands, new men, new thoughts. Let us demand our own works and laws and worship"—he posits a continuity in the evolution of the Anglo-American imperial self.[15]

If Emerson offers a relatively covert meditation on the American imperial self in *Nature*, he conjures him or her in the fullest, most overt terms in "The Young American." Ever the optimist in his early addresses, he imagined young Americans willingly enlisting themselves in "new moral causes"; the United States would become, he believed, the next agent of social and political progress around the world, and he calls upon young Americans to step forward:

> In every age of the world, there has been a leading nation, one of a more generous sentiment, whose eminent citizens were willing to stand for the interests of general justice and humanity, at the risk of being called, by the men of the moment, chimerical and fantastic. Which should be that nation but these States? Which should lead that movement, if not New England? Who should lead the leaders, but the Young American?[16]

The young American will venture abroad in order to lend his energy or expertise to others; she will not seek selfish gain; he will not seek his own power or aggrandizement. He will not be an agent of conquest or violence, but rather an agency for change and human betterment; she will possess only the highest ideals and virtues and will seek to do only what is right for the benefit of others.

The source of beneficent leadership, Emerson tells us, will be Nature. Returning to themes first sounded in 1836, he asserts a teleological force at work in the world:

> Men are narrow and selfish, but Genius or Destiny is not narrow, but beneficent. It is not discovered in their calculated and voluntary activity, but in what befalls, with or without design. Only what is inevitable interests us, and it turns out that love and good are inevitable, and in the course of things. That Genius has infused itself into nature. It indicates itself by a small excess of good, a small balance in brute facts always favorable to the side of reason.

This passage, however hazy concepts such as "Genius" or "Destiny" may remain, bespeaks a remarkable utopianism. For Emerson, human affairs move steadily toward "love and good." The United States, he suggests, cannot help but advance civilization. Nature, "the noblest engineer," tempers the desires of individuals and the state, and ensures that the United States will act in the interest of humanity: "That serene Power interposes the check upon the caprices and officiousness of our wills."[17] The romantic acknowledges the brutishness of life, but foresees—and hopes to call into being—a nation dedicated to altruism rather than rapacity. The Emersonian imperial self: agent of decency and benevolence. Taking our cue from Emerson's respect for Shakespeare, we must also note one other key quality of the imperial self: he or she must be eloquent.

As even a cursory reading of the speeches, editorials, essays, and memoirs of the mid-nineteenth-century imperial self will reveal, the agents of empire often see themselves as masters of eloquence. When impassioned—and they are almost always impassioned when speaking in defense of their ideals—they pour out gargantuan sentences and high-sounding phrases. They want to dazzle their readers or listeners with their intellectual, emotional, and poetic force. Most importantly, they want to whip them into imperial frenzies. Language serves as one of the most important weapons in the imperialist's arsenal, and Emerson offers, in his musings on the imperial self, a rather remarkable theory of language and action. Like his contemporaries, he sees language as a primary medium of the colossi.

The Genius that infuses Nature, a force from without that finds its receptive corollary within, also infuses language; the same meliorist force that pushes humanity toward acts of good also makes language an instrument, on "balance," in the service of progress. As Emerson argues, language arises from Nature: "Every word which is used to express a moral or intellectual fact, if traced to its root, is found to be borrowed from some material appearance." "Moral facts" and the words used to express them come from the same place, and, although we may live in a post-Orwellian and post-Derridean world—and therefore know language and meaning to be fixable only through force—Emerson believes that the teleological and meliorist force of Nature cannot be denied: it works to invest language with proper meanings and to freight words with appropriate courses of action. Not only does Nature work to fix the meaning of any utterance, but it somehow insures—once again on balance—that right actions come from right words and that right words come from right actions. Although the philosopher acknowledges that "the sovereignty of ideas is broken up by the prevalence of secondary desires, the desire of riches, of pleasure, of power, and of praise," he nevertheless believes that Destiny will lead Americans to discover, occasion by occasion, the true interests of justice and humanity and to act upon them.[18] In the same way, Destiny will call forth true words, and the imperial self will speak them with natural conviction.

If Emerson viewed language as a force for beneficence, the Young Americans and their follow freebooters were, despite their rhetoric, more concerned with the progress of their own ambitions than with the progress of humanity. And while eloquence may serve as one of the most formidable weapons of the imperial self, imperial eloquence differs from the eloquence of Emerson or Shakespeare. Where the philosopher and the poet may be capable of the highest forms of poetic language, of the sheer ability to conquer creation and consciousness through metaphor, image, and powerful appeals to reason or emotion, imperial eloquence must be counted as a baser—if no less effective—form of expression. Whereas the natural grandeur, ease, and poetry of Shakespeare or Emerson appeals to the finer nuances of the heart and mind, the eloquence of the agents of empire appeals to jingoistic and nationalistic fervors. In the place of the well-turned, emotionally and intellectually resonant phrase, the American imperial self has recourse, in the main, to the multiclaused, baggy harangue. Nevertheless, language remains a favored, if not exalted medium of the imperial self.

The Young Americans and other would-be imperial selves very much believed in imperial eloquence as a means to sway public opinion and to shape material practice. To take one example, O'Sullivan, in the famous 1845 article in which he coined the phrase "manifest destiny," piles clause upon clause in his attack on foreign powers for hampering the growth of America:

> Why, were other reasoning wanting, in favor of now elevating this question of the reception of Texas into the Union, out of the lower region of our past party dissensions, up to its proper level of a high and broad nationality, it is surely to be found, found abundantly, in the manner in which other nations have undertaken to intrude themselves into it, between us and the proper parties to the case, in a spirit of hostile interference against us, for the avowed object of thwarting our policy and hampering our power, limiting our greatness and checking the fulfillment of our *manifest destiny* to overspread the continent allotted by Providence for the free development of our yearly multiplying millions. (emphasis added)

The language of "manifest" and "Providence," if playing upon the Protestant sentiments of O'Sullivan's readers, nevertheless conveys in less exuberant tones Emerson's belief that Americans had a responsibility and a right to lead the world. Once again, the nation's land and fate are intimately connected.[19] Although O'Sullivan cannot match Emerson's prose—he runs his sentence into the very earth that the philosopher claimed as the source of eloquence—he suggests that big ideas require a sentence structure to match. More importantly, he shares little of Emerson's sense of benevolence: he wants the land, the power, the empire.

Eloquence and Emersonian mysticism particularly show themselves in what historians take to be Walker's two, nearly identical statements of purpose. In an unsigned October 18, 1856, article in *El Nicaragüense*—the "theme for a novelist" column that I treated briefly in the introduction—Walker (it must be Walker) describes the almost mystical moment when the self discovers, through divine inspiration, its mission. Surrounded by his favorite books—including a volume or two of Emerson?—the self experiences a sudden illumination, a sudden and fiery inflowing of empyrean insight:

> It is deeds, and not resolves and projects, that command the attention of the age. Less than two years ago, a thought sprang up in the brain of a young

man, sitting in his book-girt sanctuary, where he was wont to hold communion with the great and good of other times. He pondered upon it; he revolved it in his mind; he looked at it from all sides; he saw the obstacles that were in the way of carrying it into successful practice; he saw, too, the glorious results that might be achieved for his generation, if, in the mysterious order of God's providence, he should be permitted to triumph; and he resolved.[20]

A "thought" springs up in his soul, and he feels himself to be an agent of providence, a man chosen by God for a great purpose. This revelation transports the self out of the moment, and he sees his future; too, Walker sees his place in history, sees himself as a great leader. In this remarkable passage, Walker describes the transformation of the self into the imperial self: like Emerson in pursuit of the inward empire of the mind, he receives a sudden flash from above; so visited, he must act, must turn his energies outward toward the empires of the earth.

The article in *El Nicaragüense* rewrites an 1849 editorial from the *New Orleans Crescent*, perhaps the most famous passage in all of Walker's writing. Here, as in the later version, the Tennessean suggests that his imperial ambitions were a product of divine inspiration. Drawing upon the discourses of Manifest Destiny and Protestant election, he describes a moment where the self becomes an agent of providence, and although he does not speak in the first person, we can nevertheless read the passage as a dramatic narrative of the imperial self coming into being:

> Unless a man believes that there is something great for him to do, he can do nothing great. Hence so many of the captains and reformers of the world have relied on fate and the stars. A great idea springs up in a man's soul; it agitates his whole being, transports him from the ignorant present and makes him feel the future in a moment. It is natural for a man so possessed to conceive that he is a special agent for working out in practice the thought that has been revealed to him.... Why should such a revelation be made to him, why should he be enabled to perceive what is hidden to others—if not that he should carry it into practice?[21]

Some unnamed force—God, a spirit—calls into being "a great idea"; this force lifts the self out of the moment and unveils the individual's role in the future course of civilization. A moment of transcendence, a moment of greatness, a moment of duty. Once selected, the self must act; a divine imperative heats the self, compels it to move, to follow through on the revelation; the self becomes the imperial self. In this moment, Walker became a "special agent" of empire.

Like Emerson and O'Sullivan, Walker strives for his own dramatic language; as a capable writer and journalist, he achieves his own measure of imperial eloquence. Unlike O'Sullivan—or, say, Melville or, to a lesser degree, Emerson—he keeps his sentences brisk. He does not try to bury his reader in prodigious prose, and we do not get lost in unlovely hectoring. Rather, he describes the moment of revelation in a style that seems to anticipate the leaner mode of the twentieth century more than the extravagant and wandering style of Walker's contemporaries. Moreover, he manages some deftly counterpoised clauses—"unless a man believes that there is something great for him to do, he can do nothing great"—and repetitions—"great"—and presents a fair description of an epiphany: "A great idea springs up in a man's soul; it agitates his whole being, transports him from the ignorant present and makes him feel the future in a moment." The image of an agitated soul—though not wholly original by any means—works well, and the sentence describes a rare and towering moment of transcendence; he presents his big idea without recourse to one of O'Sullivan's trackless spumes. Of course, Walker may have had on his desk an expert model for describing such a moment.

In *Nature*, Emerson uses a language and imagery that may have inspired Walker. As Emerson writes, the poet-orator becomes "conscious of a universal soul within or behind his individual life" and experiences one of those rare "examples of Reason's momentary grasp of the scepter; the exertions of a power which exists not in time or space, but as an instantaneous instreaming causing power." A sudden influx lifts the individual out of the moment and into a fusion with a greater being. As Emerson puts it in that most famous passage in American letters, the self becomes "a transparent eye-ball": "I am nothing; I see all; the currents of the Universal Being circulate through me; I am part or particle of God." But where Emerson experiences a vanishing of mean egotism, where he finds a higher ethic or a better judgment, Walker finds filibustering. Where Emerson thinks of such illuminations in Christ and "the achievements of a principle, as in religious and political revolutions, and in abolition of the Slave-trade," Walker sees the invasion of Mexico, war against the Apaches, and the conquest of Nicaragua. If we do not know whether Walker read Emerson, we can at least say that Walker, imbued with an imperialist sense of self, fancied himself a philosopher-warrior doing precisely what Emerson called on "adventurers" to do: find some "forlorn" people and make yourself their "king."[22]

However much we might credit Walker's mystical understanding of his duty and destiny, his statements of purpose reveal the intimate connection between the inward and outward empires, between the empire of the mind and the empire of the world. Although the journalist wants to offer a dramatic tale of imperial epiphany, we can look at the articles in less ethereal terms. On the one hand, as Anderson's Emerson would have it, the self looks inward and seeks to take possession of the imperium of one's consciousness. Alone, communing with the great writers, thinkers, and figures of the past, the self pursues the inward vision, turns it over, sees its complexities and challenges. The self conjures a stage-world of the mind, peoples it, sets it into fiery motion. Armed with this vision, however, the imperial self then looks outward. The imperium of the mind is not enough; the mind and soul on fire, the self—convinced of the sacredness of its vision—must act, must pursue the outward empire. The world-stage becomes the proper forum, and he raises armies and razes cities in order to secure his dream of how the world ought to be. The self has his vision, sees it with utmost intensity and clarity, and then must "carry it into practice." The real-world imperial self does not seek transcendence through the divine within; he seeks power. He does not seek a mere empire of one; he seeks to establish his sovereignty over others. This, in the clearest possible terms, is the American imperial self at midcentury.

However formidable a figure the American imperial self may seem to be—and however deadly in actual fact—the self that Walker describes does not constitute some perfect, fully present, ultimate self. The freebooter asks us to see the imperial self as someone who possesses a God-given will and presence; God has called on him to act, and he must act: he will get the job done when others cannot or will not. He has passion, intellect, clarity; he wields words as well as he wields a sword or pistol. He stands tall (metaphorically speaking), knows no fear, holds no doubts, will not waver or be deterred. He stands apart from, yet atop the mass of humanity. The imperial self looks in and looks out, knows his mind, and bends others to his will. He will not be ruled; others will bow to him. This intense being sounds exalted, magnificent, noble. The imperial self seems to exceed all others in will and power; Walker conjures a fuller, more replete self, a self more wholly a self than others can ever hope to be. Herein lies the conundrum, however: even by his own logic, the imperial self experiences—at the very moment of apotheosis—defeat. At the moment of becoming a greater-than-self, the imperial self simultaneously becomes a less-than-self.

Emerson's moment of transcendence in *Nature*, his moment of empyrean difference, raises the question: what happens to the self when it becomes a "transparent eye-ball"? The self is no longer the self; he may be more, much more, divinely more, but he is no longer himself. A force from without—that every day, Emerson later suggests, resides within but in ruins—flows into the self, both reducing and enhancing him. The self surrenders sovereignty, becomes, in whatever happy measure, a less-than-self. If we can see this in Emerson, we can also see it in Walker. Once again, a force—the Protestant God rather than the Oversoul—reaches into the self and makes him the imperial self. Walker, like Emerson, surrenders authority to another power, loses autonomy, becomes the instrument of divinity. In a curious way, the self experiences a metaphysical conquest. The self qua self suffers defeat and becomes an instrument of imperialism. And this—as we shall see later—literally happens to Walker.

If the imperial self lacks autonomy and presence, neither does it possess an essential selfness. We can see this clearly in the performative dimensions of Walker's statements of purpose. Thinking ahead, and imagining his place in American history and literature, he begins to fashion himself as "The Gray-eyed Man of Destiny," the Homeric epithet most often attached to his name.[23] The moment of revelation works nicely as a bit of theater: we see the great man, alone; suddenly, his expression changes, and we know—from the unheard (yet swelling) music and the unseen (yet dramatic) changes in lighting—that divinity has touched him. Walker's latest and greatest role descends, deus ex machina, and he begins to act his part. He assumes the guise of the great man; he adopts the persona of what he imagines as the American imperial self. He persuades men to fund his venture, and he persuades others to join him in feats of arms and conquest. For my part, I think Walker took the inward and outward empires seriously, but he was also canny enough to realize the value of a little myth- and image-making. Too, he was both unconscious and conscious of the performative aspects of his colonizing scheme: he fashioned himself into a filibuster (a performative act in itself, as Butler and others would have it)—*and* cast himself as "the gray-eyed man of destiny." He was a deadly sober freebooter, *and* he played up the persona of the cold-blooded soldier of fortune. He was largely without affect, but he also affected affectlessness as part of his demeanor of command and intimidation. These considerations of the performative and less-than-self bring us to a reformulation of the imperial self: he is not a giant, not a suzerain of the inward and outward empires; no such pure being exists. Simply put, and setting aside mystical self-representations, the imperial self may be just a person who acts on their desires to take the wealth, land, and lives of others and who has the guns to back up those desires. The imperial self: somewhat less than advertised.

The Emperor of Anywhere

The War in Nicaragua serves as the prime focus of this section and interests us for a number of reasons. For one, Walker's memoir constitutes one of the first full-length, single-author treatments of his adventures. This work not only serves as the major source of raw material for romancers, poets, and filmmakers, but it also offers the first sustained representation of William Walker, American imperial self. Here, we see the arguments and actions of a freebooting agent of empire, and we see, in detail, his pursuit of the outward empire. Second, and perhaps most importantly, Walker offers a thorough account of the steps that must be taken to establish an American colony abroad. In his explanation of the "requisite" logic of conquest and colonization, we see the deformation of the imperial self by the processes of imperialism. Once the imperial self takes one step, it must proceed through a series of interlocking steps, each of which must be taken to ensure the success of the step before, all of which must be taken to ensure the success of the colonial venture. In Walker's case, this process takes on its own momentum, and the self becomes subject to the logic of empire. Walker, like Ahab, becomes subject to the object of his will. As Ishmael tells us, Ahab's will "created a creature" within the haggard, dismasted captain of the *Pequod:* "But as the mind does not exist unless leagued with the soul, therefore it must have been that, in Ahab's case, yielding up all his thoughts and fancies to his one supreme purpose; that purpose, by it own sheer inveteracy of will, forced itself against gods and devils into a kind of self-assumed, independent being of its own."[24] The filibuster becomes deformed by his desires, and just as Ahab pays with his life, so does Walker.

To begin, we can turn once more to Emerson. In "The Young American," the philosopher, somewhat tongue-in-cheek in his phrasing, suggests that able citizens have a responsibility to lead others: "Where is he who seeing a thousand men useless and unhappy, and making the whole region forlorn by their inaction, and conscious himself of possessing the faculty they want, does not hear his call to go and be their king?"[25] As part of the address, Emerson analyzes the transition from feudalism to early capitalism, and by no means advocates an American monarchism; rather, he means "king" to signify "leader," and believes in meritocratic society. In contrast, Walker meant to be a king in the most literal sense: he wanted to be emperor of someplace, anyplace outside of the United States. His memoir reveals, in precise detail, the route the imperial self must follow when looking outward.

In *The War in Nicaragua*, the Emersonian language of "nature" becomes the imperialist language of "regeneration." After his expulsion from Central America in 1857, Walker returned to the United States and began to organize other filibustering ventures. During this period of relative inactivity, he wrote his history, in part, not only as a commercial for his next expedition but also as a defense of his isthmian intervention. As he argues, he went to Nicaragua seeking "the regeneration of that part of Central America": "From the day the Americans landed at Realejo dates a new epoch, not only for Nicaragua, but for all Central America. Thenceforth it was impossible for the worn-out societies of those countries to evade or escape the changes the new elements were to work in their domestic as well as in their political organization."[26] Deploying the organic metaphor of "regeneration," Walker casts himself and his men as agents of civilization, as a spiritual and ethical force on a mission to strip away the corruption that Spanish and mestizo culture, Catholicism, and feudalism have wreaked in the isthmus. "Regeneration" sounds noble and natural; once again, the language of imperialism echoes not only Calvinism but also romanticism. Further, the "new elements" means not only new to Nicaragua, but new to the world; these young Americans have a responsibility to revitalize the soil and people of Central America.

In citing "regeneration" as part of his rationale for intervention, Walker drew upon the discourses of the era. Walt Whitman, for example, in a June 6, 1846, editorial in the *Brooklyn Daily Eagle*, supported the annexation of "several of the departments of Mexico" and cast the U.S. mission in strikingly organic terms: "The scope of our government (like the most sublime principles of Nature), is such that it can readily fit itself, and extend itself, to almost any extent, and to interests and circumstances the most widely different." For Whitman, the United States had a responsibility to liberate, regenerate, and populate parts of Mexico:

> We love to indulge in thoughts of the future extent and power of this Republic—because with its increase is the increase of human happiness and liberty.—Therefore we hope that the United States will keep a fast grip on California. What has the miserable, inefficient Mexico—with her superstition, her burlesque upon freedom, her actual tyranny by the few over the many—what has she to do with the great mission of peopling the New World with a noble race? Be it ours, to achieve that mission![27]

In 1847 other American newspapers, such as the *New York Herald*, called for the United States to invade Mexico: "The universal Yankee nation can regenerate and disenthrall the people of Mexico in a few years; and we believe it is a part of our destiny to civilize that beautiful country." In the imperial imagination, the self must act upon the Mexican for the Mexican's benefit; luckily for Americans, the task of liberating Mexicans from the tyranny of their government, language, and culture will prove to be less than arduous.[28]

As Albert K. Weinberg puts it in *Manifest Destiny* (1935), an important early study of U.S. imperialism, "regeneration" served as a rallying cry for the agents of empire: "Expansionist ideology changed during the strange tutelage of a war from an almost Nietzschean self-realization to a quasi-altruism. The moral inspiration of the expansionists during the war [with Mexico] was derived from the conception of a religious duty to regenerate the unfortunate people of the enemy country by bringing them into the life-giving shrine of American democracy. The imperial self, formerly a would-be *Übermensch*, becomes—at least on paper—an agent for good, and Walker, as a journalist well versed in the politics and rhetoric of his day, drew upon this popular, romantic-sounding argument to justify his isthmian adventures.[29]

If Walker drew upon nineteenth-century imperial discourses, "regeneration," as Richard Slotkin has shown, has long been a dominant American theme. In *The Fatal Environment* (1985), Slotkin dedicates a chapter to Walker and John Brown, two men violently committed to their beliefs, and argues that "Walker emerged in 1855 as the hero of the Isthmian and Caribbean Frontier":

> If it were not for the "native problem," the liberation of Nicaragua could have been seen as a classic Frontier adventure, a heroic escape from the rigors and limits of Metropolitan conditions, a new garden spot beyond the outer limits of land reached in California—a place to regenerate fortunes and soils, to aggrandize and uplift a new group of pioneers and reclaim new wildernesses for civilization.[30]

Playing upon notions of the frontier and regeneration that reached back to the Puritans, Walker presented himself as a constructive force, as an idealist dedicated to forging a new civilization in Central America. But unlike their expansionist counterparts in New England or, more contemporarily, in Texas and California, the isthmian Americans could not hope to outpopulate or displace the indigenous cultures. Faced with this "native problem," the freebooter argued for a racial hierarchy and readily cast himself as a hero of regeneration. He drew upon classic American arguments and iconography and once more demonstrated, as Slotkin puts it in *Regeneration through Violence* (1973), that the "means" to "regeneration ultimately became the means of violence."[31]

If Emerson attempts to describe the logic of beneficence at work in the world, the tendency toward "love and good," Walker reveals the imperial self to be concerned with the logic of imperialism, the tendency toward greed and power. The key term in his colonization scheme is *requisite*. The perfect word, it implies the imperative of the colonial or imperial venture: once one step is taken, then the next must also be taken to ensure the success of the first, and so on. For the imperial self, colonization consists of a series of interlinking decisions that organize the military, political, and economic lives of friend and foe alike. After the Immortals captured Granada and officially opened the way for American colonization, Walker argued that Americans must immigrate in order that the invaders acquire "the strength *requisite* for the maintenance of their privileges" (emphasis added):

> The necessity for the American element to predominate in the government of Nicaragua sprang from the clauses in the treaty of peace [signed at the end of the civil war]. In order to carry out the spirit of that treaty—to secure to the Americans in the service of the Republic the rights gauranteed [*sic*] to them by the full sovereign power of the State—it was *requisite* to get into the country a force capable of protecting it, not only from domestic but from foreign enemies. (emphasis added)

His logic abounds with the commonplaces of colonialism: the colonial venture is legal and moral; the colonizers must control the government and the military in order to protect the colonized from themselves and from (other) outsiders. With the colonization of Nicaragua well under way, the next step almost goes without saying: "It was necessary for the welfare of the Americans that a new election should be called."[32] Although he makes the faintest gestures toward the interests of the isthmians, beneficence has little to do with the imperial self's colonizing project: it is about power and profit.

With the Immortals in military and political control, Walker took the next "requisite" step and seized control of the nation's wealth. As president, he choreographed a huge land grab:

> The general tendency of these several decrees was the same; they were intended to place a large proportion of the land of the country in the hands of the white race. The military force of the State might, for a time, secure the Americans in the government of the Republic, but in order that their possession of government might be permanent, it was *requisite* for them to hold the land. (emphasis added)[33]

Once under way, the imperial self must continue to act, must do everything in its power to maintain power. Imperialism becomes an engine, a force unto itself, and the imperial self becomes swept along. Moreover, as the process unfolds, idealism gives way to power concepts, and ideals twist and deform into acts of brutality, even savagery. In order to hold the government and the land, all challenges must be suppressed, either through execution, war, or firestorm; if Walker's colonization scheme ever was about regeneration, it quickly became a matter of asserting the authority of the imperial self, of making others submit.

As one of the clearest examples of how the requisite logic of imperialism deforms the imperial self, we need only look at his attempt to reintroduce slavery into Central America. Although his mother's family had owned slaves, Walker published a number of moderate abolitionist editorials as a journalist. As Albert Z. Carr notes, "In his journalistic days Walker had taken what was then termed the 'conservative' position on slavery—against its expansion, and less overtly, in favor of its gradual elimination by law and economic measures."[34] Once dictator, however, he issued a decree—in contravention of the 1824 abolition of slavery in the isthmus—restoring the "peculiar institution" to Nicaragua. Why he did this remains a matter of some argument among historians, romancers, poets, and filmmakers—did he really support the slave trade, or was he trying to recruit men and materials from the southern slave states?—but we can once more see the requisite logic of imperialism twisting and controlling its agent:

> The introduction of negro-slavery into Nicaragua would furnish a supply of constant and reliable labor *requisite* for the cultivation of tropical products. With the negro-slave as his companion, the white man would become fixed to the soil; and they together would destroy the power of the mixed race which is the bane of the country. The pure Indian would readily fall into the new social organization; for he does not aim at political power, and only asks to be protected in the fruits of his industry. (emphasis added)

In this revealing passage, Walker hints at genocide, deploys the racist commonplaces of imperialism—Africans count only as labor, Indians need guidance—and places whites firmly at the pinnacle of society. Even more, he constructs himself as an economist and a visionary: "Slavery goes to the vital relations of capital toward labor, and by the firm footing it gives the former it enables the intellect of society to push boldly forward in the pursuit of new forms of civilization."[35] Ultimately, he reveals that the imperial self will do whatever it takes to fulfill its dream of empire. The filibuster's outward vision must be realized, and no ideals or laws will stand in his way.

In some of the most remarkable and telling passages in *The War in Nicaragua*, Walker also reveals that the imperial self believes it can do no wrong; if he did not hold Nicaragua or conquer all the isthmus, it was not his fault.

As a blueprint for American colonization schemes, the memoir not only tells Americans what steps to follow in order to colonize the poorer parts of the world but also seeks to assure its readers that Walker's colonization plan would have worked—could work again—but for a series of betrayals. Embittered (and displaying no small measure of pettiness), he spends a considerable amount of time blaming others for his failure; in fact, he blames everyone but himself. He blames, for example, Franklin Pierce's secretary of state, William L. Marcy, who refused to send the U.S. Navy to the Immortal's aid during the allied war against them: "It is difficult to imagine that an American Secretary of State would thus connive at a plan for driving his countrymen from the Isthmus; but pride of opinion and desire for office were Mr. Marcy's leading passions." He also blames his own men: when it became clear that the filibusters were going to lose the war, many of the Americans sought their own way home or accepted a British offer of safe passage. Although he could comprehend the "shameful desertion" of the Europeans who had joined his forces, he could not believe Americans could behave in such a cowardly manner: "When the fatal infection spread among the Americans, it wrung bitter tears of agony from every truehearted man who witnessed the shame and dishonor of his countrymen."[36]

In what may be taken as his ultimate act of imperialist revenge—and as an early version of the infamous Vietnam story, "We had to destroy the village to save it"—Walker blamed his impending defeat upon the Nicaraguans themselves and ordered the city of Granada razed. He argues, in his memoir, that "by the laws of war, the town had forfeited its existence": "As to the justice of the act, few can question it; for its inhabitants owed life and property to the Americans in the service of Nicaragua, and yet they joined the enemies who strove to drive their protectors from Central America."[37] The logic of imperialism leads not only to racial hierarchies and slavery but also to catastrophic acts of destruction. Once again, Walker offers a revealing example of the imperial self's logic: we destroyed their houses and buildings and murdered them because they did not want our protection and domination. Walker not only shows potential freebooters what hard actions they must be willing to take as colonizers, but he also warns potential successors about who and what to watch out for. Moreover, the destruction-by-fire of Granada reveals the true nature of the American imperial self: idealism and beneficence have little to do with his conduct; power and the assertion of the self count the most. What really matters to the imperial self is the imperial self.

Walker set out, he tells us, with the idea of regenerating the republics of Central America. While we might easily brush aside such claims as mere rhetorical gestures—a nice ribbon around an awful gift—he might have meant it. He might have wanted to improve, at least by his standards, the "civilization" of Nicaragua. He might have possessed high ideals and might have thought he was doing what needed to be done to improve the lot of the isthmians. He might have believed all of these things, but imperialism cannot sustain such idealism. It requires a sense of the superiority of the self; it requires a desire to order the lives of others; it requires, almost always, the use of force. The realities of power press down upon good intentions and grandiose dreams. Moreover, the American desires for power, for gain, for expansion—all founding principles—also work against beneficent ambitions. The push-pull of idealism and self-interest twist the imperial self, bend him more than he can control. He may go in wishing to be a knight-errant, but he comes out a deformed and monstrous figure. Ideals, in the building of empires, cannot be sustained. Imperialism deforms idealism. Walker may have wanted to "civilize" the isthmus, but he ended up a cruel, desperate, and failed conquistador.

Imperialism so distorted and twisted Walker that he could never let go of his dreams of empire. Although he had a long history of career changes, once he turned to filibustering, he never turned away. He tried again and again—after his flight from the isthmus following the allied war against the freebooters—to raise another force and to conquer another country. He sailed once more for Nicaragua, but became caught up in a dispute over the Bay Islands off Honduras. Once more asserting, if somewhat more cavalierly, the hand of God, Walker wrote C. I. Fayssoux, one of his officers, about his decision to focus his energies on Honduras rather than Nicaragua: "Always I have striven to take the course which would leave me as little as possible at the caprice of fortune, but 'man proposes, God disposes,' and I must certainly admit that in some respects we seem to have been forced by events beyond our own control." The imperial self cannot help himself; God and the demon within have conspired to drive the less-than-self into an unanticipated course of action. Just as Ahab finds "the path to [his] fixed purpose is laid with iron rails, whereon [his] soul is grooved to run," Walker descends along his own path to ruin.[38] And, just as Ahab falls victim to his will, so, too, does Walker. Quickly captured by the Honduran authorities, he was executed and, his face shot off, buried in an unmarked grave.

Ultimately, if we cannot know what the filibuster hoped to achieve in Central America from reading his blueprint, we can at least speculate. For my own part, I think Walker wanted to be emperor of anywhere. A narcissism pervades his writing and adventures. In *The War in Nicaragua*, he refers to himself in the third person, modeling his narrative after Caesar's *Commentaries*. Although he presents "General Walker" modestly and unheroically, the freebooter records his last general order to his men before their fall: "Reduced to our present position by the cowardice of some, the incapacity of others, and the treachery of many, the army has yet written a page of American history which it is impossible to forget or erase." Walker absolves himself of responsibility for the American defeat and insists upon his place in history. He still sees himself as a special agent of empire: "He is but a blind reader of the past who has not learned that Providence fits its agents for great designs by trials, and sufferings, and persecutions."[39] Others have undone him, but this only confirms his elect status; beneath the memoir's quiet tone resides Walker's sense of his own grandeur. He knows he's destined to achieve something great; he possesses a grand vision of his imperial self. He invaded Mexico and declared himself president of Sonora. When that failed, he conquered in Nicaragua (a remarkable achievement) and declared himself president. When that failed, he regrouped, sailed for the isthmus again, but never made it to Nicaragua. He went where opportunity afforded itself; he wanted to write his name in history and believed he could improvise an empire.

To conclude, we can make at least one other crucial observation: the American imperial self in the first half of the nineteenth century wanted to transform the energies of continental expansionism into overseas adventurism. The time, however, was not quite right. Walker and his fellow adventurers lacked the full backing of the state and its resources; the mainstream of American imperial energy was dedicated to rationalizing the continent and was not yet ready to turn its considerable forces overseas. Where economic ventures such as Cornelius Vanderbilt's Nicaraguan Transit Company were under way—and would eventually serve to open Central America to further commercial enterprises such as the fruit and coffee companies—and where U.S. diplomats worked to extend American influence throughout the Americas in support of the Monroe Doctrine, the swashbuckling imperial self abroad was a bit premature. Many of the conquering soldiers were still involved in subduing hostile Indians in the West and in securing the United States' southern and northern borders. The imperial self was too deeply involved in organizing the economic, military, and political life of the rapidly expanding nation to become too involved in extracontinental adventures.

The freebooters were ahead of their fully sanctioned peers, but only just. From 1850 to 1856, for example, U.S. soldiers were stationed in Panama to defend the American-built transisthmian railroad; in 1852 U.S. forces were deployed in Argentina to defend American interests during a revolution; in 1853–54 U.S. ships—the Perry expedition—"opened" Japan to the West; in 1855 U.S. troops were sent to Uruguay to protect American lives and property; in 1859 the United States sent soldiers to China to further American trade interests during the Second Opium War. The list of imperial interventions could go on, but Americans had begun to look outward, had begun to take a more and more active interest in affairs beyond their borders. More and more, the United States would seek an overseas empire. In this context, we can see Walker and other midcentury American imperial selves as the base and often vicious progenitors to the higher-sheen heroes and ventures to follow. The road from Walker leads, we could say, to Theodore Roosevelt. For that story, however, we will have to wait until chapter 3. From here, we turn to Bret Harte's refashioning of Walker's adventures into what becomes the primary vehicle for explorations of the American imperial self, the mercenary romance.

CHAPTER TWO

"What Is Good for *Them*": Harte and the Mercenary Romance

From Emerson and Shakespeare, we tumble down the slopes of Olympus when we turn to the writings of Bret Harte. Moreover, we encounter far paler visions of the imperial self than we find in Emerson and Walker's writings. Gone are the riveting, intensely inward- and outward-looking agents of empire. Gone are the fiery, fearless selves who long to toss creation like a bauble. Absent, too, is the cauldron of continental and overseas expansion that helped to call into being such intense visions. Harte, we will have to concede, is no Emerson or Shakespeare, and where Walker lived in a United States swept up in the fervors and passions of Manifest Destiny, Harte lives in a relatively quieter time. Within three years of the publication of *The Crusade of the Excelsior* (1887), Harte's Walker novel and the ur-text of the mercenary romance, and following the 1890 U.S. Census Bureau report and the massacre at Wounded Knee, the post–Civil War generation witnessed the closing of the frontier and enjoyed an era of relative expansionist and military quietude between the uproars and violences of Manifest Destiny and the Spanish-American War. We move from an age of extraordinary intellectual and political energy and tumult into a relatively more modest era, but to Harte and the 1870s and 1880s we must go: in this chapter, we take the next important steps along the filibuster's literary trail and begin our dive into romance representations of the American imperial self.

Although Harte enjoyed a considerable following early in his career, many scholars would argue that he quickly fell from his initial promise as a humorist, realist, and writer of local-color tales. Following the success of *The Luck of Roaring Camp and Other Sketches* (1870), one critical story goes, he produced some mediocre pieces for the *Atlantic Monthly;* churned out a stream of tiresome, magazine-ready tales; cowrote a play, *Ah Sin* (1877), with Mark Twain; and then, after a pair of short novels and sundry story collections, lived out his life as an American hack in London, writing stories in imitation of his early tales of "Spanish California."[1] While there may be some truth to this story, Harte rightly enjoys a prominent following among scholars and readers of western American literature, and he makes at least one serious claim on our attention here. As one of the first writers to retell the Walker narrative, he establishes, in part, one of the most important genres in the literature of the American imperial self: the mercenary romance. Not only did he supply a model for Richard Harding Davis's far more famous Walker tales—*Soldiers of Fortune* (1897) and *Captain Macklin* (1902)—but he also called into being what has become the standard plot and cast of characters for *most* American novels and films set in Central America. However tepid and boggy his later work may be, he must still be counted as a pioneer in the literature of the American empire.

Harte was a natural to write about Walker and filibustering. In his early and best tales, he depicts the lives and hardships of prospectors, gamblers, prostitutes, and adventurers in California. Set against the backdrop of mining camps, saloons, and the Sierras, the tales dramatize, however colorfully or obliquely, the settlement of lands taken from Mexico. John Oakhurst, Yuba Bill, Kentuck, Tennessee, Jack Hamlin, and other of Harte's adventurers and miscreants live (and die) on the ragged frontier, and though he only sometimes makes the displacement of the Mexicans and Indians the primary subject of his work, his sketches explore—if less deeply than, for example, Helen Hunt Jackson's *Ramona* (1884), María Amparo Ruiz de Burton's *The Squatter and the Don* (1885), or Frank Norris's *The Octopus* (1901)—the rationalization of California into the U.S. economic order. As Amy Kaplan and others have argued, nation-building and empire-building must be seen as coterminous enterprises, and, for Harte, the step from writing tales about westward expansion and the closing of the frontier to writing tales about imperial and commercial ventures abroad was a logical and easy one.

Harte's speculators and scoundrels, like their real-world counterparts, cannot go much further west, and they must look for new lands and peoples to conquer. If his early stories focus on California, his later tales—especially the two Walker narratives we are concerned with here, "Peter Schroeder"

(1875) and *The Crusade of the Excelsior*—examine the transformation of the forces of continental expansionism into overseas adventurism. Old enough to have read newspaper accounts of Walker's adventures as they unfolded (Harte was born in 1836), and at work in an era when expansionists and entrepreneurs cast about for new resources to tap and for new territories to buy, seize, or dominate, Harte weighs the turning of American energies abroad. This turning—widely documented in the newspapers and journals of the day—included both economic and paramilitary ventures. Drawing on both Walker's exploits and the events of his day, Harte recast his dubious, if sometimes poignant Californians as dubious, if sometimes admirable entrepreneurs and colonialists in Mexico and Central America.

In "Schroeder" and *Crusade*, Harte rewrites Walker's filibustering campaigns as a means to dramatize and critique different forms of American military and economic imperialism after 1865. In the decades between the end of the Civil War and the beginning of the Spanish-American War, U.S. overseas interventionism largely transformed from calls for annexation and illegal filibustering ventures to economic imperialism—supported by military force—throughout the hemisphere. In order to sound these various forms, Harte conjures a relatively modest American imperial self, alternately casting Walker as a vile con man ("Schroeder") and as a genteel, if misguided "liberator" of downtrodden peoples *(Crusade)*. Like Emerson, Harte concerns himself with young Americans and idealism. In the short story, he portrays the thwarting of American altruism in the form of a naïve would-be colonialist, Peter Schroeder; the imperial self-as-con man leads the good-natured émigré to his demise. In *Crusade*, one of the earliest full-length narrative treatments of U.S. extraterritorial imperialism, Harte lauds beneficence and casts young American entrepreneurs as the right sort of imperial selves to bring U.S. economic and political know-how to the world. The romance suggests that although filibustering was a corrupt and doomed venture, Yankee commercial savvy, tempered by democratic values, would not only improve the lot of people of color but might also foster (Harte hopes) a kind of benign American imperialism. A dream-work—a wish for how Americans ought to be in the world—*Crusade* conjures modest, self-effacing imperial selves who create a fair-minded and friendly American economic colony in Mexico. Harte saw himself, as he told his wife in a letter, as an "earnest Republican—and I think a *just* one," and in his Walker tales he examines the shifting tensions in American society between idealism and adventurism.[2]

The Nicaraguan Convulsions

If Walker's career as a representation of the American imperial self begins in an unsigned 1849 editorial in the *New Orleans Crescent*, he became a highly textualized figure long before the publication of *The War in Nicaragua* or *The Crusade of the Excelsior*. Harte, as we know, was not the first to transform the freebooter's adventures into a literary form; Joaquin Miller's narrative poem "With Walker in Nicaragua" (1871) remains one of the first extant literary treatments, but we also know that melodramas based upon his exploits were performed while he was still dictator of Nicaragua, and he was the subject of doggerel in many American and Central American publications. But even before he had life as the hero or antihero of poems, plays, and stories, he was the subject of intense, and heterogeneous, textualization in the press. He became a representation even before he crossed the border into Mexico on his first filibustering mission. He was one of the most reported-on figures of his day, and we can approach these representations in the same way we approach the more avowedly "literary" representations: as shaped, ideologically freighted portrayals that stand in an unfixable relation to the referent.

Many of the first accounts of Walker appeared in newspapers and magazines, with journalists and editorial writers beginning to formulate what would become some of the standard representations. In particular, many early chroniclers—like most recounters of his adventures—focus on his appearance and mannerisms;[3] more importantly, they also offer conflicted, even contradictory representations of him as simultaneously well meaning *and* savage, as necessary *and* criminal. Some publications, such as *Frank Leslie's Illustrated Newspaper*, championed the filibuster as an exemplum of the American imperial self, while others, such as *Harper's Weekly*, expressed ambivalent views and portrayed him as a rather less exalted being.[4]

This mix of representations was widely disseminated throughout the United States, and they very likely served, at least in part, as the raw material for Harte's freebooting tales. Unlike many later rewriters of the Walker narrative, he seems not to have read *The War in Nicaragua*; in comparison to Davis, Teilhet, Houston, or Cox, he does not seem to possess as much precise information about the freebooter's to-ings and fro-ings, and he does not concern himself with specific battles or moments in the filibuster's career.[5] Rather, in his mid-twenties when Walker died, he appears to have learned about what *Harper's* dubbed "the Nicaraguan convulsions" from newspapers and magazines; he focuses less on the particulars and more on American debates on filibustering and other forms of overseas adventurism. From its inception in *Crusade*, the American mercenary romance expresses a marked ambivalence toward both Walker and U.S. imperialism, and we can set Harte's doubts against the conflicted attitudes that were circulating in the print media of the 1850s.[6] Harte's tales seem to draw upon and work against these early representations, and for these reasons, before we turn to "Schroeder" and *Crusade*, we need to examine, albeit briefly, some of the first major textualizations of the Tennessean.

Frank Leslie's Illustrated Newspaper, to take one example of a publication that looked favorably on filibustering, celebrated Walker's conquest of Nicaragua, heralding his ascension as a boon not only to the region but to the United States as well. In a December 22, 1855, article, "Yankee Progress in Central America," the publication lauds Walker and fellow freebooter Col. Henry L. Kinney[7] as agents of civilization:

> Every thing seems to be going rapidly ahead under the management of Walker and Kinney, and unless their authority should be overthrown by some unforeseen combination, nothing can prevent this state from becoming one of the most populous and thriving in Central and South America. The measures adopted by the new government are all marked by good sense, sagacity, and a keen appreciation of the difficulties that will be surmounted before unity and strength can be imparted to its institutions.[8]

The article represents the filibuster in just the way he would have wanted to be represented: as a force of regeneration and wisdom, and as a man of practical and sound political sense. In another article a week later, "The Central American Question," the newspaper reaffirms its faith in Walker and augurs that he will join the isthmus to the republic:

> [General Walker and his associates] have established in Central America the nucleus of another powerful confederation, which, from small beginnings, may soon become a formidable rival to us in the domain, which, in our monopolizing ambition, we have been boastfully arrogating to ourselves. Are

we to pursue the course sound policy dictates, and hold out the hand of friendship and aid to this nascent power, calculating on its final absorption into our Union, or are we to wound its susceptibilities and excite its resentment by contemptuously repelling the advances which it has made to us?[9]

Critical of Pierce's refusal to meet with Walker's minister plenipotentiary to the United States, Col. Parker H. French, and supportive of the American colonization of Nicaragua, the paper conjures the freebooter as a heroic figure, one who will fashion the backward republics of Central America into an alliance to rival the United States in power and influence. They cast Walker as an outward-looking and forward-thinking imperial self—able, they imagine, to affect the destiny of the hemisphere.

If the freebooter could not have asked for better press, the newspaper also offered a sketch of Walker's life that further celebrates him as an ideal of American imperial energy. In an April 12, 1856, article, "The Nicaraguan Question—Outbreak of Hostilities in Central America," *Leslie's* asserts that "General Walker is a fortunate man. Like all bold and adventurous spirits, he is as much favored by circumstances as he is assisted by his own energy and decision of character":

> The profit to which he turned the ridiculous blunders of General Pierce; the prompt and felicitous manner in which he cut the knot of the Mosquito protectorate difficulty, and the off-hand style in which he squared accounts with the Transit Company, all show that he is eminently fitted for the mission that he has undertaken. Whether the object that he is aiming at be, as his partisans contend, the regeneration of Central America, or a purely selfish one, it seems as if Providence was directing a concurrence of circumstances in his favor.[10]

A little less certain than Walker about his elect status, the journal still asserts the hand of God in the Tennessean's career, and they represent him as a military, political, and diplomatic natural; he turns every event to his advantage, reaches the right sorts of decisions with dispatch, and knows how to deal with his rivals. He knows what to do and acts with ease; although this is the imperial self that Richard Harding Davis will imagine in his romances, Harte shares some of the doubts and ambivalence alluded to in the sketch: was Walker trying to regenerate the isthmus, or was he just a monomaniacal petty tyrant?

Leslie's continued to champion Walker as the most daring of adventurers even after his expulsion from Nicaragua, but its New York rival, *Harper's Weekly*—the self-declared "Journal of Civilization"—took an increasingly ambivalent approach to the freebooter as his Nicaraguan adventure progressed. In one of its first articles about the filibuster, "Walker and Nicaragua" (Jan. 31, 1857), the journal offers a largely negative view of Walker, casting him both as something of a romance hero and as an agent of realpolitik:[11]

> About his adventures is nothing chivalrous, no mere knight errantry of any sort. They exchange the actual for the romantic; they deal in realities practical, commercial, and political; if the horrible crops out now and then, as in tragedy and breathless tale, it is of that substantial kind which appeals rather to compassion than to ideality. Throughout, however, we are obliged to recognize a persistence, an endurance, a resolute heroism, which merit a higher place in human esteem than can be ceded to all the slayers of Paynims, felon knights, and dragons in the realms of Faerydom, or in the chronicles thereof. The difference is merely that ours is a nineteenth-century hero.

Although the article dubs Walker a "hero," it suggests that theirs is a decidedly unheroic age; little splendor can be found in freebooting, and rather than being an ideal, exalted self, the American imperial self lives very much in the world and does what it takes to secure a kingdom or empire. The writer very nicely plays with references to romances in order to highlight the hard "realities" of the "practical, commercial, and political," and he ironizes Walker as an opportunistic mercenary: "Who knows how soon he may replace the laurel of the hero for the diadem of a king?"[12]

In many other articles, *Harper's* portrays the filibuster as inept, foolish, and doomed to failure, and after his death, an October 13, 1860, article, "The End of Walker," nicely sums up their largely negative yet somewhat ambivalent regard for "one of the most wrong-headed but bravest men of the age":

> No one regrets that he has received the merited penalty of his repeated infractions of law and sacrifices of life and property. He lived by the sword, and by the sword he had perished—as was fit. One may pity him, as one may pity any wrong-doer who is justly chastised; but no one can say, that, in his case, the chastisement was undeserved or inappropriate, or that the world would have been a gainer had he escaped his doom. Mankind and civilization acquiesce in his death.[13]

Rather than being a lord of the inward and outward empires, Walker appears as a rather pathetic figure of transgression. He was a mercenary, an illegal invader, and not a paragon of American civilization. *Harper's* sees Walker for what he was: a twisted, dogged, seemingly irrational pursuer of his own dreams of power and conquest, and rather than representing the best of American energies, he represents a grotesque outgrowth of imperial desire. The world, they assert, was better for his passing. Still, they admire his bravery and persistence, and one can detect a grudging tone of respect for his accomplishments. Only an absolutely self-confident man could conquer a nation with an original force of fifty-six men; he was brave (or mad) and, for a time, realized his dream of a pocket empire. Harte, more in company with *Harper's* than *Leslie's*, expresses a similar ambivalence toward Walker and his ideals and goals. Over time, the mercenary romance as a literary form would come to express profound doubts—many of the same doubts expressed in the first representations of Walker—about U.S. adventurism and about the American imperial self.

Harte and Benevolent Imperialism

Plot, plot, plot.

In the readings that follow, I approach Harte on his terms: he likes plot. He offers fair dialogue, though it clunks along at times, and he presents more than fair descriptions of his various Mexican and Central American settings. His delineations of Todos Santos, the Mexican outpost that serves as the primary setting of *Crusade*, work particularly well; we stand in the shore-bound fogs with his lovelorn pair, and we walk the surrounding deserts with them. He does not, however, dwell much on characterization and, for the most part, does not worry too much about the interior lives of his protagonists and antagonists. We do not enjoy complex interior monologues or highly wrought representations of consciousness and being. He does not excel at presenting the nuances of human motivation, and he does not offer sustained, overarching, or complex symbolic or metaphoric structures. He will not interject excursuses; he will not offer metaphysical musings on existence, nature, or the intricate flow and ebb of love and desire. What Harte offers is plot; his work presents many different characters and many different plots and subplots. He reifies his political concerns and critiques into bits of conversation and lots and lots of to-ings and fro-ings among his casts of adventurers, travelers, and would-be American imperial selves. So we greet Harte on his own terms, and sound his themes of the young imperial self and benevolent imperialism in terms of plot.

In "Peter Schroeder," Harte rewrites Walker's Nicaraguan venture in miniature (the story runs less than twenty pages) and portrays the imperial self as a fraud. Harte, at this point in his career, does not readily admire the freebooter, and he portrays "Mr. T. Barker Johnson," his Walker character, as a wily con man who defrauds his followers and then sends them on a doomed colonizing mission to Central America. After striking it rich in the Californian gold fields in the 1860s, Schroeder, rather than return to his native Germany, enlists in "the Army of the Potomac" and serves out the Civil War fighting for "those free institutions he admired so in theory." An ardent patriot and keen admirer of Lincoln and the ideals of the Republic, Schroeder nevertheless leaves the States after the war and resettles in his native Germany. Once there, he marries and falls into a life of respectable monotony. Many years later, Schroeder receives a visit from Johnson, the self-proclaimed "president" of "the Ometepe Confederacy"—a clear geographical reference to Nicaragua—who plays upon the German's republican beliefs.[14]

Just as Walker argued that he went to the isthmus to regenerate its civilization, Johnson tells Schroeder of a country in need:

> What if I told you of another country, Peter,—newer and fresher than the one you once adopted; where the soil is virgin and the people are plastic,— a country to be moulded and fashioned into shape by men like you; a country with no predilections, few traditions, and *no* history; a republic wanting only ideas, and capital; a country that you might become president of—*as I am?*

Falling victim to Johnson's presentation of the colonial trope, as David Spurr puts it, of "negation"—the Central American has no history, is a blank slate waiting for the imperial self to arrive, to be guided and endowed with a history and purpose—Schroeder signs over his fortune and begins a "colony" in Ometepe.[15] Within a month, the Ometepeans expel the filibuster and the colonialists; although Johnson (whom the narrator characterizes as "Mephistopheles") escapes, Schroeder stands by his principles and dies (as Walker did) before a firing squad. Once abroad, Schroeder becomes enmeshed in violence he cannot control and, like the real-world freebooters, meets a bad end.

At the same time that Harte captures the sheer improbability of Walker's conquest of Nicaragua, he condemns filibustering as a corrupt form of American engagement with Central America. Before Johnson conned an unsuspecting German American, he conned the armed forces of Ometepe. As one of the characters remarks,

> It *was* a big thing he did down there. All alone, too. Got a canoe, by gum! and pulled out to a ship's yawl, and sorter revolutionizes the crew; then he takes that crew to the ship and raises a mutiny in the ship, takes command of the ship, and calls himself Admiral of the Ometepe Navy, and summons a fort to surrender! And it surrenders—blank it all!—the whole garrison and the Ometepe army surrenders.[16]

In a few hyperbolic, comic lines—perhaps the most succinct satire of Walker's unlikely rise to power—Harte reveals filibustering as a grand fraud, the theft of a nation. This kind of theft, contrary to the values Schroeder represents, violates America's republican ideals of freedom and self-determination. Moreover, Johnson's scheming undoes the potential good that a principled, if naïve gentleman like Schroeder might do. For Harte, Walker's approach to Central America was distinctly un-American. As a confidence man, the imperial self cares only for his own profit, for his own aggrandizement, and if, in his first freebooting tale, Harte does not offer a particularly complex dissection of the American imperial self, in his next effort, he dives more deeply into the philosophies and desires of the young American.

Between "Schroeder" and *Crusade*, Harte softens his take on Walker. Where Johnson appears as an icy grifter, Leonidas Bolivar Perkins (the second Walker figure) emerges as a sophisticated, charming, and philosophic man of action. In fact, Harte seems to want his readers to admire Perkins's goals, even if he does not want us to admire his freebooting methods. This apparent change in Harte's view of Walker is not an easy matter to settle upon and has been a topic of some debate among critics and chroniclers. Davis, for example, perhaps confusing—as we shall see in chapter 3—his own considerable enthusiasm for Walker's exploits with Harte's, argues that Harte offered the filibuster as a "hero" in two of his tales. In "The 'Crusade' of a Nineteenth-Century Liberal," Margaret Duckett sees Perkins as a "revolutionary idealist" and as a "persistent champion of enslaved peoples" who nevertheless mistakes his own interests for the interests of those whom he would liberate. In contrast, Gary Scharnhorst reads Perkins as a "peripatetic adventurer" who would bring a "brand of iron-fisted tyranny" to Todos Santos.[17]

My own view is closer to Duckett's than to Scharnhorst's: Harte creates a kinder, gentler imperial self less bent on conquest and empire-building than Walker. Harte's reasons for moderating his position on the freebooter perhaps can be found in history: filibustering died with Walker. As Charles H. Brown writes, after Walker, "no leader emerged with a dream of glory of establishing a tropical empire at the head of a conquering force of Americans come to free a down-trodden people."[18] With freebooting safely in the past, Harte softens his view on Walker, exploiting the romantic glamor of filibustering while downplaying its violence. In the Tennessean, he has a great character and a great story, and he sets aside such matters as Walker's propensity for executions and the razing of Granada. History might play a part, but so might the demands of fiction: Harte may have wanted a more complex, less obviously criminal antagonist; he wanted, in *Crusade*, to think a little harder about freebooting than he did in the black-and-white tale of Peter Schroeder.

Just as Harte softens his take on Walker, we could say that, in general, he offers a rather mellow take on the American imperial self. Unlike Emerson or Walker, his characters do not experience sudden, empyrean visions that compel them to venture forth into the world. Their minds and souls do not, for the most part, burn with a sense of mission or of their own self-importance. They do not, with the exception of Perkins, ache to toss creation like a bauble. They do not pour forth impassioned speeches, do not attempt to reach with all their will into the minds and souls of others. They do not—once again with the possible exception of Perkins—hold great ideals, do not make wondrous claims about wanting to regenerate the civilizations of other nations. For the most part, they lack the intellectual and martial intensity of imperial selves such as Walker and Roosevelt. This is not to say, however, that they do not possess imperial ambitions or a sense of American superiority. And this is not to say that they do not possess a certain imperial eloquence or a certain degree of willpower. They may not want to toss creation, but Perkins wants to give it a good shake, and others at least want to give it a nudge now and then. This late in his career, Harte cannot conjure a hot Henry Hotspur on fire to go; rather, he offers easygoing versions of the imperial self. Despite the often mild tenor of the romance, however, Harte shows himself to be an astute critic of U.S. imperialism.

In *Crusade*, Harte perceptively identifies and critiques the contradictory impulses in American culture between beneficence and rapacity. Based in particular upon Walker's Sonoran campaign, the romance recognizes the United States' evolving pattern of interventionism abroad, and Harte, like Emerson, hoped that kindness would moderate power. As Duckett argues, Harte shows "critical concern for American civilization and the impact of this civilization on other civilizations."[19] In his effort to explore this impact, he opposes two forms of American engagement with its weaker neighbors with a third: filibustering and economic imperialism stand in opposition to capital expansion tempered by a progressive social agenda. Harte associates each form with different characters aboard the *Excelsior*, a barque bound from New York to San Francisco, and he places his hope in a pair of American lovers, Eleanor Keene and James Hurlstone. He represents the young Americans as philanthropic agents of civilization. Since Harte largely reifies his political analysis into plot, we must follow the various story lines to observe his exploration of the struggle between idealism and self-interest in U.S. culture.

He explores the first form of imperialism, filibustering, through Perkins's exploits.[20] Based in part on Walker—and, through more than just appellation, on Simón Bolívar, "The Liberator" of Venezuela, Colombia, Ecuador, and Peru from Spanish rule—Perkins attempts to free militarily "certain distressed patriots of Todos Santos," inhabitants of a sleepy, fog-enshrouded Mexican port. He has stranded his fellow American travelers in Todos Santos after commandeering the *Excelsior* for a military mission to South America. Soon after liberating "Quinquinambo," a confederacy of South American states, Perkins returns to Mexico to save the patriots "from the effete tyranny of the Church and its government."[21] Like Walker and many other advocates of Manifest Destiny, Perkins blames the poor conditions in Mexico on an ineffectual ruling class, and he lands an expeditionary force only to be betrayed by his local contacts, captured, and executed by firing squad. Like Walker, Perkins meets a violent end.

A would-be emperor, Perkins first looks inward for a vision of how the world should be, and although Harte does not give us much insight into that vision—or into the genesis of that vision—we can perhaps infer it from his statements and actions. Like Bolívar, he possesses a grand vision of a United Latin America, and while the conquest of Quinquinambo takes place off stage, Perkins clearly believes that the nations of South America need to be taken up and organized into an effective political, military, and economic unit. Most importantly, he sees himself as the man to lead such a massive and complex reorganization. He sees himself as a man destined to regenerate the civilizations of other countries, and he shares a bit of his vision with his American shipmates aboard the *Excelsior*. He wants, he suggests, to liberate the oppressed peoples of the region and lead them to a more perfect state; as he remarks, "a little assistance and encouragement from mankind generally would help them": "And think what a proud privilege to have contributed to such a result, to have assisted at the birth of the ideal American Republic, for such it would be—a Republic of one blood, one faith, one history."[22] He imagines a rather totalitarian utopia, but he seems to mean that he will help to create a New World republic even greater and more dedicated to the good of all than the United States. Perkins looks inward for a vision of the ideal state and then looks outward to realize that vision, but rather than championing Latin American self-determination, he believes in American beneficence, in his own ability to rule with magnanimity.

For the most part, Harte portrays Perkins as a charming and eloquent imperial self.[23] The freebooter fancies himself an expert on the problems of imperialism, and, like Walker and O'Sullivan, he relies upon imperial eloquence to persuade others of the rightness of his missions. While on board the *Excelsior*, for example, he explains the impact of European colonialism on "the aborigines of the New World" to his American companions: "The modern North American aborigine has not yet got beyond the tribal condition; mingled with Caucasian blood as he is in Mexico and Central America, he is perfectly capable of self-government." Nevertheless, the "aborigine" has never obtained self-rule because "he has always been oppressed and kept down by the colonists of the Latin races; he has been little better than a slave to his oppressor for the last two centuries."[24]

Perkins rehearses the racist and anti-European arguments of the era, and promises his fellow Americans that he does not seek his own fortune but rather "the deliverance of one of those oppressed nations" of South America: "Call me a citizen of the world, with a strong leniency toward young and struggling nationalities; a traveler, at home anywhere; a delighted observer of all things, as an admirer of brave men, the devoted slave of charming women—and you have, in one word, a passenger of the good ship *Excelsior*."[25] Harte presents Perkins as a sympathetic character—many of the Americans defend him even after he strands them in Mexico—and to achieve this he transforms Walker's unswerving determination to found his own empire into the gentlemanly pursuit of someone else's good. At the same time, even if Harte wishes us to laud Perkins's emancipatory rhetoric, he wants us to reject his methods: filibustering represents a too dramatic and violent intervention into the domestic affairs of less powerful nations.

Harte's portrayal of Perkins shows the romancer to be an astute reader of Walker's career: he analyzes why freebooting, even if undertaken with the best intentions, turns from liberation into conquest. As Perkins explains in the hours before his execution, "Politics and the science of self-government, although dealing with general principles, are apt to be defined by the individual limitations of the enthusiast. What is good for *himself* he too often deems is applicable to the general public, instead of wisely understanding that what is good for *them* must be good for himself."[26] Harte shows how beneficence and rapacity become entangled, shows how the contradictions in American culture cannot be so easily separated. On the one hand, he credits Perkins for possessing a genuine sense of altruism; on the other, he reveals that the processes of empire-building can corrupt even the most noble aspirations. *Crusade* envisions an American imperial self who acts upon his caprices, losing sight of the generous impulses that first set the colossus in motion. Harte suggests that the filibuster became enamored of his own military and political triumphs and thereby failed to accomplish what he set out to do: regenerate the civilization of the isthmus. In this early treatment of the Walker narrative, he offers a balanced, perceptive take on U.S. energies overseas and on the seemingly inevitable corruption of the imperial self. Just as with Walker, imperialism overruns Perkins and leads to his destruction.

In the second form of undesirable imperialism, a group of stranded American businessmen—to be backed, it turns out, by military force—set out to take over Todos Santos's resources and thereby enrich themselves. As in the case of filibustering, Harte points to the rapacity of the imperial self—the economic agents of empire, in this case—as the reason for his opposition. Unsure about the nature of events transpiring aboard the *Excelsior*, Mexican officers arrest Brace, Crosby, Banks, and Winslow. Quintessential entrepreneurs, the four quickly scout their "open air prison" for potential business opportunities. As Banks remarks, "I don't see why we can't be pretty comfortable here, and all the better for our being alone. I shall take the opportunity of looking around a bit. It strikes me that there are some resources in this country that might pay to develop." Always on the lookout for an advantage, they turn temporary captivity into an occasion to strike it rich. Once the appropriately named Banks gets the men focused, Crosby claims his stake: "And I shall have a look at that played-out mine. . . . If it's been worked as they work the land, they've left about as much in it as they've taken out." Brace, in turn, draws "a dull vermilion-colored stone from his pocket": "That's cinnabar—quicksilver ore—and a big per cent. of it too; and if there's as much of it here as the indications show, you could buy up all your *silver* mines in the country with it." As the narrator remarks, "The fact that they were in the hands of a hostile community—appeared but as trivial preliminaries to the new life that opened before them!"[27] Armed with Yankee drive, know-how, and abundant self-confidence, they intend to own Todos Santos, and as the novel progresses, Harte reveals their underlying avidity: not only do the businessmen think they work harder and smarter than people of color, some of them also conspire with local radicals and Perkins to overthrow the government of Todos Santos.

Like Walker during his Nicaraguan venture, they want to control the region's resources and labor. Winslow, a would-be freebooter, persuades a number of local discontents to join him in a revolution: "Either Todos Santos is in rebellion against the present Government of Mexico, or she is independent of any. Her present government, in any event, don't represent either the Republic of Mexico or the people of Todos Santos—don't you see? And in that case *we*'ve got as good a right here as any one."[28] Unlike Perkins, Winslow acts from a desire for wealth and power; he wants the mines and he wants to turn the local Mexicans and Indians into a subjugated workforce. He holds no ideals of regeneration or civilization or good government, and he believes only in profits and the American right to exert authority over more and more lands and peoples. Motivated by greed, Winslow and his supporters appear much worse than Perkins: they seek only their own good.

In the process of fashioning the basic plot and cast of the mercenary romance, Harte, in an interesting move, fragments Walker. On the one hand, we have in Perkins the violent yet intelligent freebooter who meets a bad end; we have a clear representation of the Tennessean. More interestingly, we also have, as the primary romantic protagonist, the often moody James Hurlstone. As with nearly all the heroes or antiheroes in the countless mercenary romances to follow, he ventures abroad after suffering traumas in his personal life. Estranged from his wife, he seeks asylum and anonymity in Todos Santos: "He thought of the crumbling barrier, that even in its ruin seemed to shut out, more completely than anything he had conceived, his bitter past, and the bitter world that recalled it. He thought of the long days to come, when, forgetting and forgotten, he might find a new life among these simple aliens, themselves forgotten by the world."[29] Harte takes up different elements of Walker's life—in this case, the freebooter's sense of being adrift following the death of his fiancée—and attaches them to different characters; in this way, he fragments the American imperial self and fashions him into more than one sort of character. Many of the cast resemble Walker in one way or another, and any of the characters may emerge, as a figurative descendant of the freebooter, as an imperial self. The heroes and antiheroes of the mercenary romance need not be only soldiers of fortune; they may also be entrepreneurs, engineers, or lovelorn young Americans.

As models of the right sort of young Americans, Harte offers Hurlstone and Keene. Once stranded in Todos Santos, Hurlstone becomes a force for good. To atone for his past life and to find fulfillment, he builds a schoolhouse *for the Indians* who live around the town. As Father Esteban remarks to some of the women stranded at the town, "But look you: my gentleman is not satisfied with [the old building], and wishes now to bring his flock to the Mission school, and have them mingle with the pure-blooded races on an equality. That is the revolutionary idea of this *sans culotte* reformer. . . . Ah, we shall yet have a revolution in Todos Santos unless you ladies take him in hand." The connection between a bitter past and redemption through service to Indians is particularly suggestive. The good imperial self addresses the sins of the past through his mission abroad, through a sensitivity to issues of race and culture; as we almost always find in tales of American imperialism, the protagonist brings forward traces of the Indian Wars. And, as Duckett points out, Harte concerned himself with native rights throughout his life: "His defense of the Indians of Humboldt Bay against brutalities of frontiersmen had cost him his job and almost his life at the very beginning of his writing career."[30] For Harte, the right sort of imperial self addresses the failure of the New World to create a fair and racially open society; Harte links the Walker narrative with this critique of American culture and hopes that beneficence will guide American actions abroad (if it is already too late at home).

Crusade demonstrates that the American imperial self need not be a conquistador or daring mercenary. The imperial self need not swing a sword or pack several firearms; rather, the imperial self can be the bearer of everyday prejudices backed by American self-assurance. Shortly after being stranded, Keene registers a sense of American superiority: "She could not resist the impression, which repeatedly obtruded upon her imagination, that the entire population of Todos Santos were a party of lost children, forgotten by their parents, and grown to man and womanhood in utter ignorance of the world."[31] Keene embodies the colonial attitude that the Mexicans—or Central Americans, or Africans, or Asians—are children that require American or Western guidance. These people, her thoughts suggest, need our help; we must uplift them or they will stay in a fog forever. Both Keene and Hurlstone—Harte's gentle young Americans—display paternalistic, and even maternalistic, attitudes toward their hosts. The imperial self recognizes its own preeminence and knows that Americans have a responsibility in the world.

If Harte condemns what he sees as truculent forms of imperialism, he somewhat reluctantly sees advantages to an American presence in Latin America. In the face of much more aggressive forms of intercession, the romance articulates what the right sort of American interventionism should be: business alongside beneficence. Through the school and other good acts, Hurlstone and Keene win the admiration of the clerical rulers of Todos Santos. As the tale progresses, Harte transforms them from lovelorn travelers into romance versions of Emerson's young Americans. They will help others, will lead, through mild beneficence, the leaders of their tiny corner of Mexico: after the failed revolution, the good-natured and passionate duo receive an invitation to remain in Todos Santos and take over the businesses started by the American conspirators.

As superior products of a superior culture, the couple successfully import American enterprise *and* social reform into Mexico: "Hurlstone and Miss Keene alone were invited to remain; but, on later representations, the council graciously included Richard Keene [Eleanor's brother] in the invitation, with the concession of the right to work the mines and control the ranches [Keene's brother] and Hurlstone had purchased from their proscribed countrymen." As the narrator goes on to remark, "Although the port of Todos Santos was henceforth open to all commerce, the firm of Hurlstone & Keene long retained the monopoly of trade, and was a recognized power of intelligent civilization and honest progress on the Pacific Coast." *Crusade* imagines a polite form of U.S. imperialism; as Gary Scharnhorst remarks, "The solution Harte envisions to the related problems of economic exploitation and social unrest is typically mild—benign modernization through commercial trade, a kind of Better Business code."[32] A mild anti-imperialist, Harte settles on this seemingly pro-imperialist ending as a means to acknowledge the economic and military facts of his day even as he might wish to reform them: U.S. economic exploitation of Mexico and Central America was already well under way when he wrote *Crusade*.

Even as Harte conjures a romantic, genteel world of tea-sipping, poetry-reading imperial selves, he keeps a half-closed eye on events transpiring abroad. And in almost every instance, U.S. military force was used to secure American economic interests.[33] In the 1850s, for example, U.S. firms constructed a transisthmian railroad in Panama, and the U.S. government furnished troops to protect it from attacks by Panamanian independence forces; in the same years, in addition to operating the isthmian Accessory Transit Company, Cornelius Vanderbilt began negotiations with both the English and American governments for the construction of a canal across Nicaragua. In 1852 U.S. Marines were landed in Buenos Aires, Argentina, to protect "American interests" during the revolution to overthrow the regime of Juan Manuel de Rosas. In 1853, as Ellen C. Collier writes, "U.S. forces landed [in Nicaragua] to protect American lives and interests during political disturbances." In the same year, Commodore Matthew Calbraith Perry began, through a show of force, the "opening of Japan"; on July 8 he sailed a squadron of four ships into Tokyo Bay with the purpose of opening Japanese ports to American trade, and he returned with an even larger force in February 1854 to ensure that the Japanese court would sign the trade treaty. Also in 1854, the U.S. Navy bombarded and burned San Juan del Norte, Nicaragua, "to avenge an insult to the American Minister to Nicaragua."[34] In Walker's decade of the 1850s, U.S. forces were also sent to China, the Fiji Islands, Uruguay, and Turkey.

Between 1860 and 1887, the year of *Crusade*, the number of interventions in support of U.S. economic interests continued unabated. In 1860 U.S. and British ships were deployed to Angola and Colombia. Over the next ten years, American forces also undertook missions to Japan, Mexico, Nicaragua, Formosa, and Uruguay, on each occasion extending U.S. influence and protecting American lives and property. Between 1865 and 1873, U.S. forces intervened in Panama three times to protect U.S. commercial ventures. In 1871 "a U.S. naval force attacked and captured five forts to punish natives [Koreans] for depredations on Americans, particularly for murdering the crew of the *General Sherman* and burning the schooner, and for later firing on other American small boats taking soundings up the Salee River." In 1874 U.S. forces were sent to Hawaii to "preserve order" and to "protect American lives and interests" during the coronation of David Kalakaua. In 1882 American Marines landed in Egypt "to protect American interests during warfare between British and Egyptians and looting of the city of Alexandria by Arabs." And in 1885, "U.S. forces were used to guard the valuables in transit over the Panama Railroad, and the safes and vaults of the company during revolutionary activity"; in the same year, the United States sent, in yet another act of "gunboat" diplomacy, the USS *Wachusett* to Guatemala to protect—in the parlance that persists to this day—"American lives and property."[35] As Franklin Pierce made clear when he refused to assist Walker, the right to intervene abroad belonged to Washington, and the White House and Congress, venturing well beyond the hemispheric limits set forth in the Monroe Doctrine (1823), acted dozens and dozens of times to safeguard U.S. assets and commercial interests.

Harte would have known about many of these interventions and about U.S. capital expansion into Mexico and Central America. In the 1870s Minor Keith built railroads and began accumulating banana plantations in Costa Rica; he eventually founded the Tropical Trading Company, which later merged with Boston Fruit to form the United Fruit Company. In 1880 the Mexican government granted U.S. railroad companies favorable concessions, beginning the nation's "railroad boom"; this infrastructure construction led, in turn, to U.S. domination of the Mexican mining (and, eventually, oil) industries. Between 1870 and 1880, Guatemala's coffee industry tripled its exports and the U.S.-owned Pacific Mail Steamship Company held, as George Black writes, "the monopoly on the transportation of Guatemalan exports." Pacific Mail, needless to say, became one of the most successful American enterprises in Central America. And, as Lester D. Langley and Thomas Schoonover note in *The Banana Men* (1995), American entrepreneurs—often supported by small mercenary armies—capitalized on the efforts of isthmian liberals to modernize and to develop their republics' economies:

> Foreigners took advantage of the new liberalized laws to build isolated centers of extraction, exploitation, and production, which are commonly called enclaves. Before World War II three products—bananas, coffee, and minerals—constituted the bulk of isthmian exports. In the 1880s Costa Rica had enclaves for bananas, Honduras for mining, and Guatemala for coffee. The banana and mining enclaves (located mostly near the Caribbean coast of Costa Rica and Honduras, where governmental authority had traditionally been weak) came under extensive foreign control.[36]

Harte's benevolent imperial selves in *Crusade* establish just such an economic enclave in their remote corner of Mexico, but they lack the ruthlessness and guns of later entrepreneurs such as Sam Zemurray and the Vaccaro brothers (about whom we shall say more in chapter 4). American businessmen pushed their way in Mexico and Central America and carved out pocket kingdoms of substantial value and safeguarded them with private armies.

The list of banana kings, enclaves, and military interventions in support of commercial enterprises could go on, but these few examples describe the form of economic imperialism supported by military power preferred by U.S. administrations after the Civil War. As Secretary of State James G. Blaine put it, the United States sought the "annexation of trade," not "the annexation of territory." This policy persisted throughout the later half of the nineteenth century, culminating in part in the Open Door Notes of

1899 and 1900. As William Appleman Williams asserts in *The Tragedy of American Diplomacy* (1972), fin de siècle debates over the "proper strategy and tactics" of U.S. expansionism included more than just imperialists and anti-imperialists: "The third group was a coalition of businessmen, intellectuals, and politicians who opposed traditional colonialism and advocated instead a policy of an open door through which American's preponderant economic strength would enter and dominate all underdeveloped areas of the world."[37] Harte, writing at a time when U.S.-built infrastructures were opening Mexico and Central America to the establishment of U.S.-owned agricultural and mining corporations, dramatizes what he sees as the excesses of filibustering and rapacious American economic imperialism. *Crusade* rewrites Walker's exploits as a means to tilt, however tentatively, against the pattern of U.S. capital expansion supported by U.S. military or paramilitary force. At the same time, Harte cannot turn his back on the facts—the United States would continue to exert its influence abroad—and the romance strives for a degree of optimism about American culture and assures its readers that there are better, more ennobling ways to engage lesser nations. Set against the sheer number and violence of U.S. economic and military ventures, however, his tale seems rather pale: the genteel Hurlstone and Keene do look much like the real-world agents of empire who often took what they could get, by force if necessary.

The Mercenary Romance

Harte is one of the pioneering figures in the American mercenary romance, and in *Crusade*, he establishes the basic plot and dramatis personae of this romance subgenre: adrift in his or her personal or professional life, a young American (or, in later tales, a not-so-young American) travels abroad in search of redemption or a turn of fortune and becomes caught up in a filibustering scheme, revolution, coup, civil war, counterinsurgency campaign, or some other form of catastrophic violence and upheaval. Remarkably, this describes the plot and character of any number of American novels set in Central America (or Mexico or Asia or Africa) from the 1870s to the present. Harte, in part, calls into being one of the ur-narratives of American imperialism and the imperial self; Davis will cement the paradigm in the culture, but Harte set the pattern that his fellow romancer—and countless writers since—would follow.

We can see this plot and these characters in work after work. Gore Vidal's *Dark Green, Bright Red* (1950)—to choose an American novel set in Central America almost at random—offers the standard narrative. The first line takes us to one of those Latin American countries run, Theodore Roosevelt once remarked, by "dagoes," and it confirms the old prejudice that Central Americans cannot govern themselves or maintain order: "On the day of Saint Rose of Lima the revolution began." Another saint's day, another revolution; perpetual cycles of disorder and violence. We soon learn that an American, Peter Nelson, numbers himself among the conspirators and that he has agreed to join the army of the revolution after "his court-martial and discharge from the American Army." A ruined career, a need to flee, to start again if possible. Nelson travels to the isthmus and joins a plot to topple a liberal, reformist regime because, as he realizes, "it was not as if he had a future."[38] The novel offers by now familiar ingredients: an American—a soldier, mercenary, filibuster, adventurer, spook, or simply a lost soul—adrift in his or her personal or professional life, travels abroad in search of redemption, power, or profit, but finds instead brutality and death. Abundant, tropical death. We can see this same plot in works as ideologically and artistically diverse as Paul Bowles's *Up above the World* (1966), Robert Stone's *Dog Soldiers* (1974) and *A Flag for Sunrise* (1981), Philip Caputo's *Horn of Africa* (1980), Barry Gifford's *Port Tropique* (1980), Cormac McCarthy's *Blood Meridian* (1985), Oliver Stone's *Salvador* (1986) and *Platoon* (1986), and countless other texts.

The mercenary romance, for a number of reasons, remains a favored literary vehicle for the exploration of the American imperial self. In the first place, the genre isolates the imperial urge in a limited number of characters. Where real-world imperialism requires the combined efforts of political leaders, bureaucrats, diplomats, soldiers, businessmen, and so on, a writer can focalize sundry forms of American ambition, idealism, and desire in one or two figures. The mercenary can be presented with clarity, and his beliefs and actions sounded at length; the writer can dive as deeply as he or she likes into the hero or antihero's inward and outward visions. In the second, the mercenary romance allows an author to present U.S. imperialism in a rather unadulterated fashion. The mercenary does not apologize for his ambitions or interventions, does not attempt complex rationalizations if his actions belie his stated ideals. In this way, the writer can lay bare—to whatever degree he or she wishes—not only the actions, desires, and arguments of the era dramatized but also, and more importantly, the actions, desires, and arguments of his or her own era: Harte or Davis or Teilhet or Houston may write about Walker and past events, but their narratives nevertheless can be read against their contemporary periods. They can be read as soundings of the arguments for and against interventionism in the 1870s or 1890s or 1950s or 1980s; they can be read as explorations of the violences of the fin de siècle, the Cold War, or the war in Vietnam. Third, at least in some examples of the genre, the figure of the mercenary creates a space for the reader to come up against the hard truths of imperialism without, perhaps, excessive discomfort. The soldier of fortune pursues his own visions and power; he is *not*-us, *not*-me, and so we can more readily distance ourselves from the events described. We come obliquely at the truths of necessity and empire. In other examples, we are more likely to be brought up, with a cheer, against the greatness of the nation and the American imperial self.

In the fourth place, the mercenary romance offers the usual pleasures of the romance—travel to distant realms, feats of bravery, beautiful women in need of assistance—but it also differs from the classic chivalric romance: where the romance traditionally focuses on the sacred and the magical, the mercenary romance focuses on the political. Both Harte and Davis, for example, offer romances less concerned with realms of enchantment or the Manichaean struggle between good and evil than with the political worlds to which their works stand in more or less fanciful relation. In their tales about the nascent American empire, they reformulate the tropes and concerns of traditional romances, turning away in large degree from religious, transcendent, or metaphysical themes and obsessions and toward decidedly secular and material issues. Their romances feature heroes and derring-do enough to satisfy their readers' desires for adventure and exotic locales, but even as they conjure exciting realms of intrigue, action, and *affaires de cœur*, they use the romance form as a means to explore and weigh the actual workings of U.S. overseas commerce and foreign policy. Their heroes fight not dragons but villainous generals and crooked politicians; they do not swing swords but put down coups and revolutions and bring the forces of "civilization" to the Caribbean, the isthmus, South America. Their characters journey to fog-enshrouded outposts or imaginary countries, but beneath these trappings dwell very real questions of American influence and prestige. Their works worry over economic and political power; they dramatize the ascendancy of young American mercenaries and entrepreneurs in Latin American countries; they examine threats to American ventures in the hemisphere and analyze the people and policies that work against U.S. interests.[39]

We can argue that the mercenary romance emerged as a favored vehicle for explorations of the American imperium and imperial self because the romance stands as one of the primary literary forms for the expression of desire. Northrop Frye—to reach back to the venerable Canadian theorist—argues in *Anatomy of Criticism* (1957) that the romance "is nearest of all literary forms to the wish-fulfilment dream."[40] At work in the years before the Spanish-American War, Harte and Davis can only imagine the American ascendancy; as romancers they dramatize the expansionist desires at play in U.S. culture between the era of Manifest Destiny and the era of the turn-of-the-century Spectacular Empire. For Harte, the wish or utopian fantasy is for a beneficent empire guided by liberal young Americans; for Davis, it's for a world ruled by dashing, rather ruthless young imperial selves. Where Frye claims that the romancer longs for the restoration of some previous golden age, for some prelapsarian state, both Harte and Davis look forward to an impending golden era of American power in the hemisphere. The romance, for them, stands as a perfect genre for imagining an imperium; if romances are dreams, then these early mercenary romances offer dreams of a great and far-flung empire.

Although the mercenary romance may serve as a means to satisfy the reader's desire for action, mystery, and exoticism, it also embodies some of the darkest currents in American culture—indeed, these desires and dark currents intertwine. The pleasures of the romance often depend upon some form of racism—we can cheer Indiana Jones outwitting the Nazis, but he also cracks his bullwhip at Arabs, Indians, and South American tribesmen and steals artifacts from all over the world—and in many of the romances based upon Walker, the romancers express a profound disdain, even hatred of people of color. Latin Americans, these works tell us, cannot govern themselves, cannot rise above bribery and corruption, cannot change leaders without violence, cannot run commercial enterprises, cannot separate church and state. These people—a deplorable mix, the writers often lament, of Europeans, Africans, and Indians—must be organized from above. The romances recirculate, supplement, foster, or—less often—decry the antagonisms and bigotries at work in the culture.

Not surprisingly, the imperial selves of romance most often trace their familial or martial lineages back to the Indian Wars or the African slave trade, or both. The father or the grandfather of the young hero may have fought Indians in the West, or the hero himself may have served in the cavalry or worked as a scout, or he may, as a boy, have idolized Indian fighters such as Daniel Boone, Davy Crockett, and Kit Carson. The West and westward expansion and all its attendant violences circulate in the hero's blood, and he cannot escape the forces and ghosts of the past. The hero may have been an Indian killer, or he or his family may have owned slaves. He may have served as a mercenary or a trader in Africa or the Middle East or in some even farther flung colonial outpost. He may have fought for—or, less often, against—the South in the Civil War. If it is in the blood to despise and kill Indians, it is also in the blood to despise and sometimes kill Africans, and these same hatreds extend beyond continental boundaries. The violences of nation-building, in other words, are the violences of empire-building; as Amy Kaplan puts it, we must understand "United States nation-building and empire-building as historically coterminous and mutually defining."[41] The Walker narratives once again reveal, from a variety of ideological perspectives, the devastating connections between race, nation, and empire in American history.[42]

Needless to say, perhaps, the mercenary romance recalls Richard Slotkin's paradigm of "regeneration through violence." In his classic study, he offers extended readings of John Filson's *The Discovery, Settlement, and Present State of Kentucke* (1784) and James Fenimore Cooper's Leather-Stocking tales (1823–41), and argues that Filson and Cooper—among many other writers and historians—embedded the narrative of regeneration through violence in American culture. Like Daniel Boone and Natty Bumppo, the heroes and antiheroes of the mercenary romance head for the frontier (wherever they may find it) in an effort to rehabilitate themselves and their fortunes. Unlike Cooper's narratives, however, the authors of mercenary romances tend not to work so diligently at burying imperialism and its processes beneath a rhetoric of personal purification. As Slotkin argues, in "the Boone-Bumppo myth," the hero's experiences lead to "moral truth":

> Through his trusting immersion he discovers truths about himself and his world that were hitherto hidden to him; his discriminations are now more just, less the result of habit. In solitude and isolation his acts of war and hunting awaken him to his kinship with creation, to a sense of reality and of religious and social duty. His heart is cleansed of evil impulses, and his reason is clarified, strengthened, more dominant over his passions.[43]

Where Bumppo appears as an almost Emersonian romance hero, as a figure burned clean through his contact with Nature and—contrary to the bard's deepest desires—violence, the hero of the mercenary romance does not go through the same process. Rather than awakening to a "kinship with creation" and "social duty," he awakens to kinship with power and profit. The mercenary romance hero does not inhabit nearly so exalted a plane; he does not reach new realms of reason or religious sensibility. If the tenor of the mercenary romance differs from that of the early, classic examples of Slotkin's paradigm, and if the mercenary romancers tend to present their material and ideological concerns a bit more baldly, the subgenre nevertheless belongs within the longer tradition Slotkin describes: Bumppo pursues—in *reverse* order and in Cooper's painfully broken-twig way—the inward empire through its outward corollary.

Finally, if we consider the form across time—and we must acknowledge that it has not been around that long—we can say that despite a few exceptions, the mercenary romance expresses ambivalence about and even contempt for imperialism and the American imperial self. Following the unchecked enthusiasm of Davis's *Soldiers of Fortune*, the mercenary romance becomes increasingly bleak and the imperial self less and less like Emerson's benevolent young American and more and more like a murderous freak or automaton. Rather than promising great adventure, the form promises sordid escapades undertaken for dubious or morally repugnant reasons; rather than descent into realms of enchantment or spirituality, it offers trips into political wastelands where corruption, greed, and murder predominate; rather than noble ideals, it foregrounds the thwarting of ideals; rather than heroes to hope for, it offers twisted conquistadors, drug addicts, burnt-out cases, or simply the lost; rather than the triumph of good or the achievement of majesty or decency or benevolence, it gives us savagery, rapacity, and death. Over time, the form ceases to laud American imperialism and the imperial self and begins to cast the empire and its agents as forces of violence and degradation. As a form, the mercenary romance comes to promise a bad trip and a bad end; the form, in other words, finds its spirit and tenor in Walker's life and death.

From Harte to Davis

Harte establishes the Walker narrative in American literature. Newspaper accounts of the freebooter's adventures furnished many of the ingredients and arguments for and against filibustering, but Harte transformed them into story form and, crucially, splintered the Tennessean into military and nonmilitary characters. After suffering defeats at home, the young American becomes caught up in revolutions and violence abroad, and while this tale persists to this day, from Harte we have a clear—and crucial—next step: Richard Harding Davis. As Davis remarks in "William Walker, the King of the Filibusters," he admired the freebooter and knew of Harte's treatments:

> In the days of gold in San Francisco among the "Forty-niners" William Walker was one of the most famous, picturesque and popular figures. Jack Oakhurst, gambler; Colonel Starbottle, duelist; Yuba Bill, stage-coach driver, were his contemporaries. Bret Harte was one of his keenest admirers, and in two of his stories, thinly disguised under a more appealing name, Walker is the hero.[44]

With the Mexican and Nicaraguan campaigns and Harte's tales knocking around in his head, Davis in turn produces the next, and perhaps most significant, rewrites of Walker's adventures, and further complicates and entrenches the mercenary romance in American culture.

So to Davis and the crucial next steps in the evolution of the mercenary romance as a means to explore American imperialism and the imperial self. But to read Davis, we also have to read Theodore Roosevelt, the fervent champion of empire and next important theorist of the American imperial self. As we shall see, Davis forever inscribes the story of William Walker into the story of Theodore Roosevelt, and in many, almost uncanny ways, we can see Roosevelt as Walker's bright and shining twin. They were both frail as boys, they both loved literary romances, they both turned to lives of adventure following the deaths of their beloveds, and they both wanted empires; but where Walker and his fellow freebooters acted without American sanction, Roosevelt had the backing of the nation and fulfilled many of the extraterritorial ambitions of Manifest Destiny. No account of the imperial self would be complete without a consideration of the Rough Rider and his adventures, writings, and connections to the twisted filibuster. From Walker, Emerson, and Harte, then, we turn to the journalism, travelogues, romances, and essays of what we will dub the "Spectacular Empire," or the phase in American imperialism where the United States sought not only the annexation of trade but of overseas properties as well.

CHAPTER THREE

The Spectacular Empire: Davis and Roosevelt

RICHARD HARDING DAVIS may be the preeminent rewriter of Walker's adventures. Working from *The War in Nicaragua* and Harte's two freebooting tales, he wrote perhaps the most famous of all Walker romances, *Soldiers of Fortune* (1897).[1] A best-seller the year it appeared, and boasting, as Davis's work often did, illustrations by Charles Dana Gibson, the novel found a receptive audience in a nation once more caught up in imperial furors and fantasies. An astute reader of his moment, Davis reached back to the freebooter in order to fire his readers' imaginations and expansionist desires, and he gave them what they wanted: a swashbuckling tale of American triumph and ascendancy. *Soldiers* not only secured Davis's fame and fortune, but it also achieved a great deal more that makes it perhaps the most important novel in this study: with this one book, Davis firmly embedded the mercenary romance in American culture, inscribed the story of William Walker within the much greater and much more celebrated story of Theodore Roosevelt, and did his small part to push the nation toward war with Spain.[2] Not bad for a writer as likely to be mocked as praised by his peers.

This chapter explores the historical and literary connections between three key figures in our study of the American imperial self—Walker, Davis, and Roosevelt—and the novelist serves as the link that binds the other two together. As a means to excite his readers' imperial passions, Davis rewrote Walker's adventures into a slick mercenary romance; he assured his readers that the United States would soon take its rightful place on the world stage. Like Harriet Beecher Stowe's *Uncle Tom's Cabin* (1852) or William J. Lederer and Eugene Burdick's *The Ugly American* (1958), *Soldiers* stands as one of those rare novels that had an impact on the political landscape of its day, and it helped to push the United States toward its venture in Cuba, Puerto Rico, and the Philippines. Remarkably, Walker, ever the ghost in the imperial machine, did his spectral best in the acquisition of overseas territories at the end of the nineteenth century. The romancer, via the freebooter, did his part to call the imperium into being, and Roosevelt, a much greater agent of empire than either Davis or Walker, gathered up the furious and multiple expansionist energies of his day and rode them to Las Guásimas and from there, following McKinley's death, into the White House. Through *Soldiers*, Davis literally etched the story of the freebooter into the much more magnificent legend-in-the-making of the twenty-sixth president of the United States. The intersection of these three key imperialists provides us with a number of crucial permutations and combinations through which to explore the evolution of the imperial self—in American literature and in the world—from the era of Manifest Destiny to the Spanish-American War.

In the first instance, Davis provides us with an occasion to examine the striking similarities between Walker and Roosevelt. As we shall see in more detail, they were remarkably alike: as boys, they both read widely in adventure romances; frail as boys, they aspired to martial adventures to prove themselves; after suffering profound losses in their private lives, they turned to the soldier's life; once set on their imperial and political courses, they could not be turned aside; and both seemed unable to accept the loss of power. Further, both imagined an ideal American imperial self, both wrote about this self, and both did their best to become that glorious, select being. Armed with visions of conquest and individual ascension, both sought empires. Roosevelt, however, triumphed where Walker could not, and we have his copious writings, roles, and exploits to examine for his projection of the imperial self.

Davis also points us to a joint consideration of Walker and Roosevelt for another crucial reason: when the romancer reached back to the freebooter, he did not merely hit upon a lucky bit of history for a good story; rather, he clearly understood the course of American imperialism in the latter half of the nineteenth century. Roosevelt accomplished what Walker could only dream of: where the freebooter raised an army and conquered Nicaragua, but lacked the resources to hold onto power, the Rough Rider raised an army, conquered the "Pearl of the Antilles," and had the resources to assert

U.S. military, political, and economic hegemony over Cuba, the Philippines, Panama, and the Dominican Republic.[3] Where Walker operated beyond the neutrality laws and lacked the support of the U.S. government, Roosevelt operated within the bounds of U.S. law and enjoyed—if not without dissent—widespread public and political support.[4] In less than fifty years, the ambitions of Walker and the freebooters became the policies of McKinley and Roosevelt: Davis could see that many of the extraterritorial desires of Manifest Destiny and the 1850s were about to be realized in the Spanish-American War and the 1890s.[5]

If the combination of Walker and Roosevelt reveals a great deal about American history and about the intersections between the personal and the historical in the calling into being of the imperial self, the combination of Davis and Roosevelt adds a crucial dimension to our analysis: the romancer and the Rough Rider foreground *performative* masculinity as a key feature of the imperial self. In the era of the Spanish-American War, few concerns were more urgent to such imperialists as Davis and Roosevelt, and few received as much attention in their writings. Both the reporter-novelist and the politician champion and model American imperial masculinity in their writings and public lives, but whereas Davis—at least in his first rewrite of Walker's adventures—has little doubt about American prowess, Roosevelt worries that American men might not be up to the task of building and sustaining an overseas empire. The American male may be too fainthearted, too effete; as he remarks in "The Strenuous Life" (1899), "We do not admire the man of timid peace": "These are the men who fear the strenuous life, who fear the only national life which is really worth leading. They believe in the cloistered life which saps the hardy virtues in a nation, as it saps them in the individual."[6] Roosevelt has no use for what he sees as "fearful" men, and he worries that these men of "timid peace" will undo the empire. Both Davis and Roosevelt confidently act out the attitudes and behaviors of what they see as the imperial self, as the sort of man capable of conquering foreign lands; like the filibuster, they play the roles of conquerors and agents of empire, and they avidly desired a mass audience for their performances. Most importantly, perhaps, anxiety over masculinity and the American imperial self becomes an increasingly central concern for retellers of Walker's exploits.

(Literary) Agent of Empire

Not everybody liked or admired Richard Harding Davis. In fact, some of his contemporaries could be scathing in their comments on his skills and reputation as a journalist and man of action. As Arthur Lubow recounts, in anticipation of hostilities between the United States and Spain, Davis decked himself out in "an elaborate war kit" and had his photograph taken: "The publication of the picture in the *Critic* provoked nationwide comment, mainly of amused derision. 'If he were cut up into small pieces,' jeered the *Springfield Republican*, 'he would furnish the insurgents with arms and equipments for a whole winter'; without doubt, 'there will be a terrific inkshed when he reaches the front.'" Theodore Roosevelt, in letters to friends, also had unkind things to say about Davis. After a heated public exchange between himself and Davis over "A Colonial Survival," an unflattering article on the "vulgar rich" that Roosevelt had published in *Cosmopolitan* (1892), the politician-turned-cowboy complained to James Brander Matthews that Davis "was so entirely unintelligent that it was a little difficult to argue with him."[7] In a later letter to Matthews, Roosevelt declared, "What an everlasting cad R. H. Davis is!"[8] Sensitive to the criticisms, jibes, and sometimes poor reviews that came to his attention, Davis nevertheless soldiered on, earning a fortune and seeing his image and byline plastered everywhere. He traveled around the world, reporting on wars and the adventures of the men he most admired, and he published over twenty books, including romances, "histories," travelogues, and collections of stories, plays, and essays. Still, as the editorialist for the *Republican* noted, he was a bit silly and overblown, and we might not want to take him too seriously but for the impact he made as an agent of empire.

For much of his career, Davis was *the* writer of the American empire; as an imperial self, he dedicated his considerable energies to the outward empire, and if we do not have a record of his inward visions—he does not provide, like Emerson or Walker, an account of an empyrean call to action—we can say that through his many writings he did what he could to call the imperium into being. In his journalism, travel writing, and fiction, he expresses many of the jingoistic sentiments already circulating through the nation in the years before the Spanish-American War and rehearses with glib ease many of the arguments deployed by foreign-policy agents in defense of U.S. military and economic intercession in Central America, the Caribbean, and the Pacific. Collectively, his works represent a massive intervention into American popular and political culture, a sustained—if neither systematic nor ideologically consistent—effort to reshape American attitudes toward expansionism. Like Roosevelt, Davis wanted the United States to take its place among the world powers, but whereas the former took up politics, pistols, and the pen to achieve his vision, the latter relied mostly on his prolific quill. In some unquantifiable measure, he used his work to help alter the course of U.S. history, and rather than denying the United States' already imperialist practices, he wanted Americans to embrace and celebrate the idea of empire-building. An intense, if sometimes risible agent of empire, he sought to do his part in rewriting the national narrative from one of (ostensible) anti-imperialism to pro-imperialism.

A journalist and novelist, Davis was ideally situated to disseminate imperialist attitudes. As a number of postcolonial and American studies critics have argued, novels and journalism play key roles in the fostering of empires. Literary forms help assimilate readers—both men and women—into the imperial project. In *Culture and Imperialism* (1993), for example, Edward Said asserts that "cultural forms like the novel . . . were immensely important in the formation of imperial attitudes, references, and experiences." He goes on to contend that "unless we can comprehend how the great European realistic novel accomplished one of its principal purposes—almost unnoticeably sustaining the society's consent in overseas expansion . . . we will misread both the culture's importance and its resonances in the empire, then and now."[9] As Amy Kaplan also argues, American romance novels (which often featured women characters as the chief spectators of masculine achievement) and newspaper accounts of U.S. expeditions abroad sought to integrate the domestic sphere into the creation of a U.S. empire. They did so "by positioning women in the role of the jingoist": "The presence of domestic viewers in the romance links these mass-marketed bestsellers to the strategic role of the mass-circulation newspapers in the culture of imperialism. By circulating imperial adventures into the American home, the novels incorporate domestic space into that imperial network, and work with the press, which, according to [Josiah] Strong [in *Our Country* (1886)], 'transforms the earth into an audience room.'"[10] Novels and newspapers, Said and Kaplan argue, do their part in naturalizing the idea of empire and in stirring or feeding the public's desire for imperialist expansion.[11] Davis, as one of the best-selling novelists and widely traveled and celebrated journalists of his day, did more than any other writer to call the American empire into being.

Davis's fame as a daring correspondent added glamor to his pro-expansionist positions. As Christopher P. Wilson contends, successful reporters like Davis "were mythologized as masculine, globe-trotting vagabonds":

> As a "soldier of fortune"—[Julian] Ralph called the correspondent a "knight of the pen" from our "free and enlightened land"—the reporter's worldly experience ostensibly baptized him as an American representative. Thus, when he pronounced on "civilized" conduct or drew the line between genuine revolution and merely lawless "banditry," he spoke *both* to American audiences and his own "foreign" interviewees themselves.[12]

The foreign correspondent served as an imperial agent, helping to define American interests and to explain those interests and responsibilities to the public. Moreover, when Davis observes that Central Americans "are the dogs in the manger among nations," he not only provides a rationale for U.S. interventionism in the isthmus but also lets any Central Americans who read his work know what a famous American thinks of them. When he remarks that "the Central-Americans are like a gang of semi-barbarians in a beautifully furnished house, of which they can understand neither its possibilities of comfort nor its use," he warns them (he hopes) that the United States will soon set them on a better path.[13] Davis, as Wilson suggests, cast himself as an agent of civilization, as a voice of the American ascendancy.

That the reporter and his peers were "mythologized as masculine, globe-trotting vagabonds" suggests the performative dimension of Davis's public life as an agent of empire: he dressed and acted the part of the masculine imperialist. As we have already noted, his peers liked to make fun of his adventure-wear, and in the years leading up to the Spanish-American War, Davis established the wardrobe of the reporter–as–imperial self. In *Three Gringos in Venezuela and Central America* (1896), for example, Davis and his two companions, Lloyd Griscom and H. Somers Somerset (who brought along his "servant," Charlewood), all adopted British-style pith helmets, complete with colored sashes, and wore them in many of their set-piece photographs. In one of the most famous, the three gringos look dapper in their helmets, suits, and bow ties as they pose on the front of a small steam engine. Men of the world, the image tells us, they are ready for anything, and they will look good doing it. Too, the image tells us that these, indeed, are men: real men live lives of adventure and daring and will not be constrained by the life of the home and routine. Be like us, it suggests, if you can or if you dare.

In the oft-derided photo of the adventurer in his Cuban war kit, Davis once more strikes the manly pose: resting (in a studio) against a tree stump, one leg raised on a second stump, he wears tall leather boots, boasts a pistol holster on his belt and binoculars around his neck (and the binocular case on another strap also around his neck), and above one pocket on the front of his jacket appears a band of material that suggests combat ribbons. He looks like a mock-nostalgic, pastiche ad for one of our contemporary adventure clothing catalogs. Nevertheless, however silly Davis may be, he plays the part of the rugged, albeit slickly coiffed reporter-imperialist, and just as he did in his early days as a journalist—where he would dress up as a thief to "infiltrate" street gangs—he consciously constructs a persona and look. This, he suggests, is how real men should dress, and then they should act like me: go to the front, get the story, stand side by side with soldiers, and, when one of them falls, grab his weapon and start firing. For Davis, masculinity constitutes performance, not some essential core of his being.

The construction of a masculinist persona can also be seen in Davis's willingness to sit as the model for the male escort to the Gibson girl. He allowed himself to be cast as the *beau idéal* in images circulated throughout the country. As Charles H. Brown recounts in *The Correspondents' War* (1967),

> The artist Charles Dana Gibson chose Davis as the model for his male counterpart of the all-American sweetheart of the period—the high-pompadoured, clear-featured, swan-necked Gibson girl. The clean-cut, firm-jawed Gibson man was a somewhat romanticized version of Davis, who actually was rather heavy featured and solidly built—but no matter, he was the dream-hero of the sighing damsels of the time and exuded golden splendor wherever he went.[14]

As with Wilson's language, Brown's suggests the constructed nature of Davis as the agent of empire and masculine prowess. In the cultivation of his image and role, he becomes "the dream-hero of the sighing damsels"; he becomes a romance hero, an icon of adventure, and in addition to placing him in the company of the Gibson girl, the artist also drew a number of pictures of the Davis figure in exotic and dangerous locales. Masculinity became a matter for circulation and consumption, a matter of image and performance; Davis modeled manliness for his generation, and for a time, he was the best show around. However daring he may have been as a war correspondent and adventurer—and we have already seen that he was not quite as bold as Walker—he was one of the most popular performers of gender in the fin de siècle.

Before turning to *Soldiers*, if we look, briefly, at Davis's nonfiction in order to establish his themes, we can see his vision of the American empire; the imperial self, he suggests, must instruct his readers on the desirability and requisite nature of a more forceful U.S. presence abroad.[15] In his pre-turn-of-the-century journalism and travel writing, in particular, he argues for U.S. intervention in the Caribbean and Central America. A correspondent for the *New York Herald*, the *Times* (London), and numerous magazines, Davis journeyed throughout the Caribbean and Latin America, and he covered both the Spanish war in Cuba and the Spanish-American War. He collected many of his articles into books such as *Three Gringos, Cuba in War Time* (1897), *A Year from a Reporter's Notebook* (1898), and *The Cuban and Porto Rican Campaigns* (1898). In these works, he points out the political and economic failings of non-Americans, and he suggests that the peoples of the Caribbean basin could benefit from American guidance; more importantly, he argues that the United States should take its place among the world's powers.

Davis, like Roosevelt, valorizes U.S. interventionism and sees it as a rather hard-edged but nevertheless necessary elaboration of American ideals. In his travelogue *Three Gringos in Venezuela and Central America* (1896), for example, along with standard travelogue vignettes about the people he and his companions met, the means by which they traveled, and the curious customs of the "natives," he argues that Central Americans require instruction in the proper workings of democracy. They need, in other words, American guidance:

> The Central-American cannot understand that when a bad man is elected to office legally it is better in the long-run that he should serve out his full term than that a better man should drive him out and defy the constitution. If he could be brought to comprehend that when the constitution says the president must serve four years that means four years, and not merely until some one is strong enough to overthrow him, it might make him more careful as to whom he elected to office in the first place. But the value of stability in government is something they cannot be made to understand.[16]

Davis speaks as if to a child, and he portrays the isthmians as petulant children, as beings incapable of reasoning. Replete with condescension and finger-wagging—(1) do not elect the "bad man" and (2) try to understand what I am telling you—he instructs both his readers and the isthmians on the failings of Central America. As an imperial self, he knows he knows better than others about the proper workings of the world. He possesses a clear vision of how the world should be, and he knows who should run it.

He goes on, in one of his most infamous passages, to contend that "the Central-American citizen is no more fit for a republican form of government than he is for an arctic expedition, and what he needs is to have a protectorate established over him, either by the United States or by another power; it does not matter which, so long as it leaves the Nicaragua Canal in our hands."[17] Recirculating well-worn notions of the "white man's burden"—even if Rudyard Kipling's infamous poem would not appear until 1899, the ideas were deeply entrenched in European imperialist culture—Davis suggests, most importantly, that the isthmians need someone to manage not only their political but their economic affairs as well. However deeply Davis believes, as we shall see, in the exercise of masculine power as a counterforce to materialism and political enervation, matters of commerce nevertheless underlie many of his early pronouncements. If the United States does not colonize the isthmus, it should at least control—and thereby profit from—the movement of material and people.

Davis did not, of course, invent the arguments in favor of economic imperialism. His assertions echo arguments set forth as early as 1847. In an unsigned article in the *United States Magazine and Democratic Review*, for example, the editorialist argues that U.S. forces should occupy, but not annex, Mexico and start the long process of "regenerating" the Mexicans:

> Great is our reverence for the people at large, and respectful as all ought to be to their opinions, we may look in vain among the populace of the Mexican states, for that activity of intellect and vigilant intelligence necessary to those who would govern themselves. A people who are too proverbially indolent to pursue industrial employments, and too dishonestly envious to permit others to enjoy the fruit of their own industry, would make unprofitable and dangerous inmates of our political family. A long course of probation is necessary so to regenerate them in their habits and views, as to make them worthy of self-government.[18]

We once again see the naturalizing language of regeneration, and Davis's work stands firmly in this decades-old imperialist discourse. As always, the Latin American is corrupt, lazy, does not understand government, and would, if he or she could, steal from Americans. Just below these words lingers an unsaid but seemingly always present belief: unlike Euro-Americans, people with darker skins are not quite human. Davis reveals, yet again, the deep and vicious racist currents running through the nineteenth-century imperial self.

In *Cuba in War Time* (1897), Davis, ever the hardworking agent of empire, offers a different series of arguments for U.S. interventionism, this time circulating around the idea of American hemispheric dominance. As one of William Randolph Hearst's *New York Journal* reporters in Cuba covering the struggle for liberation from Spain, he recounts that although he was originally opposed to U.S. involvement in the war, he witnessed events that changed his mind. The United States, he contends, should intercede:

> We have been too considerate, too fearful that as a younger nation, we should appear to disregard the laws laid down by older nations. We have tolerated what no European power would have tolerated; we have been patient with men who have put back the hand of time for centuries, who lie to our representatives daily, who butcher innocent people, who gamble with the lives of their own soldiers in order to gain a few more stars and an extra stripe, who send American property to the air in flames and murder American prisoners.[19]

This passage merits some unpacking. First, he suggests—in the spirit of the Monroe Doctrine—that the United States can compete with the European colonial powers, that it should do so, and that it will not be a player in the hemisphere until it exercises its strength. Next, in the process of portraying the Spanish as deceitful and corrupt, he implies that while they have prevented the democratization of this part of the New World, the United States will bring Cuba out of the colonial era, or the United States will at least bring Cuba into its more enlightened sphere. In his last remarks, he also provides the oft-repeated rationale for the dozens and dozens of U.S. interventions that preceded the mission to Cuba: to protect American lives and property. For all these reasons, he suggests, the United States should go to war with Spain, but he seems less concerned about the well-being or aspirations of the Cubans than he does about American power.[20]

In his coverage of the Spanish-American War, *The Cuban and Porto Rican Campaigns*, Davis makes clear his belief that, having arrived in Puerto Rico, the United States should stay for the benefit of all: "Peace came with Porto Rico occupied by our troops and with the Porto Ricans blessing our flags, which must never leave the island."[21] He calls for the sustained construction of an American overseas empire; with Cuba and Puerto Rico will come the Philippines and other territories. Throughout his travelogues and collected articles, Davis presents different arguments for the same thing: an American imperium. If he called for these things in his nonfiction, he imagined them most fully, and most confidently, in his popular swashbuckling fiction. In perhaps the most famous of all mercenary romances, he imagines a young American descendant of William Walker calling into being, once and for all, the American empire.

Soldiers of Fortune

Although *Soldiers* is ostensibly set in South America, the American public, increasingly caught up in the Cuban struggle against Spain, could not help but make connections between the events in the novel and the war in Cuba.[22] The tale imagines that the young American can interpose himself into the political affairs of a Latin American country. Once involved, he can easily straighten matters out even as he protects, first and foremost, U.S. interests. A fantasy of American power, the mercenary romance presents a picture of the American imperial self—the swashbuckler, the handsome man, the restorer of nations—that readers readily seized upon: *Soldiers* became the third best-selling novel of the year behind Henryk Sienkiewicz's *Quo Vadis*, a story of early Christians, and James Lane Allen's *The Choir Invisible*, a historical romance.[23] Davis promised his readers that Americans could, if they allowed themselves the opportunity, triumph overseas. Moreover, they would look good doing it. The novelist, picking up on jingoistic cultural currents, told his readers what they wanted to hear.

Since *Soldiers* is not widely read these days, a brief summary may be in order. Mercifully, Davis is not so painfully plot bound as Harte; he keeps his fiction lean and brisk. Part romance, part novel of manners, the tale follows the adventures of Robert Clay, an American engineer and former mercenary, who journeys to "Olancho," a South American republic on the Caribbean, to operate the Valencia Mining Company. Once in Olancho, Clay runs the iron ore mine—owned by Andrew Langham, an American entrepreneur—efficiently and profitably. Just as Langham and his daughters arrive in Olancho to inspect the mine and to take advantage of the climate, Clay becomes embroiled in a coup d'état orchestrated by General Mendoza, the leader of the opposition in the Senate. In order to protect the mine, Clay organizes his workers into a countercoup and thwarts Mendoza's power play. Along the way, the hero falls in love with Hope, Langham's youngest daughter; rather than remain in Olancho as its "military President"—a post junior officers in the Olanchoan army offer to him—he returns to New York in order to marry Hope and to embark upon a career as an engineering consultant. Like Harte, Davis offers a romance version of Emerson's Young American as his hero of empire.

In many ways, *Soldiers* betrays a curious, Oedipal anxiety of influence. Instead of writing back against his literary fathers, however, Davis writes back against perhaps the most important figure in his life: his mother. In particular, the romance can be read as a rewriting of Rebecca Harding Davis's *Life in the Iron Mills* (1861). In *Life*, a novella famously recovered through the work of Tillie Olsen and the Feminist Press, Rebecca describes the squalid, polluted, harsh lives of immigrants and laborers in a Virginia mill town (an industrial wasteland that recalls Coketown in Dickens's *Hard Times* [1854]). A masterpiece of early American realism and naturalism, the tale recounts the lives of Hugh Wolfe and his cousin, Deb. Hugh, a primitive yet gifted artist, sculpts powerful statues from *korl*, a waste product of the iron mills. Deb, a grotesque whose body and spirit have been broken by poverty and crushing labor, works long hours in a cotton mill and attempts to care for Hugh, whom she loves. In an effort to elevate Hugh from the blackness of the mill, Deb steals a wallet from Mitchell, a wealthy visitor and friend of the mill owner's son, Kirby. After a dark night of the soul during which he agonizes over returning the wallet, Hugh is arrested and later commits suicide in prison. Deb, given a lesser sentence, joins a Quaker community once released. Thick with smoke and ash, *Life* offers a dystopic portrait of America; the New World has turned out not to be the New Eden but rather a Dantesque world of suffering and grime.

Richard, then, rewrites his mother's most famous work in order to reclaim the promise and romance of the New World.[24] Just as in *Life*, Davis centers his story around iron, an emblem of industrial capitalism. Beyond this basic similarity, however, he implicitly inverts or rejects his mother's protonaturalist critique of big business. Where Rebecca presents Kirby as a heartless capitalist, for example, Richard offers Langham as a relatively decent businessman who does what he can for his workers while leaving most of the details to Clay. In *Life*, as Kirby and his guests, Dr. May and Mitchell, wait for the rain to let up so they can leave the mill, they engage in a conversation about who is responsible for the lives and suffering of the workers. As they regard the grasping, disturbing korl statue, each absolves himself of any responsibility for the uplift or upkeep of Hugh and his fellow laborers. Kirby, the voice of capitalism and social Darwinism, states his position bluntly: "*Ce n'est pas mon affaire*. I have no fancy for nursing infant geniuses. I suppose there are some stray gleams of mind and soul among these wretches. The Lord will take care of his own; or else they can work out their own salvation. I have heard you call our American system a ladder which any man can scale." The industrialist sees the men as brutes, as subhumans who lack intelligence or a spiritual nature, and he quickly dismisses any suggestion that big business should take better care of the underclasses. "If I had the making of men," he continues, "these men who do the lowest part of the world's work should be machines,—nothing more,—hands. It would be kindness. God help them!"[25] Sounding not unlike Marx and Engels, Rebecca Harding Davis portrays capitalism as a heartless and dehumanizing mode of production, and she leaves little doubt about where she stands: men like Kirby have a responsibility whether they think so or not.

In comparison, Langham seems considerably less vicious and perhaps a little more concerned about the living and working conditions of his labor force. Before he and his daughters arrive to inspect the mine, Clay and his subordinates make an effort to spruce up the workers' village and to make themselves as presentable as possible:

> Their coming was a great event in the history of the mines. Kirkland, the foreman, and Chapman, who handled the dynamite, Weimer, the Consul, and the native doctor, who cared for the fever-stricken and the casualties, were all at the station to meet them in the whitest of white duck and with a bunch of ponies to carry them on their tour of inspection, and the village of mud-cabins and zinc-huts that stood clear of the bare sun-baked earth on whitewashed wooden piles was as clean as Clay's hundred policemen could sweep it.[26]

Clay, Davis makes clear, operates a sizable police force in order to maintain control over the mine, but he at least provides rudimentary housing and medical care for the workers and their families. Where Kirby expresses loathing for his men, Langham appears not to want his to live in absolute squalor and degradation. Moreover, the miners use the latest technology and follow Clay's carefully orchestrated procedures. In contrast to his mother's trenchant critique of industrialization and the exploitation of labor, Davis offers a relatively benign view of American capitalism, assuring his readers that the locals are much better off working for a U.S. firm than they would be if left to their own initiatives. Big business, he suggests, is not the body-, mind-, and soul-killing thing his mother described. He answers her charge that the promise of the New World, the New Eden, has been thrown aside for profit with a tale of commercial and military triumph that suggests the Americas have only just begun to yield their riches to the United States.

If Davis rewrites his mother's representations of industrialization, he also rewrites her tale of unrequited love among the lower classes into a story of upper-class adventure and passion. Deb, we soon learn, loves Hugh, but knows that he will never love her or her twisted and broken body: "She knew, in spite of all his kindness, that there was that in her face and form which made him loathe the sight of her." As if to torture herself, she thinks of herself as hopelessly ugly to his artist's eye: "She knew, that, down under all the vileness and coarseness of his life, there was a groping passion for whatever was beautiful and pure,—that his soul sickened with disgust at her deformity, even when his words were kindest." Love cannot come into being in such a polluted and dank environment, Davis suggests, and just as a life of unceasing labor and pain has worked to thwart Deb's desires, it has done the same to Hugh. Not only does he long to be a sculptor and to be free of a life of grime and toil, but he has feelings for Janey, a young girl who sometimes stays with him, Deb, and his father whenever her father goes to "the stone house." After Kirby, May, and Mitchell leave the mill, Hugh realizes the futility of his existence, and his vague hopes for a life with Janey disintegrate: "A hope, trifling, perhaps, but very dear, had died just then out of the poor puddler's life, as he looked down at the sleeping, innocent girl,—some plan for the future, in which she had borne a part. He gave it up that moment, then and forever."[27] Neither love nor life has any chance in the world of industrial squalor, and neither Hugh nor Deb achieve the family and passion they long for. Industrial capitalism has made life impossible for the starving, suffering classes.

Davis, once more rewriting his mother's narrative, offers a tale of love triumphant among the elite. Not only do Clay and Hope Langham fall in love and become engaged, but along the way they battle the Mendoza forces and Hope saves Clay's life. Where Deb desperately attempts to save Hugh from a life of torment and frustration by stealing Mitchell's wallet, Hope risks her life to rescue Clay, MacWilliams, and Ted, her wounded brother. Pinned down by enemy fire, the men—in true adventure-romance fashion—seem doomed, until salvation emerges from the darkness: "They saw the carriage plunging out of the shadow of the woods and the horses galloping toward them down the beach. MacWilliams gave a cheer of welcome. 'Hurrah!' he shouted, 'it's José coming for us.'" Clay—Davis's imperial self must be greater than other men in all regards, including eyesight—sees that, in fact, José does not drive the carriage: "Good God! It's Hope." Whereas Deb's efforts hasten Hugh's demise, Hope participates in the action, and the escape from death leaves both Clay and Hope in an excited state: "He stooped lower and kissed her, and his lips told her what they could not speak—and they were quite alone."[28] If part of the difference between Rebecca's and Richard's stories rests in class considerations and genre—where the protagonists of naturalist fictions often meet a bad end, the stars of a romance, like those in a comedy, often end up engaged or married—Davis seems, whether consciously or not,[29] to upend his mother's work in as many ways as he can.

Most importantly, perhaps, to vivify his masculinist ethos, Davis constructs Clay as Hugh's opposite. As Olsen and others have noted, Rebecca feminizes Hugh, providing a stark contrast to the groping, muscled figure of the statue; the puddler-sculptor possesses neither physical strength nor good looks, and he certainly does not have the intellectual or cultural means to elevate himself from his life of unceasing labor. Worn away by poverty, pollution, poisoned liquor, and a lack of healthy food and clean water (and education and spiritual sustenance), Hugh looks, to Deb and his coworkers, to be less than the other men. He looks, they think, like a woman: "Physically, Nature had promised the man but little. He had already lost the strength and instinct vigor of a man, his muscles were thin, his nerves weak, his face (a meek, woman's face) haggard, yellow with consumption. In the mill he was known as one of the girl-men: 'Molly Wolfe' was his *sobriquet*." Small and thin and possessing a "finer nature" than the other men, he endures taunts and isolation, and though he will fight, he is "always thrashed, pommelled to a jelly."[30] Hugh falls well short, seemingly, of a masculine ideal of size and strength and pugilistic skill. Worst of all, he cannot achieve any measure of success; he carves his statues—in itself, at least in the economy of the mill workers, an unmasculine pursuit—only to destroy them in fits of anguish and anger at his lot.

In contrast, Clay appears as the perfect masculine being. He has strength, a handsome profile, and, most importantly, he gets the job done; these constitute, for Davis, the chief qualities of the American imperial self. When Clay first takes the stage, Davis describes him as a typical romance hero: "He was a tall, broad-shouldered youth, with a handsome face, tanned and dyed, either by the sun or by exposure to the wind, to a deep ruddy brown, which contrasted strangely with his yellow hair and mustache, and with the pallor of the other faces about him." Clay is everything Hugh is not: muscular, substantial, and attractive.[31] The dinner-party guests refer covertly to him as "the cowboy," and he has, we learn later, lived a life of adventure in the great outdoors. Whereas Hugh is pale and stained with dirt and pollutants, Clay has been tanned by the sun in some far-off, exotic locale. At ease among the elite of society and possessing "the frank, quick look of the trained observer" of—we can assume—women, men, and any given situation, he quickly emerges as the sort who can handle himself and others. He has the confidence, his bearing suggests, of a man who achieves his goals and does not accept fear or defeat. Everyone else around him looks pale and effete, and he unsettles the other guests with his self-possession and charisma. Alice Langham, the narrator tells us, "felt annoyed with herself and with her friends, and resented the attitude which the new-comer assumed toward them."[32] A man's man and a woman's man, Clay sets the masculine standard; he represents, for Davis, the ideal young American self. The romancer does not want anything to do with his mother's weakling artist. We soon learn, however, that Clay could have turned out like Hugh.

Like Harte, Davis offers a representation of the imperial self who sets out on a life of adventure only after suffering traumas in his personal life. The desire to assert the self, the romancers suggest, requires a dramatic, if often painful liberation from mundane or ordinary existence. To be great, to toss creation like a bauble, the self must break free from the world and its spirit-dulling routines and expectations. Clay, in a moment of contemplation, thinks back to his childhood and to his early days as an adventurer:

> Clay's mind went back to the days when he was a boy, when his father was absent fighting for a lost cause; when his mother taught in a little schoolhouse under the shadow of Pike's Peak, and when Kit Carson was his hero. He thought of the poverty of those days—poverty so mean and hopeless that it was almost something to feel shame for; of the days that followed when, an orphan and without a home, he had sailed away from New Orleans to the Cape. How the mind of the mathematician, which he had inherited from the Boston schoolmistress, had been swayed by the spirit of the father, and which led him from the mines of South Africa to little wars in Madagascar, Egypt, and Algiers.[33]

A lost father, poverty, shame, orphaned; these experiences harden the young man, make him fearless; adrift and in desperate straits, he turns to a life of travel and adventure. He does not give in to poverty and its tolls; he will not be crushed and die an ignoble death like Hugh. Rather, he explores continents, becomes a mercenary, sees the great and exotic countries and cities of Africa. The sorrowful experiences of youth prepare him for any challenge, and he can work in a mine and kill a man, if necessary. In fanciful, romantic terms, we have in Clay the masculine imperial self, the storybook equivalent, as we shall see later, of Roosevelt's young Americans.

In this passage, Davis also cements many of the key elements of the mercenary romance. We have, in the first place, the archetypal hero: the young American, at a loss, leaves the United States in order to reclaim a sense of self and to earn his fortune. In the second, we have the plot: once abroad, and already hardened by life, the young hero becomes caught up in violence, colonial actions, coups and countercoups. In the third, we have the setting: the African or Central or South American republic—any impoverished, jungle or desert nation will do—appears as a wasteland of political, military, and economic corruption, and it clearly needs the help of the imperial self. Just as Davis argues in his nonfiction, these corrupt and ineffectual people need our guidance; despite the riches of their lands, they can do nothing well, and we must do it for them and for ourselves. The plot, characters, and setting recall Harte's *Crusade*, but Davis dresses it up much more smartly; a more adept romancer, he brings a high sheen to the basic tale, and offers up an abundance of romance thrills and pleasures. And, in this hugely popular novel, Davis embeds the mercenary romance in the culture; we can see the same elements in any number of later works set in Central America, Africa, and, eventually, Southeast Asia. Most importantly, Davis establishes the genre as one of the favored literary forms for exploring the desires and history of U.S. imperialism; he establishes it as perhaps the favored literary form for the exploration of the American imperial self.

This passage further reveals what we already knew we would find: as always, the figure of the imperial self abroad contains traces of the Indian Wars and the slave trade. Clay revered Kit Carson,[34] a famous hunter, guide, and Indian-killer. Once more, the metaphysics of Indian-hating operate in the text, and we see again the connections between continental expansionism and overseas adventurism. As Richard Drinnon argues, the scout becomes the outrider of empire. Clay's journeys to South Africa, Madagascar, Egypt, and Algiers not only evoke the pervasive slave trade in Africa—in his crisscrosses over the continent, he no doubt would have come into contact with some part of the trade—but, just as importantly, place his adventures in a colonial context. He moves through a world of intense racial hatreds and prejudices, and though he does not tell us explicitly what sides he fought on, we could wager that he stood with one or more of the colonizers and not the colonized. As a man of empire, as someone steeped in European practices, Clay brings what he learned in Africa back to the Americas. His attitudes toward, and his strategies for containing, the indigenous population of Olancho arise in part from colonialism, and he brings it all into the service of U.S. interests. As always, the old wars and racial hatreds resurface in representations of the American imperial self.

Davis, following Harte, bases Clay's adventures in part on Walker's exploits. If he never left behind a letter or notebook identifying the freebooter as a source for his narrative, we can still assert with some confidence that he had the Tennessean in mind. We know, for example, that he read Harte's Walker tales, and in *Macklin*, the novel that followed *Soldiers*, he explicitly bases the action on the freebooter's Nicaraguan campaign. Some of the characters in *Macklin*, we learn from the narrator, served with Walker in Nicaragua, and just as the Nicaraguans, the U.S. government, and his own forces "betrayed" Walker, the Guatemalans and one of Macklin's fellow officers "betray" the mercenary army. If Davis certainly bases *Macklin* on Walker's campaigns, he also celebrates Walker in *Three Gringos* and again in "William Walker, the King of the Filibusters," a chapter from *Real Soldiers of Fortune* (1906), a nonfiction book on mercenaries. In "William Walker," he quotes from *The War in Nicaragua*, offers a detailed account of the freebooter's career, and speculates on Walker's motivations and aspirations. Davis clearly knew as much about Walker as any of his contemporaries, and the various treatments suggest an abiding interest. Most importantly, *Soldiers* also supplies evidence to confirm the tale as based upon the long-dead hero of Manifest Destiny.

The filibuster figures as a ghost in *Soldiers* in at least two ways. For one, Davis links Clay to Walker through an absent father "fighting for a lost cause." As a tearful Clay explains to his love interest, "My father, Miss Hope . . . was a filibuster, and went out on the 'Virginius' to help free Cuba, and was shot, against a stone wall. We never knew where he was buried."[35] Davis casts Walker as a figurative father to Clay, and in this way links the past generation and its desires to the present generation and its desires. Moreover, the references to the father's death by execution and burial in an unmarked grave explicitly refer to Walker; executed by firing squad on a beach in Honduras—and given a final coup de grace to the face—the freebooter was dumped into a shallow grave and left without a marker. Davis provides another trace of the freebooter through a yacht, the *Vesta*, that Clay makes use of during the counterrevolution: Walker sailed for

Nicaragua in 1855 aboard a brig of the same name. And, just as Walker sailed to Nicaragua to rejuvenate the isthmus, Clay does his own part to set things right in Olancho.

Clay represents Davis's ultimate expression of the young American as the imperial self. He is cool, suave, handsome, able, effective, fearless—an Errol Flynn before Errol Flynn. He commands the respect of men and women alike, and he's not afraid to act or to intervene in the affairs of other nations. He is a self-made man, self-reliant, a rugged and robust individualist in the employ of American capital. He does only what serves his company's interests; as the mercenary-turned-engineer remarks, "I've got our concession to look after." He is young, energetic, and knows how to handle a pistol, a corrupt general, a coup, and a woman with equal ease. For Clay, most things are easy; more, perhaps, than any other hero in the literature of the era, the mercenary anticipates the American victory over Spain: Clay conquers Olancho without a protracted or particularly bloody struggle. Empire-building, the novel assures its readers, will be easy. Once the countercoup succeeds, the "native officers" spring upon Clay, "hailing him as the Liberator of Olancho, as the Preserver of the Constitution, and their brother patriot." In response, Clay casually remarks, "I guess I am the Dictator of Olancho."[36]

Whereas Emerson viewed eloquence as a primary mode of the imperial self, Davis's young American relies on a baser form of imperial eloquence. He does not so much speak with genuine eloquence as tell others what to say. With the coup brewing, he instructs his foreman on what to say to the mine workers—who are also government soldiers—in order to secure their loyalty when hostilities break out: he tells him "to point out to them how much better their condition had been since they had entered the mines, and to promise them an increase of wages if they remained faithful to Mr. Langham's interests, and a small pension to any one who might be injured 'from any cause whatsoever' while serving him."[37] He goes on to say, "Tell them, if they are loyal, they can live in their shacks rent free hereafter.... They are always asking for that. It's a cheap generosity... because we've never been able to collect rent from any of them yet."[38] Davis's young American tells his subordinates what to say while he concentrates on protecting U.S. investments; a shrewd manipulator when it comes to protecting the mine, he has no qualms about interfering with the internal politics of Olancho. He also has little more than passing concern for the welfare of his workers; in the end, these very same workers follow their American overlords without question.

Davis imagines the young American as the effortless, if manipulative hero of empire, and he represents Latin Americans in the usual ways: he presents the Olanchoan political elite as corrupt, lazy, and rapacious. When Clay has the mine running smoothly, he receives a visit from General Mendoza, who explains that he shall "move a vote of want of confidence in the Government for the manner in which it has given away the richest possessions in the storehouse of my country, giving it not only to aliens, but for a pittance, for a share which is not a share, but a bribe, to blind the eyes of the people." Rather than accepting one-tenth of the ore as agreed upon, Mendoza demands that "one-half of all the iron that your company takes out of Olancho shall be paid into the treasury of the State." Clay, defending American interests, informs the general that Olancho receives its fair share: "That's ten percent on nothing, for the mines really didn't exist, as far as you were concerned, until we came, did they?" While Davis appears to represent Mendoza as a patriot intent upon striking a better deal for his nation, he peels away Mendoza's veneer of patriotism to reveal a crooked schemer underneath: when Clay offers him sixty thousand dollars to quell opposition to the mine, Mendoza agrees, saying, "If I say 'It is all right, I am satisfied with what the Government has done in my absence,' it is enough."[39]

The only politician more corrupt than Mendoza is the president, Alvarez. At the urging of his wife, Alvarez plans on declaring himself dictator or king: "She's a tremendously ambitious woman, and they do say she wants to convert the republic into a monarchy, and make her husband King, or, more properly speaking, make herself Queen." Failing a takeover, the Alvarezes have the nation's treasury stowed in their suitcases. As the captain of the guard explains, Alvarez "has transferred every cent of it into drafts on Rothschild. They are at the house now, representing five millions of dollars in gold—and her jewels, too—packed ready for flight."[40] With these depictions, Davis dramatizes the customary assertions that Latin American elites do not understand democracy but rather plague their countries with incessant revolutions; in his romance, he enacts the observations he made in *Three Gringos*. Moreover, he stirs his reader's antagonism toward the "Spanish" (or at least those with Spanish names) and indirectly suggests that the United States must manage those nations that cannot properly manage themselves. In fact, Davis articulates—before the Spanish-American War—what will become the Roosevelt Corollary: we reserve the right to intervene in the affairs of other nations if those nations show themselves to be in a chronic state of chaos or that demonstrate, over time, a "general loosening of the ties of civilized society."

As one of his final acts in Olancho, Clay oversees the transfer of power to Alvarez's vice president, a pro-American leader. As U.S. marines land, in an act of gunboat diplomacy, to protect American lives and property, Clay ensures General Rojas's legitimate ascendancy to the presidency: "Present my congratulations to General Rojas, and best wishes." He goes on, instructing the Olanchoan officers to tell their new leader that "I wish him to promote all of you gentlemen one grade and give each of you the Star of Olancho. Tell him that in my opinion you have deserved even higher reward and honor at his hands."[41] Clay not only tells the soon-to-be president what to do but also earns the loyalty of the key players in any Latin American republic: the junior army officers, the future leaders of coups. Most importantly, Rojas will not, like Mendoza, seek a better deal for himself or Olancho from Langham; the countercoup maintains the status quo and ensures the continued profitability of the American enterprise. If Davis perfectly anticipates the Roosevelt Corollary, he also describes, with more than fair prescience, the shape and essentials of the American proxy system.

Even as Davis conjures an idealized world where the hero's will translates automatically into success, his depiction of imperialism-by-proxy heralds actual U.S. policy throughout Central America, the Caribbean, and the Pacific in the twentieth century. We need only think of U.S. support for the Somozas in Nicaragua, the ruling oligarchs in El Salvador, Muhammad Reza Shah Phlavi in Iran, Ferdinand Marcos in the Philippines, and countless other lesser (and less well known) tyrants, dictators, and kings for examples of the proxy system at work. In exchange for financial, military, and political support, the proxies support U.S. policies and investments. Above all, the proxies lend stability to the various regions; as Walter LaFeber remarks, in its support for tyrants and internal security forces, the United States found "the answer to the perplexing problem of how to maintain an orderly, profitable system without having constantly to send in the marines."[42]

Soldiers imagines a globe ready for American domination, and for Davis the shrewdness and natural superiority of the American imperial self will make the task of empire-building an exercise in easy wish-fulfillment. As Amy Kaplan argues in "Romancing the Empire" (1990), "Swashbuckling romances about knights errant offer a cognitive and libidinal map of U.S. geo-politics during the shift from continental conquest to overseas empire." In a novel like *Soldiers*, Kaplan suggests, Davis creates Clay as "the ideal American man": not only does he win the girl while defeating the revolutionaries, but he also refuses, when offered, to become a dictator. As Kaplan writes, "fantasies indeed, [novels like *Soldiers*] enact the desire for infinite expansion without colonial annexation, total control through the abdication of political rule, the disembodiment of national power from geographical boundaries."[43] I agree with much of Kaplan's argument, but *Soldiers* does stand as a fantasy of "colonial annexation"; although Clay declines to be dictator, his refusal gestures toward what remained absent as Davis wrote the novel. The young American cannot annex Olancho, even in a romance, because the United States had not yet begun to construct its official overseas empire. Davis, standing on the historical brink of the spectacular imperium, projects American hegemony throughout the Caribbean basin and beyond, and awaits real young Americans to step forward and take power abroad.

In *War Games* (2003), John Seelye offers a different argument than Kaplan, but one that does not quite capture the spirit of the novel. Seelye asserts that "aside from matters of sartorial style, the hero of *Soldiers of Fortune* demonstrated a high-minded enterprise that was never exercised in the service of the self but rather was patriotically and idealistically enlisted in that dual errand that [Walter] LaFeber identifies as the new imperialism, carrying U.S. capitalism into Central American countries and importing 'civilized' order along with it."[44] True, Clay's loyalties clearly lie with his employer, and he does not seek his own power and profit—beyond that entitled to him as the mine boss—but there remains very little that could be said to be "high-minded" about his actions. He shows little interest in the Olanchoans, and his interests in civilization run only as deep as to serve the interests of Langham's enterprise. He does not explicitly wish to foster democracy or to bring a stability to the country that would serve the long-term interests of its inhabitants. He wants the status quo and the 90 percent of the profit. On this occasion—Seelye makes a persuasive case for Davis's interest over time in an anticolonial imperialism—the romancer may well entertain thoughts of direct American colonial rule. With Walker as his inspiration, we cannot preclude the possibility.

Theodore Roosevelt and Young American Ideals

Although we are not, in this section, about to embark on a lengthy aside that makes no mention of Walker, we can safely say that no account of the American imperial self would be complete without a consideration of the adventures and writings of Theodore Roosevelt. In word and deed, he is perhaps the greatest American imperial self. Equally adept with pen, pistol, and pulpit, he accomplished a tremendous amount even as a young man. Before becoming president of the United States at the age of forty-two, he held a number of important appointments and political offices: he served as a member of the New York Assembly (1882–84), as head of the U.S. Civil Service Commission (1889–95), as police commissioner of New York City (1895–97), as assistant secretary of the Navy (1897–98), as colonel of the "Rough Riders" (1898), as governor of New York (1899–1900), and as vice president of the United States (1900–1901). He was also the first American to win a Nobel prize in any category, receiving the Peace Prize in 1906 for his efforts to resolve the Russo-Japanese War (1904–5). A sometime peacemaker and political progressive, Roosevelt possessed a clear and unapologetic vision of the United States' place in the world—he wanted to call into being a spectacular American empire—and he went after that vision with considerable ferocity. He helped to secure a U.S. victory in Cuba, oversaw the American colonial war in the Philippines (1899–1902), asserted U.S. control over the Panama Canal, and put forward, in "The Roosevelt Corollary," an amendment to the Monroe Doctrine.[45] Involved in some of the most important offices and issues of his day, he also articulated his ideals and visions in numerous addresses, essays, and books. His collected works run more than twenty volumes, and where Davis traveled and wrote, Roosevelt traveled, wrote, and led the nation. Seemingly, he could do it all.

In the context of our study of Walker and the American imperial self, we can locate a number of striking similarities between the freebooter and the

Rough Rider. For one, and perhaps most importantly, they stand as exemplars of the American imperial self. Both refused to live quiet, safe lives; both were physically daring, military minded, and, crucially, both were leaders. Through force of personality, intellect, and rhetorical skill, they won others to their side, made others believe in them enough to follow them onto the battlefield or into the political arena. Whatever doubts or anxieties they may have faced, they mastered or concealed them; to the world, they projected confidence and certainty of mission. Once dedicated to a cause or a course of action, they could not easily be turned away, and each possessed an extraordinary will. They believed in themselves, in their right to govern, and did almost anything in their power to achieve their goals.

Most strikingly, each possessed a dream of empire; they pursued the inward and outward empires with remarkable energy and ferocity. They wanted to be rulers, to be presidents, to reshape nations, to call into being American imperiums. They raised armies, crushed opponents, and conquered foreign lands. Walker seized power in Nicaragua, and Roosevelt helped to secure American interests in Cuba, the Philippines, Panama, the Dominican Republic, and elsewhere. And once they had won power, they could not quite give it up: after his expulsion from Central America, Walker tried again and again to raise another invasion force; after handpicking William Howard Taft to succeed him, Roosevelt became disgruntled with Taft's policies and in 1912 helped organize the Progressive Party for another run at the White House. By many standards, but certainly not all, Walker and Roosevelt were great achievers; one could hardly find men or women who were more imperial, more dedicated to acting in the world.

If remarkably alike as agents of empire, we can also note a number of parallels in Walker and Roosevelt's early lives and formative experiences. As boys, for example, they read romances and absorbed, as some commentators have suggested, some of their ideals from adventure tales; the deeds and literatures of American imperialism and the American imperial self grow, in part, from earlier texts. As we saw in the introduction, Walker read Walter Scott and other romancers and, as Albert Z. Carr asserts, was profoundly influenced by the notions of chivalry and great deeds he found in *Ivanhoe* and other works. If the freebooter, as a southern gentleman, suffered from what Mark Twain called the "Sir Walter Disease," Roosevelt also had roots in the southern aristocracy and particularly enjoyed adventure writers such as Daniel Defoe, Henry Wadsworth Longfellow, Frederick Marryat, R. M. Ballantyne, and James Fenimore Cooper. As he recounts in *Theodore Roosevelt: An Autobiography* (1913), he wanted to be like the great men and heroes he heard and read about as a child:

> I was nervous and timid. Yet from reading of the people I admired,—ranging from the soldiers of Valley Forge, and Morgan's riflemen, to the heroes of my favorite stories—and from hearing of the feats performed by my Southern forefathers and kinsfolk, and from knowing my father, I felt a great admiration for men who were fearless and could hold their own in the world, and I had a great desire to be like them.

As H. W. Brands remarks, "This romantic view of the world would shape Roosevelt's entire life. Repeatedly, and in diverse circumstances, he cast himself as the romantic hero, battling natural and human odds in pursuit of noble and glorious goals."[46] Both Walker and Roosevelt valorized heroic physical action, even if they were not themselves particularly robust as children, and they fashioned their visions of the American imperial self in part from models they found in adventure stories and poems. Remarkably, their reading of romances helped to call into being the American empire.

The similarities continue. As young men, both abandoned comfortable and economically secure lives in favor of strenuous careers: born into a prosperous Nashville family, Walker, at the age of twenty-nine, became a filibuster and invaded Sonora; after faltering in his political career, Roosevelt, then in his mid-twenties, transformed himself from an upper-class, Harvard-educated, New York politician into a cowboy, rancher, and hunter in the Dakota Territory. He later drew on those frontier skills as he raised the Rough Riders for their famous expedition to Cuba. Determined to be neither physically weak nor fainthearted, both men overcame physical infirmities to become soldiers and conquerors. And, curiously, both suffered early emotional traumas before turning to military gestures; they both set out to war after the premature deaths of loved ones: in April 1849 cholera took the life of Helen Galt Martin, Walker's fiancée; in February 1884 Roosevelt's first wife, Alice Hathaway Lee, died following complications arising from the delivery of their first child, Alice. On the same day, and in the same house, Roosevelt's mother, Martha Bulloch Roosevelt, died at forty-eight of typhoid fever. Suddenly and painfully adrift in their personal lives, Walker and Roosevelt cast about for something to do and turned their considerable abilities toward adventures. The American imperial self: a product, in part, of childhood frailty, early reading in romances, and the premature and personally devastating death of loved ones.

Like Walker, Roosevelt offers a vision of the American imperial self, but as a tireless writer and public intellectual, he presents a much more substantial and detailed representation than the freebooter. In adventure after adventure, career after career, address after address, essay after essay, and book after book, Roosevelt modeled and explained to his observers, listeners, and readers what it meant to be a real man and imperial self. If possessed, perhaps, of less intellectual ferocity than Emerson, Roosevelt comes well armed with his own brand of ethical insistence, and he calls for a masculine young American dedicated to family, work, and ever greater circles of political responsibility: one must first serve the community, then the state, then the nation; ultimately, the masculine young American must do his duty for the empire. In such essays and addresses as "The Duties of American Citizenship" (1893), "The Strenuous Life" (1899), "Manhood and Statehood" (1901), "The Administration of the Island Possessions" (1902), and "The Expansion of the White Races" (1909), he argues that the imperial self—a man undaunted by physical adventure, a man willing to act with force when necessary, a man unadulterated by ease or unearned wealth or weak idealism, a man unafraid to be a man and to pursue his rugged ideals and visions with utmost determination and candor—must step forward and do the hard but necessary work of the world. As with Emerson's young Americans, Roosevelt's imperial selves will lead the leaders of other nations, but they will not be too concerned with poetry and tossing creation like a bauble; when required, they will take creation in both hands and shake it roughly; they will say what needs to be said and do what needs to be done. They know, without doubt, that responsibility falls upon them, and if they are not opposed to beneficence, the term seems too feeble and decorous to describe their way of being; the masculine American self wants to stand a colossus over the nation's far-flung possessions.

In perhaps his most famous address, "The Strenuous Life," a speech given in Chicago before the Hamilton Club on April 10, 1899, Roosevelt offers his vision of the American imperial self. Writing in the afterglow of victory over Spain—and sounding like Whitman in his most vigorous, most prophetic moments—he articulates his key "Americanisms." He acclaims "all that is most American in the American character": "I wish to preach, not the doctrine of ignoble ease, but the doctrine of the strenuous life, the life of toil and effort, of labor and strife; to preach that highest form of success which comes, not to the man who desires mere easy peace, but to the man who does not shrink from danger, from hardship, or from bitter toil, and who out of these wins the splendid ultimate triumph." Following in the tradition of imperial eloquence—once again, the great work of empire-building demands equally formidable prose—he communicates his fervor for power, for masculine assertion:

> The timid man, the lazy man, the man who distrusts his country, the overcivilized man, who has lost the great fighting, masterful virtues, the ignorant man, and the man of dull mind, whose soul is incapable of feeling the mighty lift that thrills "stern men with empires in their brains"—all these, of course, shrink from seeing the nation undertake its new duties; shrink from seeing us build a navy and an army adequate to our needs; shrink from seeing us do our share of the world's work, by bringing order out of chaos in the great, fair, tropic islands from which the valor of our soldiers and sailors has driven the Spanish flag.[47]

Like O'Sullivan before him, he pours his belief in the United States' manifest destiny into a massive, multiclaused harangue and castigates wimps and intellectuals, dissenters and pacifists, anyone not up to the manly project of leading the world. Looking inward—he casts himself among the "stern men with empires in their brains"—he then looks outward and calls on young men to do what needs to be done, to be unafraid, to harden themselves for the benefit of others, to feel the thrill of empire. Always conscious of the power of the bully pulpit, Roosevelt tells young men how to think and act; he goes over the top and stages imperial masculinity in dramatic, vivid terms.

Roosevelt knew how the imperial self and the nation should behave, and in many of his essays and addresses he more particularly instructs young men on their responsibilities as workers, fathers, citizens, and imperialists. The imperial self, Roosevelt argues, must attend to his family *and* to his nation, must do what needs to be done at home *and* abroad, must accept his domestic responsibilities *and* do his best for others. As he remarks in "The Administration of the Island Possessions,"

> Just exactly as each man who is worth his salt must first of all be a good husband, a good father, a good bread-winner, a good man of business, and yet must in addition to that be a good citizen for the State at large—so a nation must first take care to do well its duties within its own borders, but must not make of that fact an excuse for failing to do those of its duties the performance of which lies without its own borders.[48]

In "The Duties of American Citizenship," a speech given before the Liberal Club of Buffalo on January 26, 1893, he sets out in even greater detail many of same ideals. Once more sounding like the Whitman of "Children of Adam," he clarions his classic themes: a father must raise robust children; the father, as a citizen, must do his duty to his family, to his community, to his name, and to his empire; real men do not fear action, and they must not be made soft by education or wealth. In the opening blast—a passage worth quoting in full for the manner in which Roosevelt weaves together his abiding concerns—he describes the "ideal citizen," his phrase for the American imperial self:

> Of course, in one sense, the first essential for a man's being a good citizen is his possession of the home virtues of which we think when we call a man by the emphatic adjective of manly. No man can be a good citizen who is not a good husband and a good father, who is not honest in his dealings with other men and women, faithful to his friends and fearless in the presence of his foes, who has not got a sound heart, a sound mind, and a sound body; exactly as no amount of attention to civil duties will save a nation if the domestic life is undermined, or there is a lack of the rude military virtues which alone can assure a country's position in the world. In a free republic the ideal citizen must be one willing and able to take arms for the defense of the flag, exactly as the ideal citizen must be the father of many healthy children. A race must be strong and vigorous; it must be a race of good fighters and good breeders, else its wisdom will come to naught and its virtue be ineffective; and no sweetness and delicacy, no love for and appreciation of beauty in art or literature, no capacity for building up material prosperity, can possibly atone for the lack of the great virile virtues.[49]

Roosevelt makes it easy for his audience. Life is not complicated, and living the right sort of life can be achieved by following some simple truths. He does not admit alternatives or opposing views, does not admit complexity, does not worry about the human costs or the desires of others. He believes in action, not in art or profit; he believes in manliness and ever-widening circles of responsibility. An *Übermensch* in a cowboy hat, an overman with a walrusy mustache, he tells young men how they must be in the world.

Like Walker, Roosevelt embodies the always in flux, never quite fixable performative imperial self. As with the freebooter, he moved rapidly through a series of careers and adventures; he tried his hand as a politician, rancher, historian, police commissioner, soldier, president, peacemaker, Bull Moose, and more. At each stage, he dressed, acted, and spoke the part, and he carried out his roles with a great degree of self-conscious flair and theatricality: we can all recall the famous photographs of him as a Cowboy in the West, a Soldier in Cuba, an Imperialist in a steam shovel in Panama, a Politician haranguing an audience from the Bully Pulpit. Always in search of fame, power, and achievement, Roosevelt calculated and cultivated his public personae; of all the American presidents, he may have been more adept at self-mythologizing than any other. He was always bigger than life, always outdoing peers, always making his name, always doing something to get his image circulated and to reach as wide an audience as possible. If Walker acted out his part as "The Gray-eyed Man of Destiny," Roosevelt, a far greater imperial self, provided the American public with numerous fine performances in his various roles as Cowboy, Rough Rider, and President.

If Roosevelt, like Walker, believed in his imperial mission even as he played the part of the conquistador in a self-conscious, made-for-public consumption manner, he also, like Davis, staged masculinity as a key component of the American imperial self. With Roosevelt, we have perpetually the effects of masculinity; as Butler puts it, "gender is always a doing, though not a doing by a subject who might be said to preexist the deed." Masculinity comes into being and is sustained through its very performance; it does not preexist its performance. And, as Butler further argues, the effects of masculinity become naturalized through repeated performances: "Gender is the repeated stylization of the body, a set of repeated acts within a highly rigid regulatory frame that congeal over time to produce the appearance of substance, of a natural sort of being."[50] Over and over, Roosevelt stages his masculinity in order to create a norm, and we can see his efforts at "stylization" in event after event and image after image.

As with Davis, we can observe the performance of masculinity in some of the most celebrated images of Roosevelt. In an 1884 photograph from his cowboy days, the young Roosevelt stands before a painted backdrop, sporting a nicely fringed buckskin suit and moccasins. Looking very much the scout or Indian killer, he boasts a suitably gigantic Bowie knife on his abundantly bulleted cartridge belt, and rests a lever-action rifle on its stock while gripping the barrel in both hands before his chest. The smooth-faced Leatherstocking gazes off at some unknown horizon or scene, but his countenance suggests no alarm or tension. So poised, so well outfitted and armed, he need fear no beast, man, or terrain. Here stands, the image tells us, the epitome of a western man. He can ride, shoot, and survive in the wilderness. Like Davis, Roosevelt has the pose and the kit down to an art, and we know that we are looking at a real man, not some eastern rube. If hardly alone, as a late-nineteenth-century American, in staging elaborate photographs, Roosevelt nevertheless took care with his masculine image.

In a famous, post–San Juan heights photograph, Colonel Roosevelt, in need of a shave, sits at a very plain wooden table, pen in hand, writing a letter or report before being mustered out at Camp Wikoff, Montauk Point, Long Island. In uniform, he also wears his hat and riding gloves against the chill, and we can see plainly the eagle on his epaulet and the crossed swords of the cavalry on his upturned brim. Quiet, alone in his tent, we have an image of the contemplative, serious soldier. Attending to final matters before leaving quarantine and returning home, his body language suggests that he does not boast about his triumph; rather, he exudes the weariness of the victor who has done his job and done it well. Here sits the genuine imperial self: tough, noble, confident yet subdued in his power, a man who knew what had to be done and who did it better than all others. Here sits a man, a man's man, a hero. If less posed and theatrical than his cowboy picture, Roosevelt is nevertheless angled slightly toward the camera, confident that this image or some other will make the rounds and add to his growing legend.

In recent years a number of scholars—including, among others, Gail Bederman, Kristin Hoganson, E. Anthony Rotundo, and Kim Townsend—have examined Roosevelt's adventures and writings in terms of late-nineteenth-century American masculinity, but not enough emphasis has been placed upon the performative dimensions of imperial masculinity. As Hoganson argues in *Fighting for American Manhood* (1998), for example, imperialists and "jingoes" such as Roosevelt, Henry Cabot Lodge, Marion Butler, Albert J. Beveridge, and others believed that "the health of the nation rested on the robust character of its men." These politicians and public figures, she contends, believed that with the passing of the Civil War generation—men who had amply demonstrated their courage and character under fire—the nation was in danger of losing not only valuable role models but also its vigor. They feared that American society would grow soft and corrupt and that its young men, lacking the benefit of character-building combat, would not know how to lead or how to make the difficult decisions. For men like Roosevelt, an empire was the solution to this waning of American valor and manliness. As Hoganson writes,

> Imperialists like Roosevelt believed that holding colonies could prove to be a longer-term solution to modern civilization's seemingly dangerous tendency to make young, middle-class, and wealthy men soft, self-seeking, and materialistic. They thought that the experience of holding colonies would create the kind of martial character so valued in the nation's male citizens and political leaders (especially in the aftermath of the Spanish-American War), and that, in so doing, it would prevent national and racial degeneracy.[51]

The imperialists, she asserts, took their own arguments seriously; they believed in the rhetoric of robust masculinity. They wanted an empire, and they believed that the United States should take its place among the powerful nations, but they also believed that wars, overseas conquests, and the management of other peoples would produce strong and vital citizens at home.

Although Hoganson overstates the role of masculinity in empire—the Rough Rider and his peers also had geopolitical and material concerns guiding their actions, and there was far more to Theodore's ambitions than masculinist triumph—and although Roosevelt believed in his own arguments and rhetoric, he also employed the bully pulpit to influence policy and win followers. He both believed in his vision of the masculine imperial self *and* staged his vision, in his campaigns and writings, in a deliberately heightened, nearly melodramatic fashion. Rather than being wholly a matter of a stern, essential belief, masculinity for Roosevelt was at least in part a show put on for the public. As much as he believed himself, he was also selling imperialism and the imperial self to the culture in a way that would make them attractive and robust. He marketed manliness as a means, in part, to achieve political, military, economic, *and* cultural goals.

If Hoganson perhaps takes Roosevelt too much at his word, Bederman argues that while the Rough Rider skillfully "constructed a virile political persona for himself as strong but civilized white man," he nevertheless believed that "the United States was engaged in a millennial drama of manly racial advancement, in which American men enacted their superior manhood by asserting imperialistic control over races of inferior manhood." As Bederman notes, as a young New York state assemblyman, Roosevelt was often mocked by his peers for being effeminate and was sometimes—because of his high voice and tight pants—referred to "by the name of the well-known homosexual Oscar Wilde, and one [of his detractors] actually alleged (in a less-than-veiled phallic allusion) that Roosevelt was 'given to sucking the knob of an ivory cane.'" Deeply offended, and believing himself to be a man's man, he worked diligently, as always, to refashion his image, and emerged within a few years as a champion of the masculine imperial self and of the natural superiority of the white race. For Roosevelt, Bederman claims, "History proved that manhood and race were integrally connected—almost identical—and the future of the American nation depended upon both."[52] Once more, although I have no doubt that the politician believed his own arguments, Bederman's language suggests the performative dimension: Roosevelt staged a "millennial drama" and "enacted" his views on masculinity. He wrote himself a great part in the imperial play and put on a splendid show, but the imperial venture was just as much about the American ascendancy and realms of influence and economic possibility as about manliness and racial Darwinism. For Roosevelt, like Davis, performative masculinity was a key part of the imperial self.[53]

Unlike Emerson and Walker, Roosevelt does not seem too interested in the intense inward gaze. Matters are not that complicated for him. Where his predecessors describe a sudden, mystical insight, a moment in which the self sees its future and its mission with absolute clarity, he refers to the "stern men with empires in their brains" but does not describe his own instance of revelation. Too busy doing, he has little time to wonder about the wellsprings of his actions, and he does not attribute his sense of mission to a divine inspiration. Rather, he readily affirms and elaborates upon the arguments and rationales of colonialism and imperialism, and although he spends a great deal of his time writing, he worries more about presenting his message in accessible and enthralling terms than about diving deeply into metaphysics or the finer points of imperial desire. He may work furiously in his study, and he may commune with the minds of the past, but he tells young men that they should set aside their books and find someone to pummel or shoot at or lead. If Roosevelt ever worried that he was not on the right path—if he ever entertained doubts about how the imperial self should behave—he kept his anxieties to himself. If Emerson had a mind on fire, Roosevelt felt the fire in his feet and fists and in the seat of his pants.

Although Roosevelt may or may not have read Emerson's "The Young American" while a student at Harvard, he targets the same audience—young men—and transforms Emerson's ideal of young Americans leading the world through kindness and generosity into a stern and athletic form of imposed guidance. In his discussions of U.S. responsibilities in the Philippines following the Spanish-American War, he offers a much more robust, much more aggressive figure; his young Americans will be tough first, and kind second:

> The Philippines offer a yet graver problem [than Puerto Rico or Cuba]. Their population includes half-caste and native Christians, warlike Moslems, and wild pagans. Many of their people are utterly unfit for self-government, and show no signs of becoming fit. Others may in time become fit but at present can only take part in self-government under a wise supervision, at once firm and *beneficent*. (emphasis added)[54]

Where Emerson imagined gentleness, an openness of spirit, a tendency toward "love and good," Roosevelt, an actual agent of empire, has little time for the nicer sentiments. We must speak plainly about the situation, must know who we are dealing with, and we must, as always, do what needs to be done. When dealing with "half-caste" Christians, "warlike Moslems," and "wild pagans," we had best set aside polite notions and dreamy airs; these people need to be put in order.

In the half-century between these two American giants, the tone of American idealism changes, becomes harsher, more about material power and the actual assertion of influence overseas. As Roosevelt's exploits and writings demonstrate, the young American cannot operate, in the real world, on an exalted plane; to lead the leaders requires the exercise of economic, political, and military power. Utopianism gives way to realpolitik, and the stepping of the imperial self from the page to the world necessitates a fall, a devolution. The imperial self as Emerson imagined it cannot exist.

If O'Sullivan and Walker represent the immediate twisting of the kindhearted Young American into a piratical adventurer, Roosevelt also demonstrates that leading the leaders requires the letting of blood, the visceral conflict between wills, peoples, nations. To "help" or "civilize" requires efforts to make Central Americans or Filipinos see economic and political matters the American way. The young American, as the agent of "uplift," must be hard first, then beneficent, must be prepared to be brutal, to kill and to confiscate. The Young American, Emerson's ethereal vision, becomes in Roosevelt—and the literature that follows the establishment of the spectacular overseas empire—a fully authorized, rugged imperialist in jungles and deserts around the world.[55]

In his writings and his life, Roosevelt embodies many of the shifting contradictions in American culture. He claimed to believe in beneficence yet was intent upon his own fame and power; he claimed to believe in democracy, yet he had little interest in extending the franchise and other rights of citizenship to those peoples he conquered. He was friendly, yet deadly. He imagined a life worth living, a great, hardy, athletic life, yet he did not really value the lives or desires or dignity of people who were not like him. He wrote of uplift, but had little use for people who were not gifted, or tough, or white. He wanted to set aside wilderness areas and to protect the environment, but he had no qualms about taking land and resources from Indians. He held progressive social and political notions, yet he was a profound racist and conquistador. He held high ideals, but these very same ideals of beneficence and manly virtue helped to push the United States into a protracted and often bloody colonial action in the Philippines. He believed in America, in new ideas, but his faith in the New World seemingly ended at the United States' borders. A peculiar mix of the progressive and the reactionary, of construction and destruction, he wanted to box and write, to wage wars, break trusts, create national parks, and spread the power of the United States around the world. He wanted to do these things, and he did, and if he was never as personally vicious as Walker, he did his part in bringing American violence to the world.[56]

Indian Wars and the African Slave Trade

If Roosevelt made major contributions to the literature of empire, we can also see in his work many of the historical and political currents circulating in romance representations of the imperial self: his essays and speeches address both the Indian Wars and the African slave trade. As a cowboy and historian of the American West, he connects the energies and desires of overseas imperialism with continental expansionism; as a politician and public intellectual grappling with "American Problems," he connects American global responsibilities with U.S. relief programs in Africa. Through whatever mechanism or combination of internal and external forces—the return of the repressed, a sense of direct or indirect culpability, a desire to confront two of the New World's greatest human catastrophes, an urge to assert a hierarchy of races, a need to say what cannot be said—the ghosts of the imperial past resurface often in Roosevelt's writings.

In *The Rough Riders* (1899), for example, he discusses the raising of his regiment, and thoroughly grounds the mission in the contexts of the frontier and the metaphysics of Indian-hating. As he remarks, "The captains and lieutenants were sometimes men who had campaigned in the regular army against Apache, Ute, and Cheyenne, and who, on completing their term of service, had shown their energy by settling in the new communities and growing up to be men of mark."[57] Joining forces with Harvard and Princeton graduates, the cowboys and soldiers of the Southwest found a new terrain for action in Cuba. In fact, his long disquisition on raising the force makes abundantly clear the relationship between continental expansionism and overseas adventurism: since the closing of the frontier and the defeat and settlement of hostile Indians on reservations, these hypermasculine men had been casting about for something worthy to do.

In "The Expansion of the White Races," an address given in celebration of the African diamond jubilee of the Methodist Episcopal Church, Washington, D.C., on January 18, 1909, Roosevelt articulates one of the primary tenets of Indian-hating: "On the whole, and speaking generally, one extraordinary fact of this expansion of the European races is that with it has gone an increase in population and well-being among the natives of the countries where the expansion has taken place." Precontact natives, such assertions suggest, amount to an affront to the white races; they lived such abominable lives that we had to take them in hand. Euro-Americans have taken Indians by the hand and made them healthy and prosperous. "Taking into account the Indians of pure blood, and the mixed bloods in which the Indian element is large," he continues, "it is undoubtedly true that the Indian population of America is larger to-day than it was when Columbus discovered the continent, and stands on a far higher plane of happiness and efficiency."[58] Current research, of course, suggests a different interpretation of events—best guesses put the Indian population in North America before Columbus at approximately ten million; by 1910, the number in the United States had fallen to about two hundred thousand.[59] Even as Roosevelt has softened his rhetoric, however, the furious energy of hatred still churns through his pronouncements.

If Roosevelt represents the forces of continental expansion turned outward, he also links the history of American slavery to future missionary projects. He argues that Americans must perform good works in Africa because of "the African slave trade, the crime of the ages": "The responsibility of America for the moral well-being of the people of Africa is manifest." The United States, once again in the colonial parlance, has an obligation to uplift not only Latin Americans and Asians but Africans as well. Nevertheless, the curious choice of the word "manifest" suggests that beneath the noble rhetoric runs an unabated current of imperial expansion and domination: Africa, too, must be rationalized into the American sphere of influence. As always, the work of empire will fall to the young Americans: "In addition to contributions in money, it is fully expected that a large number of well-prepared young men and women will consecrate their lives to service in different parts of the Dark Continent."[60] Once more, the imperial self must step forward, must do what needs to be done. Another race must be uplifted, must be regenerated, must learn the benefits of good government and hearty enterprise.

Whatever else the masculine American imperial self is about, he is—from a variety of ideological perspectives—about the metaphysics of Indian-hating and the metaphysics of the African slave trade, and Roosevelt is no exception. While we could argue that as a leader and intellectual of his day, he was likely, sooner or later, to contextualize or address the Indian Wars and slavery, the sheer recurrence of references to and traces of these two human catastrophes in the literature of the American imperial self suggests a more profound mechanism at work. Although I have no doubt that Roosevelt or Davis or Walker had little use for people of color, their declamations on race and racial hierarchies perhaps betray them. They hate Indians and have little use for blacks, yet they cannot help talking about killing Indians or Africans or about doing some good for Indians or Africans.

These traces or overt discussions represent the return of the repressed; at some level, and despite their cavalier attitudes, they recognize but do not want to accept the humanity of others. At some level, they know they want to maim or destroy or to take the lands and wealth of others—of people not unlike themselves—and while they do not come close to anything like a full articulation of the nightmare progress of history, the truth surfaces in oblique references or overbold declarations. Like everyone else, they dwell in necessity and provide glimpses into the sometimes vicious ontology of the imperial self and the imperiled other.

A Watershed

The "Spectacular Empire" marks a watershed in the literature of the American empire and the American imperial self. In Harte's *Crusade* and Davis's *Soldiers*, we have relatively positive representations of the American imperial self, and the mercenary romance, as a form, celebrates masculine derring-do and U.S. imperialism. Perkins, the Walker character in *Crusade*, earns the respect of his fellow Americans and, for the most part, operates from high ideals; he may go about trying to elevate the lives of others in the wrong way, Harte suggests, but he appears as a man of principle and action. Hurlstone and Keene, the young entrepreneurs, can do no wrong, and Harte ends up endorsing a benign form of U.S. imperialism. In *Soldiers*, Davis celebrates American manhood and power, but in his later treatment of the Walker narrative, *Captain Macklin* (1902), the text we turn to next, he offers a much bleaker view of imperialism. Macklin lacks Clay's natural abilities, and matters go badly for the American and European filibusters in Guatemala. This darker vision, in fact, anticipates the tone of many later works about U.S. interventionism in Central America, Southeast Asia, and elsewhere around the world. As the empire ages, and as the human costs become more apparent, Harte's tentative cheer and Davis's first shout seem out of touch with the sometimes brutal workings of imperialism and the imperial self. The mercenary romance takes a seemingly permanent turn toward doubt and despair, and representations of the imperial self become increasingly violent and less and less noble. Soon enough, in place of champions like Clay, we will have madmen (and madwomen) and monsters.

CHAPTER FOUR

Soldiers of Misfortune: Davis and O. Henry

Rather surprisingly, Richard Harding Davis, within five years of publishing *Soldiers of Fortune* (1897), began to look more uncertainly upon the United States' imperial project, began to question the virtues of American economic adventurism. Turning away from the celebratory spirit of *Soldiers*, Davis offered *Captain Macklin* (1902), a novel he considered his most mature work. As he told his mother, Rebecca Harding Davis, he believed the tale of a young American soldier of fortune in Central America "much the best thing I have ever written."[1] Perhaps meditating on the literary form he helped to popularize—and upon his exultant treatment of American power in his earlier fiction and nonfiction—Davis uses *Macklin* as an occasion to invert the paradigm of the mercenary romance: the imperial self does not win the girl; almost immediately after winning a foreign land, he loses it; he does not carry himself with aplomb; when it comes to battle, he fights frantically, even brutally. And, deliberately upending his own carefully constructed image as a glamorous agent of empire and the tendency of some readers to identify the author with his heroes, Davis explained to his mother that "it is rather amusing writing in the first person and making yourself out no end of a cad."[2]

Most importantly, where Davis casts Robert Clay as an exemplary agent of American military *and* economic imperialism, he presents Royal Macklin as an anti-agent of the commercial empire. In *Macklin*, a romance based more directly upon Walker's adventures than *Soldiers*, the young mercenary refuses to serve U.S. economic and political interests, becoming, instead, a rather impotent agent of "liberation." Viewing American capital and military imperialism with skepticism, Davis champions, somewhat disingenuously, a more esoteric mercenary aesthetic: combat, freedom from women and polite society, and the pursuit of masculine idealism matter more than the advancement of empire. He valorizes the paramilitary imperial self over the military or economic imperial self. Nevertheless, in this tentative critique of U.S. imperialism, the romancer cannot quite abandon the belief that Americans can do some good abroad, and, in the end, he moderates his critique of big business.

Macklin represents a temporary watershed in Davis's work (he would go back to jingoistic fluff rather quickly after the romance's relative commercial and critical failure). If Clay stands tall as the swashbuckling hero of empire, Macklin tends toward the antihero. Although Davis wishes his readers to admire the soldier of fortune's dedication to notions of political liberty and freedom from the constraints he believes women impose upon men, he portrays Macklin as a young, sometimes foolish man who cannot easily dominate his opponents and who, when under heavy attack, orders his men to fire indiscriminately upon combatants and civilians alike. Davis still admires the man of action and adventure, but he offers a more complicated and contradictory representation of the imperial self. At work on the romance during the colonial war in the Philippines—reports of brutality, including civilian massacres, began to appear in the U.S. press within a few years of Commodore George Dewey's defeat of the Spanish—and during Theodore Roosevelt's antitrust campaigns, Davis can less easily celebrate American desires and power. Creating and holding an imperium will not be the easy and relatively bloodless matter he first imagined, and big business, as his mother knew, did not often have public or national interests uppermost among its concerns. Imperial euphoria gives way to a suspicion of imperialism, and Davis attempts to describe a more complex and vexed world. The imperial self suddenly finds itself involved in bloody, even sordid affairs.

If *Macklin* marks a momentary watershed in Davis's work, it marks a truer watershed in the literatures of U.S. imperialism. In the twentieth century, and especially after World War II, the corpus takes on increasingly darker hues. Although Davis's antiromance does not single-handedly usher in a new tone in literary treatments of the empire—relatively few read it when it appeared, and it has not enjoyed much critical or commercial success since—it does prefigure many of the novels that follow. Its bleak vision and brutal representations of violence anticipate the often savage characters and plots of works such as Robert Stone's *Dog Soldiers* (1974) or Cormac

McCarthy's *Blood Meridian* (1985), important texts of what we could call the Ugly American Empire.[3] More and more, as the workings and human costs of the empire become more apparent, the literature becomes correspondingly grim and critical. Davis constructs Macklin as an unappealing, unromantic, sometimes vicious figure, and he looks a great deal like many of the antiheroes and unimperial selves who follow. Most importantly, *Macklin* is not about winning easily; it is about losing. For one of the first times, a novel of empire concerns itself with bitter defeat. Macklin, perhaps more than any other character in any other novel of its era, stands as a prototype for the defeated American abroad in the twentieth century: after suffering a catastrophe in his professional life, the hero or antihero travels to Central America and becomes caught up in violence he cannot control. In the end, he must flee for his life. Just as Michael Herr calls John Ford's *Fort Apache* (1948) "more a war movie than a Western, [a] Nam paradigm," we could call *Macklin* a paradigm for the mercenary romances of the American century.[4]

However poorly *Macklin* sold in comparison to *Soldiers*, the two did well enough to embed the mercenary romance in the culture and to earn, thereby, a mild parody in the form of O. Henry's only novel, *Cabbages and Kings* (1904). A modest comedy by most standards, *Cabbages* makes a number of modest claims on our attention. In the first place, William Sydney Porter—O. Henry's real name—mocks the conventions of the mercenary romance; he jokes lightly about the already lost American abroad becoming caught up in revolutions, coups, and countercoups. His cast includes dozens of Harte-style miscreants on the lam from the law in the United States, and they variously conspire to topple or sustain governments or large-scale commercial enterprises in Anchuria, an imaginary Central American republic based loosely upon Honduras. Second, Porter completely ignores the history of the Spectacular Empire, and focuses instead on the deeper and more sustained pattern of economic interventionism (supported by military power) and U.S. imperialism-by-proxy. In one of the first novels to describe the creation of a so-called banana republic, Porter effectively represents the truer course of the imperium and, like Davis, critiques the machinations of the economic imperial self. Third, and most importantly for our purposes here, he offers a genial satire on Walker and filibustering. In Clancy, "an American with an Irish diathesis and cosmopolitan proclivities,"[5] he offers a caricature—but a jaunty one—of the mid-nineteenth-century freebooters and their decidedly more twisted and violent ideals and ambitions. Although we will not spend much time with Porter's parodic mercenary romance, it merits brief consideration for its perceptive takes on Davis, Walker, and U.S. imperialism.

Frantic *Macklin*

Predictably, *Macklin* was not one of Davis's best-received works: few readers, with the United States embroiled in an increasingly vicious and unpopular colonial war in the Philippines, wanted either a story of failed romance or a tale that described American adventurism in negative terms. The book did not sell as well as his earlier efforts, and Davis, wanting to write a serious novel that would allow him to take his place among "literary" writers, complained that "all that was said of it was that it was 'A book to read on railroad trains and in a hammock.'"[6] In fact, the reviews fell so short of Davis's expectations that he turned from writing fiction to writing farces for the stage: "*Macklin* I always thought was the best thing I ever did, and it was one over which I took the most time and care. Its failure was what, as Maggie Cline used to say, 'drove me into this business' of play writing."[7] Not only did Davis fail to reach the highbrow audience he sought with *Macklin*, but he also alienated some of his previous admirers. As Lubow remarks, he "lost touch with his young female readers who were outraged by an 'unhappy' ending in which the girl failed to get her man."[8] Just as importantly, having built an audience invested in fantasies of empire, Davis denied his readers their jingoistic pleasure. Where readers embraced Clay, they wanted little to do with Macklin.

Generally, later critics, like the novel's early readers, have dismissed *Macklin* as an unsuccessful rewrite of *Soldiers*. In *The Richard Harding Davis Years* (1961), Gerald Langford argues that "the novel breaks down. Reverting to the juvenile swashbuckling of *Soldiers of Fortune*, it merely chronicles Macklin's derring-do amid the familiar stage-props of Central America."[9] Lubow makes roughly the same claim: "Had the Spanish-American War and Boer War not interrupted him, Davis might have written the book he wanted. The novel differs markedly in its beginning and its end—and the first half is better." Lubow goes on to remark that while Davis cut some of the "derring-do" from the novel, "he should have cut more."[10] In contrast, we can argue that this relatively undervalued novel does not "break down" or revert to tired "derring-do." Rather, a bleak tone pervades the latter half of the novel as the mercenary force suffers betrayal and defeat: confronting the serious issues of expansionism, Davis wrestled with his subject matter to create a more searching text about the American empire and about the role of the imperial self in the creation and maintenance of that empire. As John Seelye puts it, "The novel has a number of apparent inconsistencies, suggesting that the author was not in complete control of his subject and theme, but it most certainly gives an acid bath to the idealism generally associated with Davis's version of romance."[11]

Just as few read *Soldiers* anymore, fewer still read *Macklin*, and a brief summary may be in order. The mercenary romance follows the adventures of Royal Macklin, a young American who hires himself out as a mercenary after his dismissal from West Point. After suffering this setback in his professional life, and in order to redeem his vision of himself as a man and a soldier, Macklin decides to join General Laguerre and his "foreign legion" in Honduras. Laguerre's force, he learns from a newspaper, is "chiefly composed of American and other aliens, who believe the overthrow of the present government will be beneficial to foreign residents."[12] Without much reflection, Macklin takes on Laguerre's somewhat vague notions of political liberation and becomes involved in the filibuster campaign to conquer the country. Eventually, Laguerre triumphs militarily and becomes the president of Honduras—and Macklin its vice president—only to be quickly defeated. Macklin barely escapes the isthmus with his life; he leaves his troops and countless Hondurans dead in his wake. In plot, mood, and theme, *Macklin* upends *Soldiers*.

A rather debased imperial self, Macklin, unlike Emerson or Walker, does not cultivate a burning inward vision of empire. He does not recount a moment of sudden insight, a moment when he sees, with pristine clarity, his future entwining with the future course of civilization. Nevertheless, we do have access to Macklin's inner life—Davis offers the romance as Macklin's "memoirs"—and in the section the soon-to-be mercenary pens just after his expulsion from West Point, he recounts how he came to know of Laguerre and Honduras. He reads a newspaper article and, incensed, exclaims to a cousin that "it certainly isn't right that American interests in—what's the name of the place—in Honduras, should be jeopardized, is it? And by an ignorant half-breed like this President What's-his-name?" Not blessed with an empyrean call to arms, Macklin shows himself to be unschooled and impulsive. He does not know much, if anything, about Central America or about U.S. interests in the region, and he chooses his course of action on the basis of emotion and a need to reassert his masculinity and martial prowess. He has let his family down: "I am in bitter disgrace, and I am grateful that grandfather died before it came upon me. I have been dismissed from the Academy. The last of the 'Fighting' Macklins has been declared unfit to hold the President's commission."[13] Seeing himself as less than a man, as a failed son and grandson, he acts rashly and has little or no sense of mission or idealism or what it would mean to set out on an imperial venture. He sets out, at best, a haphazard imperial self.

In many ways, Macklin is Clay's opposite; the dashing imperial self becomes the frantic, ill-considered agent of paramilitary adventure. Whereas Clay is intelligent and calculating, Macklin is foolish and unthinking; whereas Clay acts to protect American interests, Macklin conflates his desire to reclaim himself as a soldier with U.S. "interests" he never knew existed. He never fully allies himself with U.S. businesses in Honduras, and—in a Walkeresque move—supports Laguerre's scheme to nationalize the American-owned isthmian transit company. He does not fully understand the situation or the forces at work in Honduras, and he lacks Clay's ability to control the republic's political, economic, and military affairs. Moreover, he possesses few of Clay's natural leadership abilities and does not command much more than a rudimentary imperial eloquence. He cannot effectively rally his troops or inspire others with his words, and he exhibits little of Clay's ease or charm, especially with women. Over the course of his adventures as a "knight errant,"[14] he develops an attraction for Miss Fiske, the daughter of Joe Fiske, a seemingly corrupt American entrepreneur and owner of the transit line, but nothing ever comes of it. Whereas Clay gets the woman and the posh job, Macklin wants neither. He remains an imperial self—he wants to help Laguerre build an empire in Central America—but he is less an *American* imperial self than an idealized soldier of fortune. He will fight for what he believes in, but he does not—*contra* Roosevelt—owe allegiance to his country or its imperial agents. More so than in *Soldiers*, Davis attempts to explore what it would mean to be a filibuster detached from U.S. desires and ambitions, to be someone dedicated to one's vision—however poorly articulated or hastily assumed—of how the world should be.

If this change in Davis's vision of U.S. imperialism arises in part from events in the Philippines and from Roosevelt's trust-busting, it also arises in part from his selection of sources for Laguerre and Macklin. More interested in the mercenary life than in celebrating the American ascendancy, he models his two principle characters after two freebooters of his acquaintance. As Fairfax Downey, Davis's early biographer notes (with some inexplicable errors), "The appealing figure of *General La Guerre* [sic] was drawn from General McIver [*sic*], a fine old veteran of many battles under many flags."[15] In *Real Soldiers of Fortune*, a collection of essays celebrating the exploits of hirelings such as Philo Norton McGiffen and Winston Churchill,[16] Davis describes the sundry swordfights, duels, and campaigns of his old friend, Major-General Henry Ronald Douglas MacIver: "Whenever in any part of the world there was fighting, or the rumor of fighting, the procedure of the general invariably was the same. He would order himself to instantly depart for the front, and on arriving there would offer to organize a foreign legion."[17] For Macklin, and even more so for Clay, Davis drew upon Charles Jeffs, a mercenary Davis met during his travels in Central America: "Jeffs is a young American mining engineer from Minneapolis, and has lived in Honduras for the past eleven years. Some time ago, he assisted [Louis] Bogran, when that general was president, in one of the revolutions against him, and was made a colonel in consequence."[18] Laguerre and Macklin, it probably goes without saying at this point, are also based upon Walker. In Davis's world of soldiers, politicians, and journalists, he seems most to have admired mercenaries and flamboyant men of action like MacIver, Jeffs, and Walker. For Davis, the swashbuckler was the ideal imperial self: daring, dashing, not bound by law or society or flag.

For the plot of *Macklin*, Davis draws in particular upon Walker's adventures. As we have seen, the romancer already had the mercenary in mind when he wrote *Soldiers*, and he patterns General Laguerre's campaigns in Honduras after the freebooter's war in Nicaragua. To cement the connection, Davis has Laguerre adopt Walker's flag as his own: "It was the flag of Walker, with the five-pointed blood-red star." As the general's men tell him, "We mean to make you President, and will not stop there. Our motto shall be Walker's motto, 'Five or none,' and when we have taken this Republic we shall take the other four, and you will be President of the United States of Central America."¹⁹ Whereas Walker sought to regenerate the isthmus—and to fashion an empire—Laguerre (like Harte's Perkins) seeks the benevolent guardianship of the isthmus. The beneficent yet well-armed imperial self will do someone else some good whether they want it or not.

Davis also models *Macklin* on Walker's adventures in one other key way: just as Walker conquered a nation and became its president only to be "betrayed" by his "subjects," Laguerre temporarily rules Honduras only to be double-crossed by some of the legion's officers and their local allies. As Macklin discovers, Graham—"the manager of the Copan mines" and Joe Fiske's representative in Honduras—has deceived Fiske and set out to destroy the legion:

> Graham offered Heinze twenty thousand dollars to buy off himself and the other officers and the men. But Heinze was afraid of the others, and so he planned to ask Laguerre for a native regiment, to pretend that he wanted them to work on the trenches. And then, when our men were lying about, suspecting nothing, the natives should fall on them and tie them, or shoot them, and then turn the guns on the city. And he *has* sent for the niggars!

In passage after passage in *The War in Nicaragua*, Walker blames the Nicaraguans, his non-American soldiers, U.S. Secretary of State William Marcy—in short, anyone but himself—for the defeat and expulsion of the American colonizers from the isthmus. Davis picks up this refrain and makes it a key theme of his novel: no one appreciates Laguerre's good intentions or understands how he will bring peace, stability, and good government to Central America. As Macklin laments, following the death of "old man Webster," a soldier who had fought with the Immortals in Nicaragua, "There he died, as his hero, William Walker, had died, on the soil of the country he had tried to save from itself."²⁰

This passage, and many others in the novel, once more reveals what we knew we would find in a tale of the American imperial self, but frantic Macklin's racial hatreds betray an anxiety that has perhaps been repressed in earlier allusions to the Indian Wars and African slave trade. The curse "niggars," and the later curse "half-breeds," suggest that Davis, like many later writers of empire, fears the possible revenge of people of color upon whites. As events begin to turn against Laguerre and Macklin, this fear surfaces over and over again. During a harrowing ride through the capital, for example, Macklin witnesses the murder of one of his men: "I saw the native guard spring like one man upon our sergeant and drive their bayonets into his throat. He went down with a dozen of the dwarf-like negroes stabbing and kicking at him, and the mob ran shrieking upon the door of the palace." Davis portrays Honduran mestizos as "dwarf-like negroes," as deformed, dark-skinned monsters who act with treachery and viciousness. He compresses the isthmians into a multilimbed, less than human predator. Later, as Macklin attempts to flee the country aboard an American steamer, he berates the ship's captain for agreeing to turn him over to "these half-breeds": "You're no American. You're no white man. No American would let a conch-nigger run this ship."[21] The racist, derogatory epithets betray, in Macklin's panicked state, a fear and revulsion at people of color achieving the upper hand over the Euro-American imperial self. He reveals that the racial violence of empire-building has always been about asserting white superiority.

Even as Davis models the plot after Walker's adventures, he also mourns the freebooter's early demise; for the apologist, the Tennessean could have been *the* American imperial self. In "William Walker, the King of the Filibusters" (1906), Davis lauds the freebooter's mission in Central America and implies that Walker's death marked the end of a near-epic potential. As he writes, after the 1856 election, "Walker was now the legal as well as the actual ruler of the country, and at no time in its history, as during Walker's administration, was Nicaragua governed so justly, so wisely, and so well." This claim points toward a larger implication: not only could Walker have ruled an "empire" in Central America, he may have gone on to rule the United States. As Davis wistfully concludes, "Had Walker lived four years longer to exhibit upon the great board of the Civil War his ability as a general, he would, I believe, to-day be ranked as one of America's greatest fighting men."[22] Since the Civil War provided heroes and presidents, Davis leaves it to the reader to wonder if Walker might have first stood in Robert E. Lee's boots, then Ulysses S. Grant's. In his novel, however, Davis backs away from jubilant veneration for the sake of a tepid anti-imperialist critique.

In *Macklin*, because he wants to acclaim filibustering over imperialism and allegiance to masculine ideals over allegiance to country, Davis writes back against Walker's history in order to separate what he deems the better ideals of freebooting from the Tennessean's imperialist agenda. He casts filibustering as a utopian venture that would improve, if done correctly, the lot of the average Central American. As Webster declares, Laguerre will be a greater, more noble man than Walker: "You will cut the Nicaraguan canal. And you will found an empire—not the empire of slaves that Walker planned, but an empire of freed men, freed by you from their tyrants and from themselves." Whereas Walker reintroduced slavery into Nicaragua, Laguerre will respect the rights of all men; moreover, he will save Central America from its true enemies, namely its own people. As Webster (sounding a lot like Davis in *Three Gringos*) exclaims, the region "is cursed with the laziest of God's creatures, and the men who rule them are the most corrupt and the most vicious." Although such remarks would seem to situate Laguerre's venture firmly in the arguments of empire, Davis, with false naïveté, implies distinctions between brands of imperialism: in one, Walker seeks an empire for his own glory; in another, as in *Soldiers*, Clay seeks control for the sake of American economic interests; in the best, Laguerre seeks to create an ideal empire of liberty. As Macklin remarks, "In his talk along the trail and by the camp-fire he had always dreamed of an impossible republic, an Utopia ruled by love and justice, and I now saw he believed that the dreams had at last come true."[23] Davis attempts to imagine a purist imperial self, a freebooting self dedicated to "love and justice"; for a moment, he faintly echoes Emerson's language in *Nature* and "The Young American."

The very impossibility of the utopian state suggests that the idea of it matters more than the reality of it; above all other considerations, the mercenary life counts the most. As Macklin finally realizes about himself, "I was no longer to be deceived; the one and only thing I really loved, the one thing I understood and craved, was the free, homeless, untrammeled life of the soldier of fortune."[24] Action above ideals, danger above security, freedom above love; these constitute the mercenary aesthetic. The men will never marry, never take regular jobs, never have to lead lives of domestic imprisonment; Macklin will not pursue Miss Fiske or his doting cousin, Beatrice.[25] Moreover, neither Laguerre nor Macklin evince much concern for the Hondurans (in fact, they do not seem to know or speak to more than a handful); rather, the intricacies of battles and alliances and the thrills of gunplay and duels consume them. Davis, however disingenuously, wants to separate freebooting from any political or economic agendas. If he constructs a fantasy of empire in *Soldiers*, in *Macklin* he builds a fantasy of blind knight errantry, a fantasy of violent adventure for its own sake. If he downplays the political realities and human costs of paramilitary conquest, he does so not only to revel in what he sees as the best sort of life but also to foreground an evolution in his thinking. In the five years between *Soldiers* and *Macklin*—the same five years in which McKinley and Roosevelt officially called the spectacular American empire into being—Davis confronted the excesses of imperialism and decided who was responsible for them: American businessmen. In a stunning reversal from *Soldiers*, he portrays American capital as the enemy.

Macklin offers a critical portrait of American imperialism-by-proxy as Laguerre's force must battle an American-backed army; the paramilitary imperial self comes up hard against the superior resources of the rapacious, corrupt, economic imperial self. As Aiken, the U.S. consul, remarks, Joe Fiske "owns" a country: "That's what I meant by saying that Joe Fiske owns Honduras. He's cut it off from the world, and only *his* arms and *his* friends can get into it." Fiske—modeled after Cornelius Vanderbilt, Walker's American archenemy—operates a transit line and mines in Honduras and indirectly backs one of the competing factions in the civil war. Earlier in the novel, when he arrives in Honduras, Macklin learns that U.S. corporations play a role in the seemingly endless cycle of coups and countercoups; suddenly, for Davis, perhaps it is not that the isthmians do not understand good government, but that Americans will not let them practice it. As Aiken tells him, "You must understand that almost every republic in Central America is under the thumb of a big trading firm or banking house or a railroad. For instance, all these revolutions you read about in the papers—its seldom they start with the people. The *pueblo* don't often elect a president or turn one out. That's generally the work of a New York business firm that wants a concession."[26]

In this dramatic turn in Davis's perspective, Clay and companies like the Valencia Mining Company are to blame for political instability in the region; the economic agents of empire seek only their own benefit and hold no ideals of beneficence or liberty. In *Macklin*, Fiske's Isthmian Steamship Line owes Honduras five hundred thousand dollars but refuses to pay; as Aiken explains, when the government came to collect its debt, the Isthmian Line "picked out a thief named Alvarez as a figure-head and helped him to bribe the army and capture the capital." In the end, these same men topple Laguerre's regime and reinstall Alvarez. Macklin remarks in disgust, "I had set out on this expedition with the idea that I was serving some good cause—that old-fashioned principles were forcing these men to fight for their independence. But I had been early undeceived."[27] Where *Soldiers's* Clay witnessed the corrupt Alvarez's murder in Olancho, Macklin witnesses the corrupt Alvarez's double ascendancy through American interference: the repetition of names points to Davis's conscious effort to explore the nature, and not the fantasy, of interventionism. Greed and economic trusts undo the "old-fashioned principles" of freedom.

Near the end of the novel, Davis seems to suffer a pang of doubt, and tries to recant his anti-imperialist heresy; he wants to hold out the possibility, however faintly, that Americans can do some good abroad. Uneasy with the conclusion that the economic agents of empire may be to blame for the perpetual political crises of Central America, Davis slips part way out from under it: Fiske, it turns out, has been duped by his own American representatives in Honduras, and he makes good on the debt. When Macklin runs into Miss Fiske in New York after fleeing Honduras, she tells him that her father's American managers in the isthmus had "deceived him dreadfully. But when he got home, he looked it up, and found you were right about that money, and so he's paid it back, not to that odious Alvarez man, but in some way, I don't quite understand how, but so the poor people will get it."[28] U.S. entrepreneurs may not be so bad after all (even if their daughters cannot quite understand how things get done); they may become responsible agents of the empire, returning some of the wealth to those who need it most. Davis still wants to believe that Americans can do good in the world, but the gesture seems facile after a sustained negative portrait of U.S. capital throughout the novel.

Davis's turn against economic imperialism perhaps has part of its roots in Roosevelt's efforts to regulate corporations. In a number of articles and addresses, Roosevelt turned his considerable energy to curbing the excesses, as he saw them, of American "trusts." In "The Control of Corporations" (1902), for example, he argues that "there are real and great evils in our social and economic life, and these evils stand out in all their ugly baldness in time of prosperity; for the wicked who prosper are never a pleasant sight. There is every need of striving in all possible ways, individually and collectively, by combinations among ourselves and through the recognized governmental agencies, to cut out those evils." Among these evils lurk some corporations: "There is clearly need of supervision—need to possess the power of regulation of these great corporations through the representatives of the public—wherever, as in our own country at the present time, business corporations become so very powerful alike for beneficent work and for work that is not always beneficent."[29] Davis, a long-time admirer of Roosevelt (if only he had known what the politician thought of him!), may have drawn upon the antitrust, antimonopoly legislation and sentiment of the era. Fiske's isthmian line acts, for most of the novel, in a less than beneficent manner, and Davis, attuned to public debates, offers a negative portrait of an American corporation. Still, few wanted to read about the evils of U.S. businesses abroad.

If Davis taps into the antitrust currents of his day, a deeper wellspring of his critique of U.S. enterprise may be found on the novel's dedication page: "To my Mother." Davis wanted to be acclaimed as a serious writer; he wanted to write something that would approach the artistry and depth of his mother's best work. In the process of writing *Macklin*, as Langford notes, he sent "a long synopsis for Rebecca to comment on."[30] Although this was not completely unprecedented, he seemed especially concerned with impressing her. Just as Rebecca, in *Life in the Iron Mills* (1861) and *Margret Howth* (1862), delved into the hardships of life and the complexities of human desire and need, Richard wanted to produce a more complex character and to confront some of the human costs of war and imperialism. He wanted, perhaps, to dive a little deeper into things than he had before. For a change, he broke the surface, but few applauded him for it.

Lubow also notes that Davis desired his mother's approval of his work. He wanted to be taken seriously as a writer—just as his mother had been early on in her career—and he seems to have been driven, at least in part, to fulfill *her* desire for the Davises to be known as a literary family:

> His mother was always on his mind. He relied on her to correct his manuscripts before publication. He valued her opinion above all others. The desire to be worthy of her overwhelming love dominated him from his childhood until his death. His hunger for public approval seems closely linked to his need for maternal sanction. He was addicted to positive reinforcement, but no one could ever match the love of his mother, a love rooted in loss:

first, the death of her father, Richard's namesake, and then, the withering of her literary career. She took great vicarious pleasure from Richard's professional success, as if seeing in it the extension of her own interrupted flight.[31]

After rewriting *Life* in *Soldiers*, Davis reverses his take on American capitalism in part to honor his mother and her critiques of big business. Although he possesses little of his mother's trespass vision, and although he reveals little sympathy or insight into the suffering caused by U.S. economic imperialism, he nevertheless, on this one occasion, offers a negative representation of capitalism and its contributions to cycles of unrest and violence. With *Macklin*, he wanted to secure, yet again, his mother's approval and wanted—even as he tried to cement the family name in American letters—to build upon her legacy. In effect, he rewrites his rewrite of *Life* in order to emulate some of his mother's ethical gravity.

Davis also offers a negative portrayal of U.S. imperialism due, in part, to the violence of the American neocolonial action in the Philippines. Following Dewey's victory in Manila Bay on May 1, 1898, Filipino insurgents soon began a guerilla war against the American occupation force; on December 20, 1900, General Arthur MacArthur, acting upon the authority of President McKinley and Secretary of War Elihu Root, declared martial law over the islands in an effort to break the alliance, as Daniel B. Schirmer remarks, "between the guerilla fighters and the Philippine people as a whole." With reports already circulating in the United States that the military was following a policy of "taking no prisoners," MacArthur's proclamation assured both Americans and Filipinos that his men would not hold back in their efforts to secure the United States' imperial interests. As numerous journalists and combatants reported, U.S. forces swept through entire villages, setting fire to the residences and firing upon men, women, and children. In November 1901 a reporter for the *Philadelphia Ledger* summarized the savagery of U.S. policies:

> The present war is no bloodless, opera bouffe engagement; our men have been relentless, have killed to exterminate men, women, and children, prisoners and captives, active insurgents and suspected people from lads of ten up, the idea prevailing that the Filipino as such was little better than a dog.... Our soldiers have pumped salt water into men to make them talk, and have taken prisoners people who held up their hands and peacefully

surrendered, and an hour later, without an atom of evidence to show that they were even *insurrectos*, stood them on a bridge and shot them one by one, to drop into the water below and float down, as examples to those who found their bullet-loaded corpses.³²

Like many of his contemporaries, Davis would have known of these reports, and although he never joined such writers as Mark Twain, William Dean Howells, or William James in the Anti-Imperialist League, the frenzied violence in *Macklin* recalls journalistic accounts of atrocities in the Philippines. Even for Davis, U.S. imperialism had become too violent and sordid, and, in this regard, we can once more see his mother's influence.

In *War Games* (2003), Seelye recounts that Rebecca "was outspokenly critical of the ongoing war in the Philippines, which the United States was pursuing with the intention of placing 'the crown of Imperialism on its brows, to gird a sword on its thighs and drive another nation into civilization and Christianity—at the point of a bayonet.'" Against the war in Cuba, and adamantly opposed to American policies in the Philippines, Rebecca wrote anti-imperialist tracts, and if Richard could not bring himself to do the same, still he did not approve of American violence against the Filipinos. As Seelye writes, "Davis was not proud of the activities of the U.S. Army in the Philippines, of which he was reminded by the actions of the British army in South Africa, noting that 'in our newspapers we give our war a short quarter of a column of space a day, partly because we are rightly ashamed of it,' while the British beat the drum and rattled the tambourine in celebrating their 'victories' over the hapless Boers."³³ Once more feeling the weight of his mother's critique of American callousness and violence against the less powerful, Davis tilts against American military imperialism but still tries to celebrate masculine feats of arms and the life of the mercenary.

If Davis deliberately attacks American economic and military imperialism, he less knowingly goes against the grain of the mercenary aesthetic that he so admires. He cannot easily sustain his idealized vision of the pure imperial self. In the final scenes in which Laguerre, Macklin, and the Foreign Legion lose power, events quickly spin out of control, stripping the glamor from their adventurous lives. In hindsight, Macklin knew at the instant of betrayal that they were lost: "The storm broke at the moment I turned from Lowell on the steps of the palace, and it did not cease, for even one brief breathing space, until we were cast forth, and scattered, and beaten." Where Clay captures Olancho with ease, Macklin flails desperately in his effort to hold onto Honduras. Under fierce attack, he orders his men to fire their Gatling gun at will: "Kill every man in this street if you have to, but get to the palace." Freebooting, for a time, becomes a harrowing experience: "And then there was a pitchy blackness through which I kept striking at faces that sprang out of the storm, faces that when they were beaten down were replaced by other faces; drunken, savage, exulting." For Macklin, the war becomes a nightmare of Indian ("savage") and African ("faces" from the "pitchy blackness") ascendancy. But just as Fiske turns out to be a good guy, both Macklin and Laguerre escape the isthmus without feeling the need to reevaluate their beliefs, and the young mercenary receives a cablegram inviting him to join his leader in a French military expedition to Southeast Asia: "Commanding Battalion French Zouaves, Tonkin Expedition, holding the position of Adjutant open for you, rank of Captain, if accept join Marseilles."[34] On the verge of a more thoroughgoing critique of economic *and* military imperialism, one that would explore the vicissitudes of armed intervention along with the problems of economic and political conquest, Davis backs away from both. On the verge, perhaps, of becoming a writer against the empire, he became a scribbler of farces.

Macklin represents a further devolution in the literary imperial self. Whereas Emerson imagined beneficent young Americans, and Harte and Davis earlier offered gentle or at least peerless young adventurers as their models of the imperial self, Macklin appears foolish, lacks dignity, and has none of the eloquence of his predecessors. The imperial self, with the United States enmeshed in a brutal colonial war in the Philippines, cannot so easily impose his will upon people of color. Davis, clearly uncomfortable with some of the critical implications of his narrative, fashions the young mercenary as a mildly ironic figure. He does not succeed with women; his men mostly despise and, occasionally, take shots at him; and he is always a step or two behind others in discovering the forces at work in Honduras. Nevertheless, Davis attempts to salvage a masculinist ethic even as he struggles with doubts about U.S. military and economic imperialism and about the imperial self. Somewhere out there, he hopes, there still exists a space for real men, men free from women, free from the desire for filthy lucre, free from obligations to the state. There still exists, he hopes, a space for the right sort of American imperial self.

Even so, *doubt* has entered the literature of the American empire; the narrative has become darker, the characters less sure of themselves, less in control of the situation. The hero is less glamorous, more willing to kill indiscriminately in order to maintain power or to save his own life. The hero has begun the slide toward the antihero. Never again will the young imperial self be quite so pristine, quite so mannered, quite so assured. The empire has become complex; it is not perfectly admirable now that it has dramatically revealed itself. As the imperium ages, it cannot maintain its bravado, its exuberant tones. Imperialism, it seems, is not quite so easy or quite so noble as it appeared. In the fall from *Soldiers*'s dream of effortless imperialism and a swashbuckling imperial self, Davis becomes—if only for a moment—a Janus-faced agent of empire.

"'Tis Elegant Weather for Filibusterin'"

If Davis followed Harte, we can take another clear step in the evolution of the narrative of the already lost American abroad. Stanhope Searles's 1905 review of *Cabbages and Kings* puts O. Henry firmly in a lineage with the two romancers, and it is worth quoting at some length:

> With his stories of life in the Central American republics Mr. Henry is seriously threatening the supremacy of Mr. Richard Harding Davis in a field in which for several years the more widely known writer has been absolutely alone. There is no resemblance whatever between *Soldiers of Fortune* and *Captain Macklin* and *Cabbages and Kings* as stories, but in their point of view and general impressions of the strange countries about which they write the two authors are much alike. One of Mr. Henry's absconding Latin-American presidents might readily be fitted, orders, uniform, accent, braggadocio and all, into any chapter of *Soldiers of Fortune*. . . . The American consul, the gentlemanly adventurer clamoring for a concession, the fakirs and hucksters of the United States, of France and Germany and England, the exiled bank presidents under a cloud, the promoters of revolutions and the derelict drunkards—these people you find in O. Henry's pages and they are much the same as in the pages of Mr. Davis. They are portrayed with much humor and sympathy and keenness, and behind them you are made to see that wonderful background of white beach and waving palm trees and sunshine and flowers and fruit and dirt and discomfort; you are made to feel all the heat and disorder and squalor, and to understand with perfect sympathy the American or European who looks out over the dancing blue waters and longs wistfully for "God's Country."[35]

As the review attests, the figure of the already lost American abroad interfering in the domestic affairs of tropical nations had become so firmly embedded in the culture that Searles readily possesses a language to summarize the novels. The tropes of "absconding Latin-American presidents," "the gentlemanly adventurer," and "the promoters of revolutions" exceed Searles's reading of Davis and O. Henry; they were already circulating, and he finds the novels exemplars of what he already recognizes and can easily delineate. By 1905 American involvement in Central America had already been largely fixed in the American *imaginary:* remarkably, if we inserted different titles, we could use Searles's review to describe the plots and characters of a great many American novels set in the isthmus and beyond.

A loosely plotted, episodic satire on American economic imperialism and a parody of the romances of Harte and Davis, *Cabbages* depicts the power of U.S. companies and adventurers in Central America at the turn of the century; like Davis, Porter offers a (mild) critique of the economic imperial self. The patched-together book—the author reworked several stories into a "novel"—teems with American imperial selves who take up "political intrigue as a matter of business" and who control Anchuria's resources and influence its politics.[36] Nearly all the American characters have fled the United States after shady business deals or collapses in their professional or personal lives, but many come to enjoy positions of authority and earn great wealth in Anchuria. American scoundrels—or a very debased and rapacious form of the imperial self—find their proper field of play in the United States' backyard, a place to try out schemes and desires without the legal constraints of home. If Davis first celebrates the fantasy of American power and then condemns the excesses of American businessmen, Porter mocks banana-republic politics and offers a satire on "filibusterin'" as a failed form of imperialism: the real power in the region, he asserts, rests with the American banana kings.

Although Porter's work and life have been the subject of a number of book-length critical and popular studies, not much has been written about him since the 1970s. My take on *Cabbages* differs somewhat from earlier critics who have tended to emphasize Porter's mastery of comic effects and local color, often comparing him to Guy de Maupassant, Washington Irving, Bret Harte, Robert Louis Stevenson, and Rudyard Kipling. In *O. Henry: The Man and His Work* (1949), for example, E. Hudson Long finds the novel "cleverly designed": "The stories may seem theatrical and exciting, but life in Honduras was strange and sometimes turbulent."³⁷ In his detailed study of Porter's fiction, *O. Henry* (1965), Eugene Current-Garcia argues that *Cabbages and Kings* has little to do with the political realities of banana republics. Instead, Anchuria represents a dreamlike "lotus" land: "In largest measure, these stories represent wish fulfillment, romantic escape—and were so intended." Condemning "academic snobbery," Guy Davenport praises the book as an exemplum of New Comedy and compares it to the works of Joyce, Dostoevsky, and Dickens: "It was as brilliant an invention in narrative technique as *The Pickwick Papers* or Victor Shklovsky's *A Sentimental Journey.*"³⁸ Though I am not sure that Davenport and I read the same novel, I agree with Current-Garcia's assertion that the satire foregrounds the narrative pleasures of mistaken identities, romances, jokes, and surprise endings. At the same time, the parody interests us here precisely because of its *worldly* affiliations, its representations of U.S. interventionism in the isthmus.

A literary descendant of Harte and Davis, Porter parodies the narrative of the American imperial self abroad. He knows the constituent elements of the narrative so well, he lampoons it by overstuffing his novel with thieves, provocateurs, and freebooters. Frank Goodwin—an American expatriate and "a banana king, a rubber prince, a sarsaparilla, indigo, and mahogany baron" all in one—tells Miss Wahrfield, the daughter of an insurance company embezzler, about the "American colony" in Anchuria (Porter's name for Honduras): "Some of the members are all right. Some are fugitives from justice from the States. I recall two exiled bank presidents, one army paymaster under a cloud, a couple of manslayers, and a widow—arsenic, I believe, was the suspicion in her case."³⁹ Porter exaggerates Harte's and Davis's themes of loss and flight, giving his characters even better reasons for hurrying abroad. The idealized, benevolent imperial self has been replaced, in Porter's comedy, by wastrels and robbers. Porter reads Harte and Davis closely and, in the act of taking up the already familiar elements of the mercenary romances, signals their embeddedness in the culture. Parody requires that the writer and the reader share a knowledge of the subject being parodied, and *Cabbages* acknowledges the place of *Crusade, Soldiers,* and *Macklin* in turn-of-the-century America.⁴⁰

In *Cabbages*, the imperial self continues its decline toward antiherodom. The characters have checkered pasts and involve themselves in a variety of crooked schemes. They do not act from particularly ethical ideals, did not set out from home with good intentions, and do not seek to help the Central Americans. They rather clearly, if humorously, seek their own good. No one speaks of beneficence, neighborliness, or good will. None of the characters, finally, appears as evil, or exceedingly brutal, and they come across as mild interlopers. Still, they bear little resemblance to Emerson's young Americans, and their primary connection to Nature comes in the form of raw materials and bananas. Porter's characters stand as neither heroes nor antiheroes, but represent another small step toward the truly mean-spirited, violent, desperate characters of the Ugly American empire.

If *Cabbages* recalls *Crusade* in its conjuring of a mild world of romance and intrigue that concerns itself more with humor than hard-edged political analysis, Porter nevertheless portrays the growing influence of American capital in Central America. The most ambitious of the sundry American exiles interpose themselves into the domestic affairs of Anchuria, always conspiring to profit from the seemingly endless cycle of coups and countercoups that plague the nation. Goodwin—Porter's paradigm of the economic imperial self—especially masters local affairs:

> He was the most successful of the small advance-guard of speculative Americans that had invaded Anchuria, and he had not reached that enviable pinnacle without having well exercised the arts of foresight and deduction. He had taken up political intrigue as a matter of business. He was acute enough to wield a certain influence among the leading schemers, and he was prosperous enough to be able to purchase the respect of petty-officeholders. There was always a revolutionary party; and to it he had always allied himself; for the adherents of a new administration received the rewards of their labors.[41]

Goodwin represents the leading edge of an "invasion" of American intriguers, and he finds kindred spirits in the corrupt officials and politicians of Anchuria. Even as Porter downplays the seriousness of events, the tongue-in-cheek events point to the very real importance of the United States' commercial empire in the isthmus.

Porter knew firsthand about the lost American abroad, and he witnessed firsthand the power of U.S. corporations in Central America.[42] Once in Honduras, he observed the dealings of American companies and freelance soldiers. At the time, as Walter LaFeber recounts,

Honduras probably gave the term "banana republic" its negative connotations of dependence on foreigners, a one-crop economy, and all-around corruption. By 1907 Honduras had suffered through seven so-called "revolutions" in fifteen years. The country's foreign debt of $124 million dwarfed its national income (largely from duties on trade) of $1.6 million. Honduras was less a nation than a customs house surrounded by adventurers.[43]

Porter captures the influence of businessmen such as the Vaccaro brothers of New Orleans (owners of Standard Fruit Company) and Samuel Zemurray (founder of Cuyamel Fruit Company and later head of United Fruit Company). These men and businesses ran the Honduras of Porter's exile, and as he jokes in the novel's "proem," the formidable combination of economic and military imperialism was too much for the isthmians: "The little *opéra-bouffe* nations play at government and intrigue until some day a big, silent gunboat glides into the offing and warns them not to break their toys."[44]

We can see the influence of the banana kings—real-world imperial selves—in an evolving subplot that deals with the intrigues of the American-owned Vesuvius Fruit Company in its bid to seize control of Anchuria's plantations. In his yearly report to the State Department, Geddie, the U.S. consul, urges U.S. firms to follow through more aggressively on the Monroe Doctrine: "Most unaccountable is the supineness of the large exporters in the United States in permitting the French and German houses to practically control the trade interests of this rich and productive country." Vesuvius fully intends to act more aggressively, and in order to gain favorable concessions—and to push out European competition—it backs Ramon Olivarra, the son of "Anchuria's most popular ruler," in a bloodless coup against President Losada, a "despot" who sanctions "the outrageous oppression of citizens by the military." After Olivarra's assassination, his widow "went to the States, and educated her son at Yale. The Vesuvius Company hunted him up, and backed him in the little game."[45] Just as Standard Fruit ran Honduras, Vesuvius takes over Anchuria; as a company agent wryly concludes, "It's a glorious thing . . . to be able to discharge a government, and insert one of your own choosing, in these days."[46] Like Davis, Porter points toward American capitalists as the agents of U.S. imperialism, but unlike Davis, he does not attempt to soften his portrait of the banana kings: the bosses in New Orleans firmly direct the political and commercial traffic in their backyard. Still, even as Porter mocks American corporations, he mocks so gently that he appears to accept their machinations as a given.

We can perhaps get a clearer sense of the mildness of Porter's take on the manipulations of American fruit companies by looking at Pablo Neruda's angry, bristling poem, "The United Fruit Co." (1950). Writing forty-six years after Porter, the Chilean poet had the unfortunate luxury of witnessing the consequences of U.S. imperialism throughout Central America and the Caribbean. Curiously, he uses the same phrase as Porter to describe the condition of countries under Zemurray's control—"ópera bufa"—but offers a far more scathing critique. Seizing control of "the delectable waist of America," United Fruit turned nations into "Banana Republics":

> Estableció la ópera bufa:
> enajenó los albedríos,
> regaló coronas de César,
> desenvainó la envidia, atrajo
> la dictadura de las moscas,
> moscas Trujillos, moscas Tachos
> moscas Carías, moscas Martínez,
> moscas Ubico, moscas húmedas
> de sangre humilde y mermelada,
> moscas borrachas que zumban
> sobre las tumbas populares
>
> (They established an opéra bouffe:
> they ravished all enterprise,
> awarded the laurels like Caesars,
> unleashed all the covetous, and contrived
> the tyrannical Reign of the Flies—
> Trujillo the fly, and Tacho the fly,
> the flies called Carías, Martínez,
> Ubico—all of them flies, flies
> dank with the blood of their marmalade
> vassalage, flies buzzing drunkenly
> on the populous middens)[47]

Neruda finds the genesis of the violent, dictatorial reigns of Rafael Trujillo (who, trained by the U.S. Marine Corps, ruled the Dominican Republic for thirty years), Tacho Somoza (who, funded by the U.S. military, established a dynasty that ruled Nicaragua from 1936 to 1979), Tiburcio Carías (who ran Honduras for seventeen years), Maximiliano Hernández Martínez (who massacred thirty thousand Salvadorans in the 1932 *matanza*), and Jorge Ubico (who controlled Guatemala for thirteen years, aggressively suppressing leftists and unions) in coups orchestrated by United Fruit. For bananas and dollars, an American company helped unleash catastrophic brutality. Neruda, writing from a Latin American position with the weight of history upon him, finds little to laugh at, little that could be construed as the proper matter for a mild satire.

If *Cabbages* mocks American economic adventurism, it also offers a successful if lightweight satire of filibustering as a failed form of imperialism. On a lazy tropical evening in Anchuria, Clancy remarks to his recumbent companions that "'Tis elegant weather for filibusterin'. . . . It reminds me of the time I struggled to liberate a nation from the poisonous breath of a tyrant's clutch." Whereas Davis holds onto utopian fantasies about mercenaries, Porter nicely deflates such pretensions, sniggering at the improbabilities of paramilitary adventuring. While working as a stevedore in New Orleans (a focal point for a number of American filibustering projects), Clancy comes upon a broken-open crate filled with Winchester rifles. When the box's owner arrives, he assures the "little brown man" that his secret is safe: "Whenever you hear of a Clancy obstructin' the abolishment of existin' governments you may notify me by return mail." After much wine, Clancy agrees to join General De Vega's cause, and when he arrives in Guatemala he thinks to himself, "Here will Clancy, by the virtue that is in a superior race and the inculcation of Fenian tactics, strike a tremendous blow for liberty."[48] Like Davis's Macklin, Clancy claims to believe in "liberty"; what he really believes in is the superiority and intelligence of whites and the inferiority and unreason of everyone else.

Filibustering, however, turns out for Clancy to be an unsuccessful venture. Rather than joining the revolution, we discover that he has been duped into serving on an enforced railroad-building crew. As he confesses to his listeners, "Yes, 'twas [Guatemala] I sailed against, single-handed, and endeavored to liberate it from a tyrannical government with a single-barreled pickaxe, unloaded at that."[49] Porter tells the tale with considerable humor and pokes fun at the idea—shared by Davis and Roosevelt—of whites as the "superior race." The brown man outmaneuvers the white man, and puts him to work for the profit of the other for a change. De Vega's attempted coup fails, however, and he ends up fleeing Guatemala aboard a banana boat bound for New Orleans. The fruit companies continue to function no matter who is in office and no matter how many revolutions come and go. The real power rests in American corporations.

As political satire, *Cabbages* critiques its moment of empire. Whereas Davis fantasizes about American commercial and imperial power, Porter acknowledges that the United States seems destined (to borrow a phrase from Simón Bolívar) to "plague and torment" Latin America. He notes current realities but leaves it to the reader to decide whether condemnation may be in order. Porter pokes fun at American power, yet he lacks the jagged edges and darkness that make Mark Twain or Jonathan Swift great satirists. Although Wahrfield commits suicide, leaving his daughter stranded in Anchuria, she eventually marries Goodwin, and they live happily ever after. And although De Vega tricks Clancy, the American has the last laugh as he arranges for the Guatemalan to be arrested in New Orleans. In the end, no one really suffers that greatly, and revolutions and American intercession are things to be joked about. And, as in Harte's *Crusade*, love wins out, and Goodwin and other American characters appear favorably. Porter gently pokes fun at the growing American empire; he shows considerable wit and captures in a less fantastic way than Davis what U.S. economic power can do in the hemisphere.

The importance of *Cabbages* can perhaps be located in its deliberate nontreatment of the Spectacular Empire. The novel makes little mention of events in Cuba or the Philippines. It neither celebrates nor condemns McKinley's and Roosevelt's exploits, and it does not concern itself with battles or assaults on the presidential palace. It jokes about gunboat diplomacy in its Lewis Carroll–like "proem," but it does not show any U.S. warships in the harbors of Anchuria; we can, however, see plenty of banana boats. It does not focus on emergent U.S. martial power; it does not show marines landing to protect American lives and property. Instead of focusing on military imperialism, it concentrates on the already more established form of economic imperialism and indirect rule-by-proxy. The novel elides the big stick in favor of exploring less public modes of interventionism.

Davis and Roosevelt (Redux)

In *Macklin*, Davis attempts to conjure an imperial self divorced from U.S. political and economic interests. Instead, he describes a young American dedicated to vague notions of liberation, love, and justice. Macklin wants to lead a life untrammeled by responsibilities to family or nation or empire. He wants to be a filibuster, to partake in military action almost for its own sake. He wants to be a rough and ready man, a man unbeholden to women or to a paycheck. He does not want to settle down and buy a house and have a family and a job. He wants to travel to dangerous and exotic locales, wants to see the world and make his mark upon it, wants to live a life of physical extremity. He wants to be free to ride and to shoot, and to be involved in great and daring affairs. He wants to hang out with other men who think just as he thinks. Perhaps most importantly, he does not want to sacrifice his masculinist vision to the wrong sort of men, men working within existing institutional and economic structures. He does not want to defer to U.S. politicians or diplomats, and he most certainly does not want to obey or give in to what he sees as the chicanery of businessmen and their agents of economic imperialism. America, Davis seems to suggest, does not leave much room for real men. Society and commerce and women continually make demands upon them, and in the face of these demands, he offers a dark fantasy of men desperately seeking to reclaim their masculinity, desperately seeking to assert male power. The world, he contends, always works to compromise their ideals and to strip them of their robust activities. Where, he seems to ask, can a real man be a real man?

This question leads us to another: what is all this whining about how hard it is to be a real man, a man's man, a man given over to the strenuous life? On the one hand, Davis makes clear his complaints against the mundane routines of everyday life. At a deeper level, however, his anxieties perhaps cut as much against the masculine imperial self as against jobs and wives. Macklin fails. He cannot get the job done; he cannot create the ideal republic in Honduras; he cannot call into being the ideal pocket empire of liberty. Real men, it seems, may not have what it takes. Whereas Roosevelt worried that American men were growing soft and irresponsible, Davis worries that the agents of empire will not be strong enough or smart enough or cunning enough to be able to command an imperium. Maybe, just maybe, the problem is not that we will grow fluffy and too rich and too educated and too afraid of action, but that we do not have what it takes under any circumstances. This fear of ultimate masculine inadequacy perhaps explains, in part, Macklin's panic: What will we do? What if we show ourselves to be too weak? What if we are not men enough?

In their different ways, Roosevelt and Davis worried about American masculinity and the imperial self. They worried that American men were not up to the task of building and maintaining an empire, and this abiding fear in the literatures and cultures of U.S. imperialism points us toward the next chapter and the Walker-inspired mercenary romances of the Cold War era. If the fin de siècle agents of empire had their doubts, then their Cold War counterparts positively tremble and gnash their teeth with anxiety. Not only may real men be too weak, but they may not be real men at all. They may be, in our contemporary parlance, queer; they might conceal their true natures and thereby corrupt the body politic from within. They may be homosexual, but worst of all, they might be *women disguised as men*. The challenges of the Cold War serve to heighten the abiding perturbations and laments over American masculinity and the enterprises of empire. From here, then, we step forward fifty years—although a number of Walker romances were published in the intervening years, they are, in the main, highly conventional and do not offer much in the way of twists and turns on the mercenary romance and do not see particularly deeply into their own eras—to the period of McCarthyism and the almost hysterical fear of the enemies within the body politic of the United States.

CHAPTER FIVE

"The Female of the Species": Teilhet and Cardenal

From Richard Harding Davis and the Spanish-American War, we step forward fifty years to the Cold War and the Walker narratives of Darwin Teilhet and Ernesto Cardenal. The retellings from the intervening years—Joaquin Miller's long narrative poem, "Walker in Nicaragua" (1906); Edgar Young's short story, "William Walker, Filibuster" (1922); Arthur D. Howden Smith's mercenary romance, *A Manifest Destiny* (1926); and Merritt Parmelee Allen's colorful history for boys, *William Walker, Filibuster* (1932)—draw upon the relatively muted imperial ambitions and energies of the 1920s and 1930s and do not add much to the genre of the mercenary romance or to our understanding of Walker, Manifest Destiny, or the American imperial self. In contrast, Teilhet, an American romancer, and Cardenal, a Nicaraguan poet and revolutionary, draw considerable energy from the Cold War era, and they add a great deal to our understanding of the genre, to our study of Walker, and to our investigation of masculinity and the imperial self. From the fin de siècle, therefore, we move to the 1950s and the next crucial era in American imperial history; once more, Walker takes the stage just as U.S. foreign policy and interventionism heat up and meet with disaster. We move, in other words, from the war in the Philippines and doubts about American imperialism and masculinity to the wars over "enemies" at home and abroad and the deep-seated fear of masculine imperial failure. To once more get our bearings, we can turn for a moment to Theodore Roosevelt.

As we have seen, Roosevelt, as much as any writer or public figure, planted the ideal of the masculine imperial self in American culture. In "The Strenuous Life" (1899), a classic of imperial eloquence, he champions American manhood and imperialism. As always, he piles clause upon clause and sentence upon sentence in celebration of his vision, and he calls on young Americans to accept their responsibilities:

> I preach to you, then, my countrymen, that our country calls not for the life of ease but for the life of strenuous endeavor. The twentieth century looms before us big with the fate of many nations. If we stand idly by, if we seek merely swollen, slothful ease and ignoble peace, if we shrink from the hard contests where men must win at hazard of their lives and at the risk of all they hold dear, then the bolder and stronger peoples will pass us by, and will win for themselves the domination of the world. Let us therefore boldly face the life of strife, resolute to do our duty well and manfully; resolute to uphold righteousness by deed and by word; resolute to be both honest and brave, to serve high ideals, yet to use practical methods. Above all, let us shrink from no strife, moral or physical, within or without the nation, provided we are certain that the strife is justified, for it is only through strife, through hard and dangerous endeavor, that we shall ultimately win the goal of true national greatness.

Indeed. For Roosevelt, the ideal citizen—his vision of the imperial self—must embrace strife, must lead the nation and the world; the namby-pamby, overcivilized types must leave the hard work of empire-building to their masculine betters. Although he argues that both men and women have roles to play—"The man must be glad to do a man's work, to dare and endure and to labor; to keep himself, and to keep those dependent upon him. The woman must be the housewife, the helpmeet of the homemaker, the wise and fearless mother of many healthy children"—the imperium belongs to men.[1] If Roosevelt has few doubts about the desirability of the masculine self and about the desirability of the empire, his writing nevertheless betrays considerable anxiety. To borrow a phrase, he doth protest too much: all his cheering about masculine power suggests that he is afraid that American men may not be up to the task, that there might be too many wimps out there. Even as he touts the masculine, he worries about the unmanly—which brings us back to Walker and to a theme found in much of the literature arising from his adventures.

In *Destiny and Glory* (1957), a book about the "epidemic" of filibustering "which broke out in the United States between the Mexican and Civil Wars," Edward S. Wallace turns away from the exploits of men to tell the story of Jane McManus, "The Female of the Species." McManus—or

Mrs. Storm, or Mrs. Cazneau, or Cora Montgomery, as she also called herself—"turned her energies to the cause of Cuban annexation to the United States," and later married William Leslie Cazneau, a business partner of Henry L. Kinney, the Texas businessman who attempted to establish an American colony on Nicaragua's Mosquito Coast at the same time Walker sailed for Realejo in 1855. Wallace links McManus circumstantially to American filibustering and commercial ventures in Texas, Cuba, Nicaragua, and the Dominican Republic, and offers a rather grandiose claim for her place in a forgotten history: "Never did this captivating woman actually participate in a pistol-shooting charge of the filibusters; in fact, she was probably never under fire. But as a behind-the-scenes wire-puller, as a power behind the throne, she well deserved [Henry] Watterson's title of 'filibuster' and a place with López, Walker and others of that lost profession."[2] Wallace delights in reports of McManus's beauty, and he seems to like the idea of a woman filibuster to round out his cast. But McManus was not, as at least one American writer would have it, the most famous woman filibuster. That honor resides, Darwin Teilhet claims in *The Lion's Skin* (1955), with William Walker. The romance, however, does not really explore the possibility of Walker as a nineteenth-century androgyne; rather, it expresses a profound anxiety over the ability of American men to win and hold an empire.

Walker's story has everything: adventure, intrigues, *affaires de cœur*, crooked business deals, millionaires, murders, assassinations, battles, conquests, empires—all the ingredients of colorful mercenary romances and novels. As it turns out, it also has currents of gender concealment and confusion. These seemingly unexpected currents arise most clearly in Teilhet, but they direct our attention to what has perhaps always been a feature of the mercenary romance: whispers of queerness or the androgynic in *The Lion's Skin* lay bare deep-seated fears over masculine power and the authority of the imperial self. What if, for all our shouting and posturing, we cannot get the job done? What if we cannot live the strenuous life? What if we are not men enough to command an empire? These fears manifest themselves in Teilhet in effeminate, queer, or androgynous representations of the imperial self, but many of the mercenary romancers worry over, mock, scorn, deny, repress, and in many other ways deal with the possibility that American men might not be, as Roosevelt feared, ideal agents of empire. If

Teilhet's relatively obscure treatment of the Walker narrative merits our attention precisely for how it worries over the less than masculine imperial self, then another, perhaps better-known rewrite of Walker's adventures from the 1950s also merits our attention for how it treats the same issues, but to rather different ends. The differences no doubt lie in the nationalities and experiences of the two writers.

If we have thus far considered only American writers in our exploration of the American imperial self in the world and on the page, we turn in this chapter to the writings of Ernesto Cardenal for a number of reasons. For one, if few Americans recall Walker, he remains one of the most well-known and understandably vilified *gringos* in Central America. He has been the subject of numerous isthmian histories, novels, stories, plays, and poems, and we can number Cardenal's narrative poems among the very best of these.[3] Moreover, not only does the Nicaraguan enjoy an international reputation as a poet and literary historian, but among Central American writers he stands uniquely qualified to write about the American imperial self. He lived in the United States and studied at Columbia University (1947–49) and with Thomas Merton at the Trappist Monastery at Gethsemani, Kentucky (1957–59), and, as a liberation theologist and Sandinista, he battled against the Somozas and their American allies.

Deeply influenced as well by American poets such as Ezra Pound and Walt Whitman, he modeled his techniques of documentary poetry and *exteriorismo* in part on their work and translated a number of their poems into Spanish.[4] In 1951 he cofounded a small press, El Hilo Azul, and brought out as its first book *Lincoln de los poetas* (Lincoln of the poets), translations of American poems about the American president. As Jonathan Cohen writes, the poet collaborated with fellow writer José Cornel Utrecho on the translation of "poems by Whitman, Masters, Bynner, Sandburg, Lindsay and others, which shared the theme of the memory of Lincoln, whom Cardenal considered the most poetic and heroic figure in U.S. history."[5] A student not only of American poetry but of U.S. history, culture, and political life, Cardenal, perhaps as much as any American writer, possesses the experience and knowledge to dissect the American imperial self. Moreover, by turning to the Nicaraguan, we not only gain a valuable non-American perspective on the imperial self (and thereby broaden the terrain of our study), but we also add a powerful, humanist reply to Teilhet's doubts over masculinity and the imperial self; much more is at stake, the poet suggests, than American anxieties.

Both Teilhet, in *The Lion's Skin*, and Cardenal, in "Con Walker en Nicaragua" (1952), ascribe feminine qualities to Walker, and they both take up the question of his gender and sexual orientation. Teilhet worries about the potential failure of American masculinist will. At the onset of the Cold War, the romancer (and literary descendant of Harte and Davis) fears that American men lack the resolve to carry out the United States' imperialist mission, and he casts Walker as an example of a treacherous unmanliness: the filibuster, he suggests, sought an empire for the wrong reasons, and he ascribes a gender and sexual "deviance" to the Tennessean not only to call into question his overall character but, in particular, to highlight his political sedition. Effeminacy and homosexuality come to signify both disloyalty to the nation *and* masculine failure. In contrast, Cardenal notes Walker's seemingly less than masculine bearing not in order to impugn the filibuster's failure as an imperialist but rather to portray him as a nearly affectless automaton dedicated to death. The problem with Walker is not that he might be homosexual or a woman in disguise, but rather that he murders Nicaraguans. Whereas Teilhet worries about the United States' ability to sustain its empire, Cardenal worries about the human costs of that empire and, by implication, about the isthmians' right to self-determination. The imperial self, he implies, is deeply broken and inhuman; dread and loss have deformed him into a monstrous killer.

Masculine/Imperialist Failure in *The Lion's Skin*

Was Walker a woman?

Probably not.

By most historical accounts, Walker was a diminutive, abstemious, and quiet individual. No historian, however, credits the theory that Walker was a woman; such speculations belong to romance writers. At the same time, the freebooter does not fit the popular image of the soldier of fortune as a large and powerful man. In *Agents of Manifest Destiny* (1980), for example, Charles H. Brown compares Walker to other freebooters and demonstrates that his appearance continues to fascinate commentators almost as much as his actions:

Filibuster leaders—López, Quitman, Flores, Raousset-Boulbon—were bold and flamboyant soldiers, commanding in physique, eloquent in speech, magnetic in their attraction for other people. Walker had few, if any, of the these assets. Only five feet, five inches tall, weighing less than 120 pounds, soft-spoken, withdrawn in the company of others, he was an insignificant figure among the boisterous and rough-and-ready men of San Francisco.[6]

For Brown, as for many others, Walker was not as masculine as other men, especially not as masculine as his fellow swashbucklers. Walker did not drink, did not smoke, did not curse, did not appear to pursue women—in short, he did not behave the way a mercenary should behave. As a young New Orleans woman—who seems to have possessed an unrequited passion for Walker—writes in a September 22, 1860, letter, "He is no 'lady's man' and lived but for 'Central America and Freedom.'"[7] In his mercenary romance, Teilhet picks up on these representations of Walker's size and deportment: he was small enough, and seemingly feminine enough, to be a woman.

More than any rewriter of the freebooter's adventures, Teilhet worries about the filibuster's masculinity. While we might expect him to represent the freebooter as an icon of violent masculinity, he offers competing representations of Walker as an effeminate man, as a homosexual, or, at the extreme, as a woman masquerading as a man. He depicts Walker as a *disfrazada* (a transvestite) in order to condemn the mercenary: the Tennessean betrays his men and his nation in an effort to fulfill his true, yet devious ambition; he wants to break apart the United States. The less than manly imperial self seeks an empire, but for the wrong reasons. Moreover, Teilhet casts "the gray-eyed man of destiny" as a homosexual or an androgyne not only to impugn Walker's politics but also to explain why an American won Nicaragua only to lose it: a woman or a half-man or a homosexual cannot do a man's work of filibustering and empire-building. In Walker's stead, Teilhet offers John Sanderson as the classic young American and romance hero. Tall, good looking, loyal to family and nation, he honors his imperial obligations. Whereas the feminized man participates in gender and political subterfuge, the man's man—a man from the pages of Roosevelt's essays and addresses—envisions the right sort of imperialism, one in which the United States paternally accepts Nicaragua as a protectorate. Despite the valorization of Sanderson's version of expansionism, however, the novel fails to establish the masculine ideal: Walker loses control of Nicaragua, but the hero never sees it become part of the United States; the step from the effeminate to the imperial masculine never occurs. While we might argue that Teilhet cannot quite get around history—Walker failed, after all, and no one succeeded him in Nicaragua—the truer reason for his failure to imagine a masculinist triumph may rest with deep-seated Cold War anxieties about American imperial resolve.

Just as we read Harte's and Davis's romances as narratives of Manifest Destiny *and* their respective eras of composition, we can do the same with *The Lion's Skin*. As we shall see in this chapter, the romancer—steeped in the homophobic and interventionist discourses of the McCarthy era—writes about not only the 1850s but also the 1950s. Like many of his contemporaries, he suffers from the Red Scare, and he fears that the Soviet Union and China will usurp U.S. power and influence in Asia and around the world. But even as he fears external forces, he also fears—once again like many of his contemporaries—enemies within. The romance betrays anxieties about the (supposed) internal corruption being wrought by communists inside the State Department and other branches of government. Worse still, homosexuals pose a serious risk to the vigor and security of the nation. They are both too effete to do the work of men and too open, because of their "predilections," to extortion and exposure. Through his look back at Walker's defeat, Teilhet expresses a profound fear of the internal and external forces that could lead to U.S. failure in Asia; at the deepest levels, he fears the defeat of the American imperial self and the collapse of the imperium.

The author of over forty mystery, science fiction, adventure, and children's books, Teilhet probably does not have much of an audience today, and a brief summary of his novel may be in order.[8] Based upon the author's researches and travels in Central America—and written on the occasion of the one hundredth anniversary of Walker's landing at Realejo—*The Lion's Skin* follows John Sanderson's adventures in Central America. After prospecting for gold in Honduras, he makes his way toward Nicaragua to catch a steamer bound for the United States. Soon after crossing the border, however, he comes upon a "tawny-haired girl" beset by a soldier with an eyepatch; a hero-in-the-making, he intervenes and rescues Tarra Manning. Manning's father, it turns out, has been influential in persuading the Leonese to bring Walker to the isthmus, and the old man explains his "progressive" sentiments to Sanderson. Already an admirer of the filibuster's Sonoran campaign, the young American avidly supports Walker's goal of bringing "Nicaragua into the Union": as he enthusiastically remarks, "'The Nicaraguan Territory of the United States!' It sounded wonderful saying it."[9] Out of admiration not only for Walker and Manning but also out of an attraction for Tarra, he joins the Immortals. As the action progresses, however, he grows disillusioned with Walker for what he takes to be the filibuster's hidden agenda. After a series of adventures, daring escapes, and battles (closely based upon Walker's account of the Immortals' campaigns), Sanderson does his part to defeat Walker while still holding onto his dream of American control of the isthmus. As the novel ends, Sanderson marries Tarra, settles on a ranch in Nicaragua, and dedicates his life to his family and his religion.

Following in the literary footsteps of Harte's Hurlstone and Davis's Clay and Macklin, Sanderson fits the paradigm of the already lost American abroad. And, once again, the circumstances of his departure from the United States foreground the metaphysics of the slave trade (if not, on this rare occasion, the metaphysics of Indian-hating). Sanderson's father, the publisher of a newspaper in Jacksonville, Illinois, suffers a brutal death because of his political views: "One drowsy August afternoon, about dusk, a dozen Missouri raiders spurred into town and reined up in front of my father's newspaper shop, shouting, 'We'll give that goddamn Abolitionist editor something to print!'" Sanderson, out "courting" on the fateful day, blames himself for his father's death: "I remembered seeing my father on the floor of his office, a bullet through his eye, his body torn by other bullets, the windows smashed. If I had been where I should have been, that afternoon and evening, being on guard, my father might not have been surprised. He might not have been killed by the slavery men from across the river."[10] Where Harte's Hurlstone seeks, through his school, to redress in small measure some of the harm done Indians, Sanderson sets off for the isthmus burdened with the history and violence of slavery. Once he has the chance to do what he sees as some good in the world—join Walker's forces for the liberation of Nicaragua—he jumps at the chance. He seeks to redeem his earlier defeat and refashions his father's abolitionist beliefs into a doctrine of benevolent imperialism. Like Harte, Teilhet wants to believe in a gentle sort of empire, run by the right sort of right-minded imperial selves.

In many ways, Sanderson stands as a romance version of Roosevelt's ideal citizen. Like the politician's young Americans, Sanderson pledges his fervent allegiance to ever-widening spheres. For one, he feels a deep bond and responsibility toward his father and his father's business; despite his feelings of guilt, he has been a dutiful son. Once in Nicaragua, he also forms a deep attachment to Manning and Tarra, and he never abandons this second family or their economic or political concerns. And if he values family first—just as he should—he also supports his nation and its empire. He believes in the United States as a firm, yet beneficent force for the advancement of civilization, and he does what he can to secure American influence in Nicaragua. Like the ideal imperial self, he is also not inclined toward too much introspection; although he questions American motives in the isthmus on one or two occasions, he does not probe too deeply into his political assumptions.[11] Like Roosevelt, he has made up his mind. Moreover, he has not grown soft through the debilitating effects of too much education or the irresponsible pursuit of wealth. An exemplum of American masculinity, he is an open, honest, patriotic, passionate, virile, brave, and—above all—robust man. He enjoys physical activity and physical danger, knows what must be done, and he will sacrifice his life, if necessary. He is both the ideal citizen and the ideal romance hero,[12] and if Teilhet presents his young American as the masculine imperial self, he presents Walker as the treacherous converse.

From the outset of *The Lion's Skin*, Teilhet speculates on Walker's ultimate goal for the Nicaraguan expedition. While historians and Walker enthusiasts do not agree on what the freebooter wanted to achieve through his incursion—did he want to be emperor of the Isthmus? did he set out, imbued with the spirit of democracy, to create the United States of Central America? did he lack a goal or plan beyond a desire for conquest?—Teilhet offers one of the most perceptive readings: Walker invaded Nicaragua in order to break apart the United States. The filibuster, he argues, wanted to reintroduce slavery to the isthmus in order to join the region to the southern U.S. slave states and thereby sunder the Union. The invasion was part of an elaborate secessionist plot. After Walker abrogates Cornelius Vanderbilt's transit franchise, Will Doubleday, Sanderson's friend and one of the novel's lesser heroes, offers his take on Walker's scheme:

> I submit that Walker was leagued with these California secessionists from the very beginning. I submit that he never was a filibuster in the sense of Houston and Fremont and others of kindred spirit were. What were Walker and his California secesh friends after if not to establish a slave empire in the Caribbean to bulwark the eventual establishment of a separate Southern Confederacy?[13]

For Teilhet, Walker was not the right sort of imperial self; he pursued American annexation of Nicaragua for the wrong reasons. He set out to take away from the body of the United States rather than to add to it; unlike Roosevelt's ideal man, he did not honor his obligations to nation and empire.

Walker, Teilhet suggests, also betrayed his men. When they first land, the Tennessean makes it known to his officers that the Immortals are in the isthmus not to colonize but to annex Nicaragua. When Sanderson asks if the Nicaraguans will not resist Walker's efforts "to bring this gateway to California under the American flag," Charley Hornsby, an old friend and one of the filibusters' leading officers, responds:

> Resist? Johnny, where you been? These Nicaraguans haven't been free from Spain long enough to think of themselves as a nation. They're scared of Mexico, not us. The progressives are looking *our* way for a protective treaty and alliance. Why, that's just a step from annexation. And Walker's too smart to discuss the whole scheme, yet. He says he's only here to help regenerate Nicaragua. When the war's finished, let the people make up their own minds and vote what way they want.[14]

Hornsby and Sanderson believe in notions of regeneration and American exceptionalism. The United States, as the good neighbor, charges into the isthmus not to plunder and conquer but to improve the civilization of Central America. To annex Nicaragua would not be an act of belligerent imperialism but rather one of uplift. Nevertheless, Hornsby's arguments reveal the usual prejudices: the childlike isthmians do not understand government; they tremble in fear; they require paternal guidance. For Sanderson, this would be the right sort of imperialism: American men would show their masculinity through the benevolent leadership of the hemisphere's lesser nations. But Walker lied to his men, and Teilhet wants to show the filibuster as a deceiver in more than just political matters.

Walker's treachery provides the novel with its central metaphor and title. Teilhet, quoting Plutarch, represents the freebooter as a leader whose seemingly noble rhetoric and actions conceal a cunning and deceitful nature: "For where the lion's skin will not reach, you must patch it out with the fox's."[15] Something, he insinuates, was wrong with Walker to make him behave in this manner. But what? Was he just a political schemer, or did his trespasses stem from deeper, more personal currents? The image of skin points the reader's attention to the body: there's something wrong or unnatural about his body, his self, his very being. More than merely devious, he was skewed from within, and his political transgressions flow from that internal twisting. He not only covered up his true political nature, but he was also covering up much more basic matters of his identity: his sexuality or even his gender.

Teilhet expresses his contempt for Walker by attacking his masculinity. Like many readers of the Nicaraguan invasion, he wonders why the filibuster failed. He suggests that the freebooter's military weakness and political deceitfulness stem from a warped body and soul. When Sanderson first meets Walker, he characterizes him as "a meticulous little alderman" and puzzles—as many of the Immortals do—over why their leader never "looks" at women. But Teilhet cannot make up his mind about what exactly was *wrong* the Tennessean, and so he offers a variety of takes that all assail the freebooter's manhood. First, he speculates that Walker covered up his true gender: as Tarra Manning remarks, "Even in Coyólar they whisper it. General Walker is a disfrazada. A woman masquerading as a man. It is why he seeks no woman here for himself and will not look at one."[16] Teilhet offers a strange misogyny, in which ethical and political corruption stem from the androgynic. The fact that Walker executed a number of his political adversaries—and was responsible for a great many other deaths—barely rates a mention: what was really wrong with him was that he was a woman pretending to be a man.

Teilhet, however, appears uncomfortable with this reading of Walker, and so modifies his position. If Walker was not a woman, Sanderson implies that he was at very least homosexual. He makes this plain in the usual, derogatory way; the freebooter surrounds himself with sissies: "With his long silky hair flying, Captain Davidson came running up to me as I approached the main plaza. While I waited for him to demand why I was absent without permission, I wondered why the slimmest and most girlish-looking young devils to join up usually ended as Walker's aides-de-camp."[17] Once again, he portrays Walker as less than a man; his queerness—his sexual deviance—bespeaks an entire range of perversions and deceits. A homosexual cannot be trusted to behave in the proper way. A homosexual would want to destroy the nation rather than build a greater one. His treachery stems from his sexuality, and, simultaneously, his sexuality prevents him from maintaining power. Just as a woman cannot do the job of empire-building, neither can a homosexual. For Teilhet, a homosexual could not be a true man, could not be the true imperial self.

Teilhet's reading of Walker-as-queer perhaps stems in part from a passage in *The War in Nicaragua*. Reflecting upon the American losses during the Falange's first attack against Rivas, Walker mourns the passing of Timothy Crocker. The freebooter seems once more to reassert the "sensitive" nature of his younger self:

> The death of Crocker was a loss hardly to be repaired. A boy in appearance, with a slight figure, and a face almost feminine in its delicacy and beauty, he had the heart of the lion; and his eye, usually mild and gentle, though steady in its expression, was quick to perceive a false movement on the part of an adversary, and then its flash was like the gleam of a scimitar as it falls on the head of a foe.... To Walker he was invaluable; for they had been together in many a trying hour, and the fellowship of difficulty and danger had established a sort of freemasonry between them.[18]

The romancer picks up upon the feminized description of Crocker, no doubt noting that, of all Walker's descriptions of his men, this stands as one of the most flowery, the most personal. The language of "flashing" eyes, "scimitars," and "a sort of freemasonry" could, alongside Walker's well-publicized indifference to women, lead to a reading of the filibuster as a closeted homosexual.

Teilhet, of course, is not the only student of Walker to make this assertion; just as many of the freebooter's chroniclers complain that no one remembers him, many note his "deviant sexuality." In *The Filibuster* (1937), a history of Walker's exploits, Laurence Greene sums up the soldier of fortune's personality: "He was biased, egocentric, monominded, quite possibly the victim of a sexual disorder, utterly unfair in his motives, acts and conclusions."[19] Greene does not spell out what he means by "a sexual disorder," but he does not have to: Walker was queer. In the foreword (1985) to a reprint of *The War in Nicaragua*, novelist Robert Houston makes the point more explicitly:

> No material I've encountered has mentioned the word "homosexual" in relation to Walker, though there is sufficient evidence at least strongly to suggest the possibility. Throughout his brief life, his strongest attachments—with the exception of those of his mother and one other woman—were to men, and he avenged wrongs against his favorites with a passion that often went beyond common reason (you'll find those in this book).

The list of those who hint at or name Walker as homosexual could go on, but even if we cannot definitively determine Walker's sexual orientation, we can at least agree with "one Guatemalan general" who suggested that although Walker may have been asexual or impotent, he loved "the sensuality of power."[20]

Although Teilhet sees Walker as a *disfrazada* or as a homosexual, in yet another curious move in the author's note appended to the end of the romance, Teilhet claims that Walker *did* have a mistress while in Nicaragua, but she was not Nina Yrena Ojaran, as some historians have suggested: "I am also indebted to Pablo Antonio Caudra, Nicaragua's principal playwright, who is working on a play whose subject is the tragedy of Walker's mistress. Because descendants of Walker and the young Granadina woman still live in Nicaragua I have avoided giving her true name, making her La Nina's sister which suffices."[21] No other American account of Walker's life in Nicaragua asserts, however, that he sired any children. Teilhet perhaps wishes to suggest that Walker had an affair in an effort to conceal or deny his own sexuality. Whatever the case, he has already done the work of explaining why Walker behaved as he did, and why he failed in his treasonous secessionist plot. Walker was not man enough to hold Nicaragua and take the rest of the isthmus. Perfidious, he was not the right sort of American imperial self.

If Teilhet, in his reading of Walker, does not attempt an early postmodern deconstruction of gender, the romance does suggest some serious gender trouble. But rather than exploring gender as performance, Teilhet, whether he means to or not, suggests that the reception of gender poses its own set of problems. An expert reader in some ways of Walker's adventures, the romancer cannot seem to make up his mind about what, precisely, was *wrong* with Walker. Was he a woman disguised as a man? Was he an androgyne? Was he a homosexual? Was he a homosexual who attempted to conceal his homosexuality through a heterosexual affair with a Nicaraguan woman? While we can be fairly certain that the freebooter was no Pope Joan, Teilhet cannot make sense of Walker's performance of gender. If he was the "gray-eyed man of destiny," why did he look and sound like a woman? If he was a freebooting agent of empire, why did he not drink whiskey and chase women?

In a converse manner, the romance confirms Butler's analysis of gender. Once the performance transcends normative limits, it reveals its lack of ground, its state of flux. Teilhet seems uncomfortable with his different takes on Walker, abandoning them almost as soon as he comes up with them; he cannot get a fix on the filibuster. Reading gender causes him considerable anxiety, and he does not know what to make of his insights. Nevertheless, if he cannot fix Walker's gender, he has little doubt that queerness poses a serious threat to the nation.

Rife with anxiety about homosexuality and about American power, *The Lion's Skin* is very much a novel of its time. Written at the peak of McCarthyism and in the wake of the Soviet blockade of Berlin in 1948, the fall of China to Mao's communists in 1949, stalemate in Korea in 1953, the fall of Dien Bien Phu in 1954, and the fear of the "domino effect" throughout Asia, it vilifies homosexuality as a menace to U.S. imperialism. Joseph McCarthy, along with his allies on the House Un-American Activities Committee (HUAC) and elsewhere in the government, sought to root out all sorts of "un-American" activities. Along with charging that the State Department had been infiltrated with communists (a charge never substantiated), he and others argued that homosexuals must be forced out of government not only for ethical reasons but also because their behavior exposed them to blackmail and manipulation by foreign powers. As Stephen J. Whitfield notes,

> Sexual "deviants," it was assumed, were so readily equated with security risks because they were so readily susceptible to seduction and then subject to blackmail, or—since they were so bereft of willpower or moral control

anyway—they were easily drawn to subversive organizations on their own. A 1950 Senate report, *Employment of Homosexuals and Other Sex Perverts in Government*, confidently asserted, for example, that "those who engage in overt acts of perversion lack the emotional stability of normal persons. . . . One homosexual can pollute a Government office."

Homosexuals, the Senate thought, posed a threat to the nation from within. Sexual treachery as political and national treachery; Americans imperiling American power. Teilhet offers his own spin on the tenor of the day: Walker, as an un-American deviant, threatened American power in the isthmus. Just as McCarthy wanted to get rid of homosexuals, Teilhet devises a scheme to push the freebooter from office. When Walker's secessionist plan becomes clear to him, Sanderson dedicates himself to "replacing Walker with Charlie Hornsby."[22]

As McCarthy and Teilhet make clear, the attacks on homosexuals and the State Department (and the secretary of the army) were not just about identifying threats from within—they were also about American imperialism. After "losing" China and suffering defeats in Korea, McCarthy and his allies wanted to promote an aggressive foreign policy. They attacked members of the State Department in order to intimidate them or to replace them with policy architects who shared their truculent beliefs. As he remarked in his first attack (1950) on the State Department, "Today we are engaged in a final, all-out battle between communistic atheism and Christianity. The modern champions of communism have selected this as the time. And, ladies and gentlemen, the chips are down—they are truly down."[23] In McCarthy's apocalyptic vision, the struggle for control of the planet had begun, and he called for an American holy war against communism. He wanted the United States to take aggressive control over other nations and world affairs. At the deepest levels, McCarthy and his cohorts worried about American defeat; as policy agents of empire, they wanted to ensure the continued power of the imperium. The United States, they argued in their particularly vicious and divisive ways, was in the process of losing the war, of defeating itself.

Teilhet, for all his attacks on Walker and homosexuality, never quite succeeds in establishing the imperialist masculine, leaving the reader with the defeat of what he sees as U.S. interests in the isthmus. After Sanderson turns against his one-time hero, he refuses to abandon his belief that Nicaragua should become a U.S. protectorate: "It was worth saddling Nicaragua with Walker to obtain annexation. But what happened to the long view if Walker went forward and attempted to conquer Central America or by his ambition raised a coalition of forces strong enough to throw out not only him but all the Americans out of Nicaragua?" Longing to see his dream come true, he even vows to assassinate Walker if Will Doubleday fails in his plot to lure Walker into a duel: "Will . . . if you should get yourself rubbed off, I'd like you to know I'll go at Walker myself in true Central American fashion. With a pistol."[24] The masculine, desperate to establish dominance over the androgynic or the queer, takes the phallus in hand to settle the matter. Sanderson never gets his chance; despite the hero's willingness to commit murder to protect American power, the allied forces of Central America expel Walker and his army.

Responsibility for American defeat, Teilhet suggests, rests with the Americans themselves. The freebooter's sexual and political duplicity contributes to the undoing of the Immortals, but the masculine, would-be imperial self fails to take power in his place. Sanderson cannot triumph, cannot undo Walker's treachery, cannot push back the allied forces of Central America. He cannot rise to the imperial occasion; he cannot be the ideal man, the robust imperial self. Like Roosevelt and McCarthy, Teilhet worries that Americans, through their own corruptions and weaknesses, will defeat themselves, will be unable to fulfill the nation's imperialist responsibilities. Whereas Davis's Robert Clay found conquering a nation a relatively easy matter, a mid-twentieth-century romancer cannot offer the same fantasy of empire. Read in the context of the early 1950s, *The Lion's Skin* stands as a cautionary tale: we had better watch out, or the Reds and their allies will overrun us. We had better be vigilant and ready to act with force, or our softness and potential for corruption from within will lead to defeat. If we lose, we will only have ourselves to blame.

As a descendant of *Captain Macklin*, *The Lion's Skin* also confirms the shift in the mercenary romance toward gloom and loss. The form no longer promises dashing heroes and rousing adventures; rather, it promises increasingly less glamorous, less able characters caught up in violence they cannot control. It also promises increasingly sordid and vicious American antagonists and antiheroes involved in increasingly corrupt schemes. The mercenary romance no longer promises quaint, fog-enshrouded outposts or semi-edenic jungles replete with natural resources and a largely untapped, albeit lazy and unskilled labor force; rather, it promises death-haunted journeys into sweltering backwaters, corrupt and villainous fiefdoms, and corpse-strewn wastelands. More importantly, rather than victory, the form promises defeat; it promises the defeat of the imperial self and the failure of American masculinity. The allied forces of greed, corruption, and deceit begin to overwhelm the strength, cunning, and good intentions of the less-than-spectacular protagonist. Adrift in his or her personal affairs and seeking redemption, the protagonist no longer finds an ennobling purpose in life. He or she can no longer count on making a positive difference in the lives of others or in the growth of American capital; he or she can no longer cast themselves as agents of regeneration, uplift, or industrialization. Increasingly, the mercenary romance represents the thwarting of American ideals; visions of beneficence, economic development, and *la mission civilisatrice* give way to acts of savagery, confusion, and regret. And, rather than promising American ascendancy, the form warns against American weakness and the collapse of U.S. imperial might; it promises the defeat of national interests and imperial aspirations. In not many more years, it will promise that America was never the beneficent agent of progress and civilization it claimed to be.

An imperialist fiction, *The Lion's Skin* is not without ambivalence about the rightness of U.S. interventionism. Throughout the novel, Sanderson remains committed to the building of an American empire, but on the last page, he seems to have a change of heart. After his marriage, he goes "great ways in seeking God" and settles upon a less belligerent view of politics: "And we will then find the true peace that St. Augustine tells us is that . . . 'when all that [the pilgrim] does for the obtaining hereof is by himself referred unto God, and his neighbor withal, because being a citizen, he must not be all for himself, but sociable in his life and actions.'"[25] In this rather convoluted coda, Teilhet seems to advocate a more benign approach to U.S. dealings with its neighbors, and it situates Sanderson in a more mellow masculinity of fatherhood. Although the novel overwhelmingly presents U.S. domination as desirable, Teilhet here seems to hint that the spiritual and human costs of imperialism may be worth considering. Nevertheless, a tone of regret pervades *The Lion's Skin:* because of Walker's deceitful nature, an opportunity was lost; the United States could have become an even larger, greater nation if Walker had practiced the right sort of imperialism.

Cardenal's Walker

Ernesto Cardenal's treatment of Walker and his Nicaraguan adventures offers a telling, non-American counterpoint to Teilhet's romance. In *With Walker in Nicaragua and Other Early Poems, 1949–1954* (1985), Cardenal confronts the American conquest of his country. A leading Latin American poet, a proponent of liberation theology, a Sandinista and former Nicaraguan minister of culture, Cardenal is perhaps the ideal anti-imperialist to confront U.S. interventionism. Not only does he possess a profound sense of history, but he also knows firsthand the costs and consequences of the U.S. proxy system. In the title piece, "Con Walker en Nicaragua"—a narrative poem and example of what Robert Pring-Mill has called Cardenal's "documentary" style—the poet notes Walker's feminine appearance and manners, but rather than attacking his masculinity, he foregrounds the violence of filibustering.[26] Whereas Teilhet glosses over the human costs of conquest, Cardenal focuses on destruction and death. He presents the American imperial self as a murderous, deformed automaton, and he offers a searching explanation for Walker's chilling violence: the imperial urge arises not from some empyrean inspiration—as Emerson and Walker would have it—but rather from a confluence of dread and loss. The poet dives deeper than perhaps any other reteller of the freebooter's life into the wellsprings of Walker's imperialism.

If we can read *The Lion's Skin* as a Cold War novel, we can see Cardenal's Walker poems as about both the Cold War and, more importantly, American imperialism-by-proxy. Although U.S. policymakers in the late 1940s and early 1950s focused primarily on the Red Threat in Europe and Asia, this did not mean that they had lost sight of American interests in Central America, and successive administrations did their best to keep leftist or reformist forces out of power in the isthmus. In Nicaragua, for example, following the assassination of Augusto César Sandino and the ascension of Anastasio Tacho Somoza in 1934, the United States had reliable, if vicious allies until the Sandinista revolution of 1979. In Costa Rica in 1948, José

Figueres—with the support of the CIA—overthrew the elected government of Picado Michalski and became acting president. As the officially elected president of Costa Rica (1953–58), he ensured the safety and productivity of lands controlled by the United Fruit Company. In Guatemala, under the reign of Jorge Ubico (1931–44), Sam Zemurray developed vast tracts of land and owned the railroad, the ports, and the telephone and telegraph operations; in 1954, with the cooperation of United Fruit, the CIA, and the White House, Carlos Castillo Armas seized power in the coup against the legitimately elected, reformist government of Jacobo Arbenz. Following, as we have seen, the entrenchment of the Vaccaro brothers' Standard Fruit in 1899 and Zemurray's Cuyamel Fruit in 1907, Honduras became the model "banana republic"; following the Hay-Bunau-Varilla Treaty in 1903, the United States enjoyed a dominant military, political, and economic presence in Panama for most of the twentieth century. In country after country, the United States exerted its preponderant economic, military, and political power and worked to suppress Marxist, socialist, or progressive movements; the Cold War, if less spectacularly, was waged unceasingly in the isthmus, and Cardenal rewrites Walker's adventures as a means not only to explore the age of Manifest Destiny but also—and more importantly—to confront the continued U.S. presence in Central America.

In a complex move, Cardenal focalizes the poem through Clinton Rollins, an American who looks back upon his service in Walker's Nicaraguan expedition. Rather than telling Walker's story from the perspective of a Nicaraguan, Cardenal takes the step few American writers ever take: to tell the story from the other side's point of view. He does so for several reasons. First, it draws attention to the fact that Americans rarely take the perspective of the Central Americans. (Pick up most American novels set in the isthmus and count the number of isthmians who even have speaking parts, let alone anything like psychological complexity or depth.) The poet suggests that to tell any story, you must see it from more than one perspective. Second, it hard-wires into the poem—to borrow a phrase from Said—the *positional superiority* of the United States over Central America. If American writers sometimes feel little need to understand history from the perspective of the Nicaraguans, the Nicaraguans can little ignore the presence of the United States in their history. Third, the selection of an American narrator suggests that Cardenal has not given up on the United States. The poet, despite U.S. support for the Somozas, seems not to despise the United States or Americans but rather, through a generosity of spirit, holds out the possibility that regardless of past violence, Americans and Nicaraguans can coexist peacefully.

Cardenal offers a portrait of the imperial self as an automaton, as an affectless killer. Like Teilhet, he attributes feminine aspects to Walker, but he does not do so to attack his politics; like Teilhet, he hints that Walker may have been queer. Just as the romancer notes Walker's fondness for Crocker, the poet implies it as well—"y Crocker, el afeminado, / que murió jadeante en Rivas" (and Crocker, the pretty-boy, / who died gasping for breath at Rivas)—but he does not do so to attack his masculinity. What is most important about Walker is not his small physique, his unmasculine voice, or his possible queerness, but rather his blankness, his lack of human emotion:

> . . . sus modales de clérigo,
> su voz, descolorida como sus ojos, fría y afilada,
> en una boca sin labios.
> Y la voz de una mujer no era más suave que la suya:
> la de los serenos anuncios de las sentencias de muerte . . .
> La que arrastró a tantos a la boca de la muerte en los combates.
> Nunca bebía ni fumaba y no llevaba uniforme.
> Ninguno fue su amigo.
> Y no recuerdo haberlo visto jamás sonreír.
>
> (. . . his clergyman's ways,
> his voice, colorless like his eyes, cold and sharp,
> in a mouth without lips.
> And a woman's voice was hardly softer than his:
> that calm voice of his announcing death sentences . . .
> that swept so many into the jaws of death in combat.
> He never drank or smoked and he wore no uniform.
> Nobody was his friend.
> And I don't remember ever having seen him smile.)

The poet portrays Walker as less than human, as an isolated, yet vicious machine dedicated to death. The soldier of fortune's "woman's voice" amounts to one more incongruous feature of his seemingly unaccountable personality. He seems not to see, or value, the life around him—"sus ojos grises, sin pupilas, fijos como los de un ciego" (grey eyes, without pupils, fixed like a blind man's)—and he offers no generosity, no warmth.[27] But why, Cardenal wonders, was Walker this way? Why this murderous numbness?

Hollow and cruel, Walker seems to be dead inside; in turn, he projects that inward deathliness outward and exemplifies David Spurr's colonial trope of "negation." As Spurr argues in *The Rhetoric of Empire* (1993), a void within Western consciousness has fueled the imperialist project:

> The representation of non-Western reality as nothingness in various forms actually serves as a projection of a more radical absence in Western consciousness. As the work of Conrad so eloquently demonstrates, there is a void at the center of consciousness that must be named or given an image in order that it be contained. The terror of this void produces the fugitive inauthenticity that Heidegger ascribes to modern existence, a constant fleeing in the face of death.[28]

This fear of death—of the meaninglessness of life in an alien universe—opens a gnawing void within the imperial self. Rather than confronting this fear of annihilation, the imperial self denies the absence within and projects it outward onto the space of less powerful peoples. The life and land of others become a nothingness, a space to be filled with desires and corpses; it becomes a space in which to combat the dread within through acts of violence. As Cardenal suggests, however, no amount of barbarity will ease the terror, and it consumes the imperial self, turning him into an automaton, an abjection, a thing dead within and deadly without.

The razing of Granada constitutes Walker's penultimate act of negation. In 1857, during the allied war against the Americans, Walker ordered one of his generals, George F. Henningsen, to remain behind with a small force in order to protect the filibusters' withdrawal from the city. Once the Tennessean and the bulk of his men had escaped, Henningsen was to destroy the Legitimists' former capital. As Walker recounts in *The War in Nicaragua* (1860), he wanted to punish the Nicaraguans for turning against him—he had never, in fact, enjoyed much support—and he argued that the city had forfeited its right to be: "As to the justice of the act, few can question it; for its inhabitants owed life and property to the Americans in the service of Nicaragua, and yet they joined the enemies who strove to drive their protectors from Central America." On the last day of the siege, as Henningsen prepared to extricate the last of his decimated cohort, his men detonated powder trains and leveled the center of the city. As his final act, the general drove a lance, bearing a rawhide flag, into the ground. The flag read "Aquí Fue Granada" (Here was Granada).[29]

Cardenal records, through Rollins, the destruction of the city. Walker's men turned it into an inferno:

> ¡Y si hubiéramos podido entonces embarcarnos
> y dejar la desolada Granada
> —*el Castillo Blanco*, como nosotros le decíamos—
> con sus calles ensangrentadas y sus pozos hediondos llenos de muertos,
> y las muecas de los muertos a la luz de los incendios en las calles!
> Nos defendíamos de las balas tras montones de muertos.
>
> (If only we could have sailed off right then
> and left that ruined Granada
> —*the White Castle*, as we used to call it—
> with its bloodstained streets and its stinking wells full of corpses,
> and the dead's grimaces lit by fires in the streets!
> We protected ourselves from bullets from behind piles of corpses.)[30]

Cold and lifeless, Walker projects outward the void within; he calls into being a wasteland without to equal the wastes within. Granada becomes a ruin of fire and corpses, and, to make matters worse, cholera infects both the Immortals and the surviving Nicaraguans. The terrain of the less powerful becomes an Old Testament city of pestilence and death, and the poet takes his reader into the streets to witness the monstrousness of conquest and defeat. Too bad, Cardenal suggests, for the imperial self and his dread; he may suffer his existential angst, but others will have to pay for it. While Spurr argues that "negation combines elements of the psychological and the metaphysical," it remains profoundly material: the poor, brown-skinned people of the world fall once more into the scarifying march of history.[31]

In the end, the poet asserts, the death Walker most sought was his own; negation leads to self-annihilation. Whereas Walker could have abandoned filibustering after his expulsion from Nicaragua, he raises force after force, seeking not to reestablish a pocket empire—the task was hopeless; the Central Americans would never allow him to return—but rather to meet death. He wants a bullet to the head, wants his face shot off, and he will keep going until it happens. As the poem closes, Rollins recounts Walker's execution:

>   Podían ver desde donde estaban
>   una fosa cavada en la arena,
>   y a Walker junto la fosa, que seguía hablando
>   calmo y sereno.
>   Y el hombre dijo:
>   "El Presidente
>   el Presidente de Nicaragua, es nicaragüense . . . "
>
>   (They could see from where they stood
>   a newly made grave in the sand,
>   and Walker, who kept speaking, calm and dignified,
>   beside the grave.
>   And the man said:
>   "The President
>   the President of Nicaragua, is a Nicaraguan . . . ")[32]

Walker speaks calmly and with dignity not because he wishes to appear noble and untouchable, but because his anguish will soon end. He looks upon his own grave and finally feels peace. In a moment, he will be undone, will have crossed into the void, and he will no longer have to endure the churning dread within. The poet represents the imperial self as Thanatos, as a radical turning away from pleasure and toward destruction, decay, and death.

While "Con Walker en Nicaragua" provides a chilling portrait of the imperial self and negation, Cardenal attempts to humanize—at least in some measure—the freebooter's inhuman behavior. Like many of his North American counterparts, he portrays Walker as an already lost American abroad and asserts an early emotional trauma as partial explanation for the freebooter's murderous actions: the death-urge arises in Walker not because he loathes his own desires or sexuality, but rather because all life drained from him after the death of his beloved, Helen Galt Martin. We catch a glimpse of her and the faintest trace of compassion during his one act of "kindness." After arresting General Ponciano Corral, a leader of the Granadians, for treason, Walker seems to see her ghost and delays the execution: "Como si una compasión fugaz como el vuelo de un párpado / hubiera cruzado entonces sus incolores ojos de hielo, / dijo levantando la mano: /—que Corral no sería fusilado / a las doce del día . . . sino a las dos de la tarde" (As if a fleeting compassion like the batting of an eyelid / had then crossed his colorless eyes of ice, / lifting his hand he said: /—that

Corral would not be shot / at noon ... but at two in the afternoon).[33] His act of generosity provokes laughter among the Immortals, and shows the depth of his emptiness; for a brief moment, he thinks of Helen, but the absence within brought about in part by her death—how could God let his love die?—quickly reasserts itself and he adds insult to murder. In Walker's case, the imperial self has transformed from a subject to an object, from a person to a nearly lifeless thing.

Cardenal offers a rather stark counterpoint to most of the American representations of the imperial self that we have examined in this study. Whereas Emerson imagined a beneficent young American, dedicated to idealism and altruism, the poet sees a haunting machine of subjugation and erasure. His Walker does not believe in the rhetoric of regeneration; he believes in murder, in asserting the power of the self even if it only masks the death instinct. The imperial self does not, for the pure pleasure of the mind and soul, toss creation like a bauble; in an effort to quiet the howling within, he executes foes, razes cities, and awaits the firing squad. He does not speak as a poet; he dispassionately orders the deaths of others. He does not experience a sudden flash of insight and see the future in a moment; rather, he sees unending darkness ahead. Whereas Harte hopes for a mild benevolence, Cardenal hopes for an end to American interference; even the best intentions and gentlest desires represent a thwarting of autonomy and self-determination. Whereas the romancer wishes for benign commercial ventures, the poet has seen banana companies, fincas, proxy wars, death squads, and assassinations. Whereas Davis imagines a youthful swashbuckler, Cardenal gives us the real thing, a man willing to raise a force and invade a foreign land. Clay may, with ease, put down a coup and win the girl, but the actual workings of power have little of charm or grace or fine adventure about them. We cannot, perhaps, ask too much of a romance, but even Davis, in *Macklin*, began to see through the genre and into the darker workings of empire. Whereas Roosevelt conjures the ideal citizen, a man dedicated to family and nation and empire, Cardenal sees a twisted, deformed figure that values neither family nor life nor greater political, military, or economic purposes. Walker serves only the basest desires for power and the obliteration of others. The imperial self, he suggests, holds no ideals, no superior ambitions, no sense of the value or rights of others. The imperial self covets, takes, kills, and waits around for his own destruction. No other writer or theorist of the imperial self comes close to Cardenal's portrait (with the possible exception of Cormac McCarthy in *Blood Meridian*), and while we cannot posit essential differences between Nicaraguans and Americans that would preclude an American from offering similar representations, we can at least say that the poet's experiences—and the experiences of many Central Americans—have much to do with his critique.[34]

Despite his black vision of the imperial self, Cardenal offers a balanced, even somewhat hopeful portrayal of Americans. In "Los filibusteros," a companion piece to "Con Walker en Nicaragua," he argues that not all the Americans were miscreants: "Hubo rufianes, ladrones, jugadores, pistoleros. / También hubo honrados y caballeros y valientes. / Reclutados por la necesidad y las ilusiones" (There were scoundrels, thieves, gamblers, gunslingers. / There were also honest men and gentlemen and brave men. / Fellows enlisting out of necessity and illusions).[35] Like many other writers, he captures a structuring tension, a biformity or deformity, in American culture: not all the filibusters acted from greed or viciousness; some thought they were doing the right thing, that they could "regenerate" Nicaragua for the good of its people. However misguided he thinks they may have been, the poet holds onto the possibility of some form of reconciliation between two peoples.

Rollins, for example, thinks back on the isthmus as an almost idyllic place—"Y aquel olor tibio, dulzón, verde, de Centro América. / Las casas blancas con tejas rojas y con grandes aleros llenas de sol, / y un patio tropical con una fuente y una mujer junto a la fuente" (And that warm, sweet, green odor of Central America. / The white houses with red-tiled roofs and with wide sunny eaves, / and a tropical courtyard with a fountain and a woman by the fountain)—and he notes that some of Walker's men remained behind after the war:

> Los que pasaron todos esos peligros y aún viven todavía.
> Los que se quedaron para casarse allá después
> y vivir en paz en esa tierra
> y estarán esta tarde sentados recordando
> (pensando escribir tal vez un día sus memorias),
> y su esposa que es de esa tierra, y los nietos jugando . . .
>
> (The ones who survived all those dangers and are even still alive.
> The ones who stayed there afterward to get married
> and to live in peace in that land

and who this afternoon probably sit remembering
(thinking about how one day they might pen their memories),
and their wife who is from that land, and their grandchildren
   playing . . .)[36]

In this representation of domestic peace, the poem recalls the ending of Teilhet's novel, in which Sanderson settles down with Tarra to raise a family. Both writers sound notes of hope, but where Sanderson muses over what might have been, Cardenal portrays Rollins as someone who lost faith in Walker and his imperialist mission. The Americans who remain in Nicaragua (at least through what little glimpse we get) seem to long not for U.S. dominance of the isthmus but for peace and a healthy family. Men do not have to kill others and take their land, the poet insists, to show themselves to be men. The gentle life, not the robust life; decency, not imperial beneficence; friendship, not invasion.

Given the viciousness of the Somozas and the violences of the American proxy system, Cardenal's treatment of Walker remains all that much more remarkable. Through Rollins, the poet refuses to give up completely on Americans, and if he sees plenty of evidence of Walkerisms throughout Central America in the 1940s and 1950s, he refrains from a sweeping condemnation of the United States. He finds an emptiness, a brutal lack in Walker—and, by implication, in American culture—but he does not abandon hope for a better, more just, less savage neighbor. As an admirer of Lincoln, as a writer (and, later, political activist) dedicated to justice and liberty, he believes in the promise of the American experiment in democracy. If the United States could battle its way out of slavery and toward equality between the races (and, later, between the sexes), then perhaps it could battle its way out of empire-building and toward a more constructive, less violent and bullying relationship with its less powerful neighbors. The United States may have its latter-day Walkers—Theodore Roosevelt, Woodrow Wilson, Minor Keith, Sam Zemurray, Lee Christmas, and many others—but it also, Cardenal hopes, may have some Lincolns.

From Havana to Saigon

If the fin de siècle was the first great era of Walker's literary resurfacings, the 1950s and the rise of the Cold War were a less promising, less clear-cut era for the freebooter's return to American literary and popular cultures. On the one hand, and as in the late 1890s, U.S. foreign policy began to heat up during the final years of the Truman administration, and, sure enough, the Tennessean shows up in yet another mercenary romance and—in a vast improvement over Miller's doggerel—in a sophisticated narrative poem. The rise in imperial energies suggests that the freebooter was due for yet another return engagement. Nevertheless, even as the United States was becoming increasingly involved in conflicts in Asia, disaster seemed to be looming on several fronts.

While a writer in the 1950s could have resurrected the filibuster as an exemplum of imperial daring and fortitude, the omens were far less auspicious for American imperial victories than they were in the 1890s. The world had changed, and with the Soviets and the Chinese seemingly intent on world domination, the thwarting of American imperial desires seemed as likely, or more likely, than the satisfaction of imperial ambitions. Teilhet, then, focuses on the filibuster not as the ideal imperial self but rather as an example of imperial miscalculation and defeat. Still, the United States had emerged as a world power during World War II, and if the signs were bad, the global situation was far from hopeless. Unlike Walker, the United States had not yet gone down to utter imperial defeat, and the time was not quite right for Walker either way: the American imperial narrative in the 1950s was neither one of failure nor triumph. The freebooter would have to wait a few more years before his second great resurfacing. As we see in the next chapter, Walker returns with a vengeance to American letters following the fall of Saigon: in less than one hundred years, the United States had gone from imperial ascendancy to imperial desolation, and the stage was set for the freebooter's return.

CHAPTER SIX

Walker, with a Vengeance: Cox and Didion

In the wake of American defeat in Vietnam, Walker resurfaces repeatedly in literature and film. As the list in the introduction suggests, he stars in at least three American novels, Joan Didion's *A Book of Common Prayer* (1977), Robert Houston's *The Nation Thief* (1984), and Albert J. Guerard's *The Hotel in the Jungle* (1996), and one British-American-Nicaraguan movie, Alex Cox's *Walker* (1987). He also serves as a historical touchstone in two of the most important American literary interrogations of U.S. expansionism and imperialism of the 1980s, Robert Stone's *A Flag for Sunrise* (1981) and Cormac McCarthy's *Blood Meridian* (1985).[1] A star of the nascent imperium in the 1850s, and a star again in the booming 1890s, he reappears as the grim grandfather or mad ghost in the imperial machine in the post-Vietnam era.

Of these exemplary narratives, Cox's *Walker* and Didion's *Book of Common Prayer* offer the most sustained and provocative revisions of both the mercenary romance and literary representations of the American imperial self. In radically different ways, both the director and novelist dive into the darkest currents in American culture and represent American imperialism as a spiritually and ethically twisted and deforming process. Whereas the freebooter once served as an exemplum of imperial pluck and triumph or of imperial energies gone slightly astray, he now serves as an emblem of imperial catastrophe and American excess and savagery. Whereas Davis reached back to the freebooter as the right sort of fearless American imperialist, Didion and Cox cast him as an emblem of the corrosive and deadly effects of American power both at home and abroad. For them, he serves as a literary and cinematic representation not only of American imperial collapse in Southeast Asia and the reassertion of imperial rule in the United

States' backyard but also of the bloody trajectory and downward spiral of the empire from Manifest Destiny to Vietnam.

Rambo, Ronbo, and Ollie

Cox—director of *Repo Man* (1984), *Sid and Nancy* (1986), the astonishingly terrible *Straight to Hell* (1987), *El Patrullero* (1991), and *Death and the Compass* (1996), among other films—makes no apologies either for his sometimes sophomoric sense of humor or for his blistering critique of the Reagan era. Like a crude, punk-influenced Michael Moore, he refuses to play nice and offers his film as an upheld middle digit to the conservative majorities in 1980s American (and British, Canadian, and German) politics and culture. He portrays Walker as both a madman of the 1850s *and*, as he would have it, an insane contemporary of Ronald Reagan, Oliver North, and John Rambo. These three icons of imperial resurgence following the fall of Saigon embody, for Cox, the abiding, furious American desire to control an empire—through whatever means necessary—and he sees Reagan, North, and their associates as latter-day Walkers. For Cox, the imperial self little resembles the exalted being found in Emerson or the robust, manly specimen found in Davis or Roosevelt; rather, he is a demented, flesh-eating fiend who not only wants power and fame but who also, for pathological reasons arising in part from the process of imperialism itself, torments and destroys as many less powerful souls as he can. The imperial self is a cartoon figure, a vicious joke, an empire-crazed, gun-toting lunatic. To say the least, the filmmaker does not hold a high opinion of either the Reagan White House or the American empire, and he does not go in for subtlety.

An astute reader—in his satiric manner—of Walker, Cox represents the freebooter as a zealous yet decent man made mad by ambition and the logic of imperialism. As the film opens, we see Walker's defeat in Sonora, and at his trial back in the United States for violating the neutrality laws, he stands in his own defense and speaks the key lines from his 1849 declaration of purpose in the *New Orleans Crescent:* "Unless a man believes that there is something great for him to do, he can do nothing great. A great idea springs up in a man's soul; it agitates his entire [*sic*] being, transports him from the ignorant present and makes him feel the future in a moment." Goggle eyed and twitchy, Walker (played by near dead-ringer Ed Harris) struggles to explain his empyrean moment, and if wound as tight as a seven-day clock, he nevertheless evinces complete faith in his vision and feels the hand of the divine on his shoulder. He knows himself to be an agent of destiny.

After these lines from the *Crescent*, Cox and American screenwriter Rudy Wurlitzer take a page from John L. O'Sullivan and the *United States Magazine and Democratic Review*. The freebooter continues his speech: "It is the God-given right of the American people to dominate the Western hemisphere. It is our moral duty to protect our neighbors from oppression and exploitation. It is the fate of America to go ahead. That is her Manifest Destiny." Although he plays to the courtroom packed with his supporters, he also fervently believes in what he says, and, in a later conversation with Cornelius Vanderbilt (played as a brutish madman by Peter Boyle), he says that he would gladly die in the defense of American ideals. He believes in freedom, liberation, and democracy, and even if megalomania bubbles just beneath the surface, waiting to erupt, a desire for a personal empire seems not to be his prime motivation. Harris plays him as a caring, if troubled imperial self, and when his fiancée (played by Marlee Matlin) objects to another man's defense of the "Southern institutions," the filibuster attempts to reassure her and responds with passion to her assertion that "Manifest Destiny" is just another way of saying "slavery": "Ellen—you know I despise— I despise slavery!" High strung but not yet mad, he holds high ideals; he wants to do his part in regenerating the civilizations of Central America.

Once in power, however, the process of imperialism takes over the freebooter, and he becomes increasingly unstable and violent. Imperialism drives him insane. Not long after becoming president, and in an effort to solidify his power and to earn support from plantation owners in the American South, he reintroduces slavery to the isthmus. As we have already seen, the requisite logic of colonization becomes its own engine, and Walker sacrifices his deepest convictions. In a later scene, as the pressure upon him increases following military setbacks, he begins to lose his grip on Nicaragua and himself. In a moment of anger, he has his brother executed for disobedience. He remarks, "Mother never liked you, anyway." He will do whatever it takes to protect his imperial venture; the process has taken control and twists him into a fratricide. Later, during the siege of Granada, Walker (a trained doctor) performs surgery on a wounded American, cuts out part of the man's stomach, and pops it in his mouth. Harris, savoring the moment, grins with grotesque, bug-eyed delight. The strain and the ethical, spiritual, and material violence of conquest and imperialism have warped and deformed the freebooter, and he has lost complete control of his mind, ideals, and kingdom. The imperial self cannot withstand either the forces of empire-building or the forces allied against him, and he finally knows only madness and savagery.

Made in Nicaragua during the *contra* war, *Walker* does more than any other late-twentieth-century retelling of the freebooter's adventures to link the 1855 invasion of Nicaragua with the Vietnam War and Oliver North's clandestine war against the Sandinistas. Very much concerned with the politics and events of the Reagan era, Cox—like Harte, Davis, and Teilhet before him—reaches back to the filibuster as a means to sound not only the desires and history of Manifest Destiny but, more importantly, to explore the long history of the empire and to critique the actions of its contemporary agents. Sympathetic to the Sandinistas and strongly opposed to Reagan's war in Central America, Cox suggests that little has changed over the course of the imperium; the United States, in one form or another, has exerted influence in the region, using force time after time to secure its political and economic interests. And just as it has exercised power in the isthmus, it has deployed a steady stream of agents to secure those interests. In 1855 it was Walker; in 1985 it was North. Before, in between, and after, there have been countless others. For the filmmaker, the imperial urge that has always operated in U.S. culture leads, with many vicious twists and turns, from Walker's campaigns to wars in Asia to attempts, following the liberation of Saigon, to repair the damage done to U.S. prestige and influence. *Walker*, in its sometimes juvenile and often uneven way, provides an ironic, bitter synopsis of empire.

If, in the Tennessean, Cox finds a deranged exemplum of the American imperial self, he likewise finds contemporary examples of the same sort of derangement. Walker, he insists, may have been viciously mad, but so were Reagan and North. In a conversation with Wurlitzer, he makes clear his position on "the worms that work for Reagan and the worms that will come after Reagan to continue the fascism—they're just gray little men. They're not like Walker, because Walker in the end would never had pled the Fifth": "I was reading about one of those guys, that scammed all this money off the arms deal with Iran to finance the contras, and it was in the *Miami Herald*, and it said some call him a saint and a patriot; others call him a wily con man, and . . . how about raving asshole? Or fucking murderer?"[2] Cox, we could say, has made up his mind about a few things. Outraged at the Reagan administration's war in Nicaragua, he sees North as the reincarnation of Walker, and he attributes a psychopathology to the imperial self. Personal and national defeat in Vietnam and the logic of empire compel the hangdog marine to undertake a clandestine war financed through a covert and criminal operation. He wants to resecure the backyard, and he envisions and carries out his monstrous, murderous scheme. Cox leaves little doubt where he stands: Reagan and North, filibusters who tried to conquer a nation with their own private army, represent contemporary examples of what he sees as the madness of American imperialism and the American imperial self.

The poster for *Walker* makes clear that Cox wants his audience to see contemporary figures when it sees Walker: "Before Rambo, Before Oliver North: WALKER." Rambo and North, the two mercenary icons of the Reagan era, represent the re-flexing of America's might after defeat in Vietnam. As J. Hoberman remarks, a "close identification" exists between "Rambo and Ronbo," and while Rambo tried to refight (and win) the Vietnam War on the big screen, Reagan and North focused U.S. energies close to home.[3] The American overseas empire began in large measure in Central America, and to rebuild it, the White House returned to familiar ground. And to make explicit the connection he sees between the *contra* war and Walker's filibustering, Cox makes jokes out of time: after the filibuster establishes himself as president, a number of Nicaraguan leaders discuss his elimination; as they consult, one of them reads an issue of *Time* with Walker on the cover. Walker, Cox implies, is as much a part of the 1980s as he was of the 1850s; like North, he would be popularized as an American hero.

The most startling and effective use of anachronism to link Walker to the Vietnam and *contra* wars occurs near the end of the film. With the allied forces of Central America closing in, U.S. Marine helicopters land to rescue the Immortals. An excerpt from the screenplay captures the scene:

> Everything is chaos and confusion as William Walker and what is left of his men try to break out of their encampment in Granada. Suddenly a strange and deafening sound is heard. Red and green flares hurtle into the plaza. The Immortals are frozen in searchlights as a helicopter descends.
>
> Marines deploy, encircling the plaza.
>
> COMPANY MAN: I have instructions from the United States of America to return all American citizens to their homeland.
>
> The Immortals frantically whip out their U.S. passports, leaping aboard the chopper.[4]

Cox constructs the scene simultaneously as a parody of Walker's surrender to the U.S. Navy in 1857 and of the infamous images of the American withdrawal from Saigon in 1975. Just as the Marines could not airlift out all the Vietnamese that supported the Americans, Cox's CIA agent turns away anyone without an American passport.

The parody of the fall of Saigon and the recasting of the historical context from the 1850s to the 1970s also allow us to reinterpret the scenes just before the helicopter arrives. In the climactic, apocalyptic moments, the Immortals raze Granada; running wildly through the streets, they set fires and shoot civilians unlucky enough to fall into their field of vision. The burning of Granada functions as a cinematic replay of the massacres at My Lai and elsewhere in the Quang Ngai. Just as American forces punished Vietnamese civilians for the Viet Cong's successes during the Tet Offensive, Walker's men torched Granada as punishment for their impending defeat. The movie portrays the imperial self as psychotic and savage, and while I would not argue for *Walker* as an aesthetic triumph—it received almost unanimously poor reviews[5]—it nevertheless stands as a caustic if sometimes juvenile critique of U.S. imperialism before and after Vietnam; it stands, especially, as a caustic critique of the agents of empire.

With *Walker*, Cox confirms the ever-darkening hues of the mercenary romance. While the genre no longer promises the gentle heroes of Harte or the swashbuckling mercenaries of Davis, a midcentury romancer like Teilhet could still offer a handsome protagonist who held the right ideals even if he could not triumph over the schemes of jackals like Walker and his secessionist allies. In the wake of Vietnam, however, the genre no longer has any redeeming figures or elements. With the exception of Ellen, few of the characters hold anything like an ethical vision—and she dies in the first act—and most of them are mad or murderous or both. None of the action seems heroic; Walker's men fight poorly, have sex with sheep, and run amok until he begins to execute them for insubordination. Moreover, no one really knows what he should be doing or why he should be doing it; they seem to excel only at murder and dying. In the end, even if a few Americans escape through the airlift, the freebooter and most of his men die. The mercenary romance now promises the bleakest portraits of American power and the most savage portrayals of the imperial self. It offers no hope, promising only death. Imperialism, the form suggests, destroys ideals and takes an incredible toll on not only its agents but particularly its non-American victims. Catastrophe in Vietnam has put the lie to American rhetoric and faith, and only despair and defeat remain.

The American Making of "Harmonic Tremors"

In *A Book of Common Prayer*, Didion offers a far more subtle and complex revision than Cox, not only of the mercenary romance and Walker narrative but also of literary representations of the American imperial self. Unlike all the other writers we have considered thus far, she offers two women—Charlotte Douglas and Grace Strasser-Mendana—as her central characters, and she concerns herself not so much with the triumphs or failures of the masculine imperial self as she does with the toll imperialism takes on the United States and its citizens. Although Grace manages to hold her own against the Machiavellian manipulations of her son, Gerardo, and the other members of the ruling elite of Boca Grande, an imaginary Central American republic very much like Nicaragua and El Salvador in the 1970s, Charlotte, as a no-longer-so-young American caught up in the turbulence and brutality of the Vietnam era and particularly as the sometime victim of the schemers and agents of empire around her, has little defense against her time or the predations of men both at home and abroad. Charlotte, the inverse of the masculine imperial self, suffers so much that she seeks her own annihilation. Ultimately, Didion suggests that American imperialism has contributed not only to the incessant violence in the isthmus but also to the ethical dissolution and brutality rampant in the United

States in the 1960s and 1970s. The savagery of the imperium and its agents has backlashed on the culture, leaving its citizens dazed and death haunted. The ambitions and schemes of Walker, Roosevelt, and their successors have led, Didion intimates, to ruin.

Although Didion's novel stands as one of the few Walker rewrites to remain in print since the time of its publication, a brief summary may be in order. Grace, the narrator and would-be witness, tells the story of Charlotte during her time in Central America. As soon as Charlotte arrives in the Boca Grande—"Boca Grande is the name of the country and Boca Grande is also the name of the city, as if the place defeated the imagination of even its first settler"—she becomes an object of sexual desire, suspicion, and hatred among the ruling elite, the Strasser-Mendanas. She has affairs with Grace's brother-in-law, Victor, the present minister of defense and ruler of Boca Grande, and with her son, Gerardo, a playboy who plots a coup against his uncle and plans to replace him with Antonio, another of Grace's brothers-in-law. Grace, an American anthropologist who "worked with Lévi-Strauss at São Paulo" and who later married Edgar, the oldest brother of the Strasser-Mendana oligarchy, seeks to understand Charlotte's motives for coming to Boca Grande and for staying, even though she knows the impending coup may put her in harm's way. As part of her act of witness, Grace attempts to understand Charlotte as an American woman of her time, and finds out what she can about Charlotte's husbands, children, and upbringing in California. Despite Grace's warnings, Charlotte refuses to leave Boca Grande, and dies of a gunshot to the back: "The moment and circumstances of her arrest are matters of record but the moment and circumstances of her death remain obscure. I do not even know which side killed her, who held the Estadio Nacional at the moment of death." Grace, battling pancreatic cancer, remains matriarch of the family, still trying to understand Charlotte's life, and her own. In the last line of the novel, she confesses, "I have not been the witness I wanted to be."[6]

The rulers of Boca Grande owe their position and wealth to the schemes and manipulations of the novel's Walker-like figure. The oligarchs, Grace tells us, trace their power back to

> a St. Louis confidence man named Victor Strasser who at age twenty-three floated some Missouri money to buy oil rights, at age twenty-four fled Mex-

ico after an abortive attempt to invade Sonora, and at age twenty-five arrived in Boca Grande. Upon his recovery from cholera he married a Mendana and proceeded to divest her family of the interior of Boca Grande.[7]

Although Didion does not name Walker explicitly, she clearly has him in mind. Like the freebooter, Strasser attempted to conquer Sonora but ended up "conquering" a Central American republic instead. Just as Davis, in *Soldiers*, casts Clay as Walker's figurative son, Didion casts the Strasser-Mendanas as the sons and grandsons of a filibuster–turned–confidence man. The novelist reaches deep into the American past and retrieves Walker as her exemplum not of imperial achievement but of sordid personal ambition and crooked scheme after crooked scheme. The brutality of the oligarchs has its roots not only in the isthmus but in Manifest Destiny and, Didion makes clear, in the long history of U.S. political, military, and especially economic interventionism in the nineteenth and twentieth centuries.

The tale of Victor Strasser connects not only the novel and its central players to Walker but to other American freebooters and adventurers in Central America as well. Strasser, like characters in Harte's *Crusade*, Davis's *Soldiers*, or O. Henry's *Cabbages*, resembles nineteenth- and twentieth-century American shipping magnates, banana kings, and entrepreneurs in his acquisition of the land and resources of Boca Grande. As we have already seen, and as Lester D. Langley and Thomas Schoonover recount, U.S. speculators descended upon the isthmus in the nineteenth century and soon took control of major resources and infrastructure in Costa Rica, Honduras, Guatemala, and Nicaragua: "By the early twentieth century, isthmian states had virtually surrendered control of major elements in their internal communications, public utilities, national debt, currency, state revenue, and other economic activities that generated national wealth."[8] Like Cornelius Vanderbilt, Sam Zemurray, Minor Keith, the Vaccaro brothers, and many other Americans, Strasser assumes control of most of Boca Grande's arable land and scattered mineral resources. More importantly, he assumes control of the government and military as well. Like the banana kings, he creates an American fiefdom in the isthmus.

As the inheritor through marriage to Strasser's fortune and influence, Grace oversees half the country: "You will have gathered that I married into one of the three or four solvent families in Boca Grande. In fact Edgar's death left me in putative control of fifty-nine-point-eight percent of the arable land and about the same percentage of the decision-making process in La República (recently La República Libre) de Boca Grande." Grace, the titular head of the family, manages Edgar's trust, but his brothers, the violent inheritors of Victor's estate, command the guns and key ministries. The "Americans" have become the local tyrants. Grace admits that she behaves as a colonial overlord: "You will notice my use of the colonial pronoun, the overseer's 'we.' I mean it. I see now that I have no business in this place but I have been here too long to change."[9]

As the lineage of the Strasser-Mendanas makes clear, Didion takes America as the subject of her fiction. The clan is more American than Central American. Gerardo, for example, "persists in tracing his line to the court of Castile," but only one of his grandparents has any "Spanish blood": "Gerardo is the grandson of two American wildcatters who got rich, my father in Colorado minerals and Edgar's father in Boca Grande politics, and of the Irish nursemaid and the *mestiza* from the interior they respectively married."[10] The brothers-in-law can be counted half-American, and Didion offers few, if any, characters that might be said to be isthmian in cultural or linguistic background. Central America matters in the text for what it reveals about American attitudes and practices. The novelist is not as interested in what the actual isthmian elites think about the United States—or in exploring their attitudes toward life in their nations—as she is in understanding how the U.S. influences others. She does not delve deeply into the complex histories and politics of the actual oligarchs, but concentrates instead on dramatizing the consequences of American imperialism, on literalizing that influence in the form of the Strasser-Mendanas.

The United States, Didion implies, has exported violence and rapacity and supplemented the isthmus's homegrown varieties. The seemingly endless cycle of "harmonic tremors"—the same problem that Davis complained about in the 1890s—arises in Boca Grande not from ideological struggle but from a desire for as big a slice of the (American-subsidized) pie as possible: "The *guerrilleros* here spend their time theorizing in the interior, and are covertly encouraged to emerge from time to time as foils to the actual politics of the country. Our notoriously frequent revolutions are made not by the *guerrilleros* but entirely by the people we know. This is a hard point for the outsider of romantic sensibility to grasp."[11] Strasser's act of piracy proves an inspiration to his descendants, and they expend their energies stealing the country back and forth from one another. Although Didion would surely agree that Central America has produced its own share of tyrants, she suggests that much of the perpetual unrest besetting the isthmus since the mid–nineteenth century has at least part of its roots in the long history of U.S. interference. The American imperial self, as Davis began to realize in *Macklin*, has been one of the leading causes of sorrow and death.

Like Davis's *Soldiers* and O. Henry's *Cabbages*, Didion's novel dramatizes the interconnectedness of indigenous elites and American agents of empire. To say the least, the Strasser-Mendanas enjoy close ties with the United States. The brothers make deals with U.S. companies interested in Boca Grande's resources: "The second Progreso was another new city, in the interior, built on leased land (ours) by an American aluminum combine during the bauxite chimera here." Tuck Bradley, the American ambassador, routinely attends parties thrown by members of the clan, and the Strasser-Mendana wives and girlfriends travel to the States for their educations, to get their teeth fixed, or to see psychiatrists. They read American magazines and gossip about Jackie Onassis. To further accentuate the connection between the United States and Boca Grande, Grace remarks, "There is a local currency but the American dollar is legal tender."[12] The free republic amounts to a satellite of the United States, run by local tyrants who serve their own interests first, and American interests a close second.

Didion captures perfectly the workings of imperialism-by-proxy: American entrepreneurs and government agents support those among the elites who support U.S. political, military, and economic interests. In El Salvador, one of the models for Boca Grande, the so-called "Fourteen Families"—or ruling oligarchs—controlled nearly all the fertile soil and about 60 percent of all the land as late as the 1980s. Throughout the 1970s, the U.S.-trained and -supported Salvadoran military seized some of the power away from the families, but the key players in both the oligarchy and the military supported U.S. anticommunist policies in the region. Many of the leaders in the internal security forces and government were involved in the death squads and terror campaign against land reformists and left-wing revolutionaries. As Didion puts in her later work of journalism, *Salvador* (1983), the United States allied itself with mass murderers and neofascists like

Arturo Molina and Roberto D'Aubuisson in an effort to suppress Salvadoran socialists and communists: "I experienced for a moment the official American delusion, the illusion of plausibility, the sense that the American undertaking in El Salvador might turn out to be, from the right angle, in the right light, just another difficult but possible mission in another troubled but possible country."[13] Like Walker, the latter-day agents of empire perhaps imagine they hold high ideals, but imperialism erodes them to the point—if they were sincere in the first place—where making deals with tyrants and mass murderers seems like the right, or at least best or most expedient, thing to do.

In Nicaragua, the other model for Boca Grande, the Somozas backed U.S. policy in the isthmus and Caribbean basin from the 1930s until the Sandinista Revolution in 1979; Didion makes the connection explicit in a reference to Victor and Antonio's efforts "to turn a profit on the Red Cross." In 1972, following an earthquake that devastated Managua and left five hundred thousand Nicaraguans homeless, Tachito Somoza, the then-dictator, profited from the ruin. Eduardo Galeano, always sensitive to the ironies of dictators, sums up Somoza's scheme: "He sells in the United States the blood donated to victims of the quake by the International Red Cross. Later, he extends this profitable scam: Showing more initiative and enterprising spirit than Count Dracula, Tachito Somoza founds a limited company to buy blood cheap in Nicaragua and sell it dear on the North American market."[14] The Strasser-Mendanas stand as Boca Grande's Somozas; and as with the Somozas, responsibility for their viciousness rests in part with the United States. The proxy system grew out of the original military and economic interventions of the nineteenth and early twentieth centuries, and in *A Book of Common Prayer*, Didion explores the legacy of this system.

If Didion takes Walker as a representative figure of the havoc and violence wrought in Central America by the American imperial self and the long history of U.S. interference and intervention, she also takes up, and revises, the narrative form that has grown from his life, adventures, and death: the mercenary romance. To this point, I have been careful to call *Book* a *novel* since it exceeds in stylistic, structural, psychological, and narrative complexity all the other works we have thus far examined. By almost any literary standard, Didion can be said to be a far more sophisticated writer than Harte, Davis, O. Henry, or Teilhet; nevertheless, the novel reworks, in terms of plot, setting, and interest in the American imperial self, all the usual elements and concerns of the mercenary romance. For all Didion's relative sophistication and late-modernist skill, she cannot escape the hold of the form on the American imagination. Harte and Davis embedded the mercenary romance in the culture, and it continues to operate as perhaps the favored literary vehicle for consideration of the agents of empire. With Walker comes a ready-made tale. Not all scholars, however, see Didion's novel in the context of Walker and the mercenary romance.

In *Late Imperial Romance* (1994), for example, John McClure explores the influence of the literature of British imperialism on American writers. As McClure puts it, he focuses on "the manifest role of European writers such as Joseph Conrad in shaping contemporary American constructions of American imperialism." In particular, he focuses on the fiction of Didion, Robert Stone, Don DeLillo, and Thomas Pynchon, and shows how their works variously excoriate or valorize or—in Pynchon's case—transcend romances of imperial adventure, liberation, or reenchantment. As McClure remarks, he is not interested in "the American antecedents of contemporary American imperialism," and few would dispute the influence of Conrad (and Kipling and Forster) on Didion and her contemporaries. Rather than arguing for *Book* as a romance arising from an American tradition, he dubs it and works such as Stone's *Dog Soldiers* (1974) or DeLillo's *The Names* (1982) "late imperial romances," or texts that "sharply interrogate the popular romance of civilizing mission or 'development' and relate in its stead a counterromance of descent into realms of stubborn strangeness and enchantment."[15] Although McClure rightly asserts Conrad's influence on Didion, and although he offers a fascinating reading of Charlotte's journey as a form of hagiography, our focus on Walker and the American tradition of the mercenary romance emphasizes not realms of enchantment but rather very material realms of masculine imperial violence.

Just as Harte, in *Crusade*, fragments Walker into different types of characters, Didion reworks the elements of the freebooter's life and adventures into two primary characters. On the one hand, in Charlotte Douglas, we have yet another instance of an American adrift in her personal life traveling abroad; once outside the United States, she becomes caught up in violence she cannot control, and she dies a violent, chilling death. Like Harte's

Hurlstone or Keene, or like Davis's Clay or Macklin, Charlotte has suffered traumas that cause her to flee her past, and like Cardenal's Walker, she ultimately seeks her own destruction. On the other hand, in Gerardo, a descendant of the Walker figure, we have the brutal orchestrator of coups and countercoups. More American than Central American, Gerardo emerges as Didion's "American" imperial self: ruthless and petty, he indulges in savage gamesmanship for his own amusement and power. Like Harte's Perkins or Teilhet's Walker, the murderous Gerardo seeks his own aggrandizement, and he ousts his uncle to become the tyrant of Boca Grande. In Charlotte, we have the self destroyed by American imperialism; in Gerardo, we have the vicious imperial self called into being by U.S. empire-building. In both instances, they can be read as Harte-like reworkings of Walker.

A number of forces work against Charlotte, shaping her into the inverse of the masculine imperial self and pushing her toward death. Male power and domestic violence, the war in Vietnam and the armed counterculture, Third World revolutions and the money to be made from them, and, perhaps most of all, the death of a child, have all taken an immense toll on Charlotte, and she winds up in Central America hoping to ease her shock and pain. Life in the United States in the 1960s and 1970s has disintegrated into cruelty and sexual and political brutality, and the characters closest to her—her first husband, Warren Bogart, her second husband, Leonard Douglas, and her first daughter, Marin—abuse her physically or take part, either directly or indirectly, in wars and terrorist bombings. Nearly everywhere Charlotte goes, she encounters some form of individual or widespread suffering; nearly everyone she meets tries to harm her or endures the harm of others. Society teeters on the edges of ethical and political dissolution; as Stone puts it in "We Are Not Excused" (1989), an essay on political fiction, the early 1970s were "a particularly evil period in this country. The cities were ruined, crime was rampant, all the due bills extended from the sixties had come up for presentation."[16] In this America, Charlotte does not stand a chance, and she flees, heading southward, arriving in the even worse wasteland of Boca Grande. Once there, she waits for the abundant, tropical death to overtake her. Imperialism has warped and destroyed the powerful and the weak alike, and just as it has taken its monumental toll on the United States' neighbors, it has also taken a vicious toll on Americans.

Charlotte lives and dies as the paradigmatic already lost American abroad. Adrift in her personal life, she charts an erratic course—"from New Orleans to Mérida and Mérida to Antigua and Antigua to Guadeloupe and Guadeloupe to Boca Grande"—perhaps hoping for some form of redemption, but waiting more for death. Grace captures the ruin of Charlotte's life:

> Here is what happened: she left one man, she left a second man, she traveled again with the first; she let him die alone. She lost one child to "history" and another to "complications" (I offer in each instance the evaluation of others), she imagined herself capable of shedding that baggage and came to Boca Grande, a tourist. *Una turista*. So she said. In fact she came here less a tourist than a sojourner but she did not make that distinction.[17]

By the time she arrives in Central America, she could not be more lost. Her marriages have disintegrated, she has lost her children, and she has left the States because she does not know what to do and has no more emotional resources. Charlotte, perhaps of all the other characters we have seen in this study, carries the deepest wounds and possesses the least ability to defend herself.

Of all the forces working against Charlotte, none takes a more immediate toll than the physical and political power of men. During their marriage, Bogart, an academic hanger-on, physically and emotionally abused her, carried on multiple affairs, and forced her into his sexual games. In his petty measure, he attempted to dominate her life. Once she arrives in Boca Grande, she falls into this same pattern with abusive men, Victor and Gerardo. She succumbs to masculine predation, and Didion suggests that sexual violence and imperialism must be understood as currents in the same stream of desire; men, and especially imperial selves, seek to dominate and control the lives (and deaths) of others. Victor and Gerardo prey on women and one another with equal ferocity; they differ from Bogart only in that they have access, through accidents of birth, to considerable firepower. As Lynne T. Hanley puts it, Didion "cannot disentangle men at war from men at home. In *A Book of Common Prayer*, Boca Grande is the historical correlative of the war zone the American home has become, and sexual relations between men and women in America mirror the internecine warfare waged so incessantly by the Strasser-Mendana brothers in Boca Grande."[18]

Although Leonard, "a very well-known lawyer," does not abuse Charlotte, and so seems in contrast to be a relatively gentle man, he runs guns for Third World revolutionary movements and profits from violence, just like Victor and Gerardo. He emerges as a minor American imperial self. In fact, Leonard had once been a partner of Edgar's in a scheme to fund and supply the Tupamaros, Uruguayan revolutionaries who kidnapped their enemies in the 1960s, hoping to exchange them for political prisoners.[19] Edgar, however, does not believe in the Tupamaros' struggle for freedom; like Gerardo, he finances the guerrilla movement in order to use them as pawns in a bigger power struggle. As Grace realizes, "I prided myself on listening and seeing and I had never even heard or seen that Edgar played the same games Gerardo played."[20] If Leonard appears to be more sincere in his political beliefs, he nevertheless serves the interests of men like Edgar. Little exists to distinguish the Americans from the isthmians—they are all would-be imperial selves, all prone to violence and hatred—and Didion suggests that given their attitudes and behavior, Charlotte was lost before she was born and could only lose more and more.

History also works against Charlotte, making her into an already lost American abroad. The novel takes place in the milieu of the Vietnam War and explores what Didion takes as the violent, petty, and fraudulent extremes of the antiwar, antiestablishment counterculture. Marin, Charlotte's first daughter, grows disillusioned with her upper-middle-class California life and takes part in a pipe-bombing of the Transamerica Building—"one of many symbols of imperialist *latifundismo*"—and the subsequent hijacking of a flight out of San Francisco. As part of her escape, they sacrifice Mark Schrader, one of their own. As Leonard remarks, "They'll ditch the harelip.... The harelip's the fresh meat they'll throw on the trail, they can't afford him, Marin's not stupid."[21]

Grace makes it clear that Marin does not really believe in or understand revolutionary movements; on a tape circulated to the media, Marin explains the nature of her cell to the world: *"The fact that our organization is revolutionary in character is due above all to the fact that all our activity is defined as revolutionary."* The statement describes a nice circle, and Charlotte "could parse the sentence but she could make no sense of it, could find no way to rephrase it so that Leonard and Warren would understand." Grace mocks Marin as she records "that the sentence was not original with Marin but had been lifted from a hand-book by a Brazilian guerrilla theorist named

Marghela." The bombing amounts to a sordid act of boredom and resentment. The forces of war, protest, and disillusionment interweave, taking their toll on Charlotte. In a state of shock over Marin's actions and flight underground, she hopes, irrationally, that if she stays in Boca Grande, Marin will somehow appear (and perhaps be reborn): "In a certain dim way Charlotte believed that she had located herself at the very cervix of the world, the place through which a child lost to history must eventually pass."[22]

The event that perhaps most devastates Charlotte, that most prompts her flight toward death, is the death of her second daughter, Charlotte. In despair, she wants another child to fill the emptiness in her life; she wants someone to love. Sadly, Charlotte is "born prematurely, hydrocephalic, and devoid of viable liver function." Determined to escape from Warren, Charlotte takes her slowly dying baby with her as she flees the United States. Grace captures the scarifying and haunting scene of the child's passing:

> The baby did not die at the Mérida airport but an hour later, in the parking lot of the Coca-Cola bottling plant on the road back into town. The baby had gone into convulsions and projectile vomiting in the taxi and Charlotte had made the driver stop in the parking lot. She walked with the baby on the dark asphalt. She sang to the baby out on the edge of the asphalt where the rushes grew and a few trailers were parked.[23]

Few could survive such an event; by the time she lands in Boca Grande, she could not be more lost, more in need of some easing of her pain. Charlotte, we come to understand, unconsciously wants to die a wretched and bloody death, and she knows, at some level, that if she waits around long enough, she will get her way.

Didion suggests that the responsibility for Charlotte's susceptibility to predation and spite rests in part with her upbringing. Affluence and mild weather have made a woman of Charlotte's class and place open to harm, to the domination of men and their weapons. As Grace remarks, "She was immaculate of history, innocent of politics":

> As a child of comfortable family in the temperate zone she had been as a matter of course provided with clean sheets, orthodontia, lamb chops, living grandparents, attentive godparents, one brother named Dickie, ballet

lessons, and casual timely information about menstruation and the care of flat silver, as well as with a small wooden angel, carved in Austria, to sit on her bed table and listen to her prayers.

Such a life, Didion suggests, makes a woman weak, deferent, unable to know what would be in her best interest. Post–World War II American affluence and optimism have conspired against women to make them vulnerable, blithely sexual, sheltered from the workings of poverty and cruelty: "She understood that something was always going on in the world but believed that it would turn out all right. She believed the world to be peopled with others like herself." As Grace concludes, "A not atypical *norteamericana*. Of her time and place."[24]

Charlotte's journey toward death inverts the journey of the masculine imperial self; rather than seeking the death of another, she seeks her own death. The forces in her life have reduced her to a state of shock, and she refuses to listen to Grace's warning to get out of the country: "I just want to see what happens." Grace tells her, "All that happens is that people get hurt. People get killed. You're maybe going to get killed if you stay here." Charlotte wants death. Life has eaten a hole in her, and she has no religion or spiritual base to sustain her, to salve the wounds within; when Grace explains to her "about a village on the Orinoco where female children were ritually cut on the inner thigh by their first sexual partners," Charlotte replies, "That's pretty much what happens everywhere, isn't it? . . . Somebody cuts you? Where it does not show?"[25] She possesses nothing like the Anglican Book of Common Prayer to guide her through this world of violence and death.

Charlotte, despite her losses, tries to do some good while abroad; she carries a measure of Kennedy's missionary enthusiasm. During a cholera outbreak, she volunteers "to give inoculations, and she did, for thirty-four hours without sleeping, until the remaining Lederle vaccine was appropriated by one of Victor's colonels." Later, she volunteers at a birth-control clinic, and refuses to abandon the notion that a film festival—the "Boca Grande Festival de Cine, First Annual"—might help put Boca Grande on the international media map. Charlotte has the confidence and assurance of an American; Americans do their part, bring good ideas, help others, are good neighbors.[26] Nevertheless, she falls prey to almost everyone, and she stands—in her allure—as the sexual object of the masculine imperial self. Warren abuses her, Victor sets her up as his mistress, and Gerardo takes her and the country away from his uncle. In Charlotte's world, ideals and missionary zeal do not amount to much. The imperial selves have the power, and they could care less about anyone or anything as flimsy as good intentions. Money, guns, power, prestige, and sexual prowess matter most.

Gerardo, the mostly American player, emerges as the novel's "American" imperial self. As Grace observes, her son takes pleasure in plots and power. He has a vision of how the world should be, and he risks destroying the clan's grasp on Boca Grande in order to realize his vision. He expertly uses everyone around him in "his game, the object of which seemed to be to place his marker in Victor's office in as few moves as possible. His marker that year happened to be Antonio, but who it was mattered not at all to Gerardo. Gerardo plays only for the action."[27] A schemer like his grandfather, Gerardo holds no ideals, believes in no higher purposes, and does not bother to pretend that he has anyone else's good in mind. The imperial self, after more than a century of visions, interventions, and conquests, has become wholly petty and self-absorbed. All that matters is personal power, gain, and the game. Emerson's ideal young American has become a brutal and twisted plotter of coups, and Roosevelt's masculine imperial self has become a sexual predator who takes no interest in the safety or well-being of his family, nation, or region. The imperial self, in the post-Vietnam era, may have fallen as far as possible: from Emersonian heights to self-made isthmian wastelands. The ambitions of Walker and his peers, Didion finally suggests, amount to little more than thievery and savagery for its own sake.

Didion's achievement rests not only in her critique of imperialism and the American imperial self but in her reworking of the familiar plot and characters of the mercenary romance. Instead of focusing on masculine achievement, she explores masculine predation and cruelty. More importantly, she foregrounds women characters and sounds not only the costs of imperialism at home but the suffering inflicted by men and the imperial self upon women. All along, the story of the American imperial self has been the story of a man and his inward and outward visions of how the world should be. In *A Book of Common Prayer*, Didion examines the human costs of masculinity and imperialism, and finds that the story includes the often neglected or excluded lives of women. The first other to the imperial self, women must be made to suffer; while the men take to the field to battle it out among themselves, women must be around to be, at the outset, spectators, and then collateral damage. Didion makes clear what has been implicit in the mercenary romance at least since Davis's *Macklin*, and she adds one more layer to our understanding of the imperial self in American literature: not only must he participate in the metaphysics of Indian- and African-hating—as Gerardo does through his manipulation of the mestizo and Indian *guerrilleros* of the interior—but he must also participate in the metaphysics of woman-hating.

CONCLUSION

William Walker, Redux?

WILLIAM WALKER, I hope I have argued convincingly, makes a number of claims upon our attention. Through his story and his many resurfacings circulate a number of the most important currents, energies, and desires in American history and culture. His is a tale of continental expansionism and overseas adventurism, of Manifest Destiny and the Spectacular Empire, of the Cold War and the war in Vietnam, of capitalism and imperialism-by-proxy. Remarkably, his story reappears across time; it is a story about the 1850s, the 1870s, the 1890s, the 1950s, the 1970s, and the 1980s. It is a tale of beneficence, idealism, and regeneration; it is also a tale of invasion, executions, destruction, chaos, and defeat. It is also a story of masculinity and, conversely, one of queerness and the abiding fear of not being man enough to rule an empire. His story, as we have seen throughout this study, is about the American empire and the American imperial self. Most profoundly, perhaps, it is a tale of death. An exemplum of imperial energies and desires, he pursued the inward and outward empires and, surprisingly, conquered a nation.

Walker's story and resurfacings also connect him to a number of famous and infamous American politicians, adventurers, and writers. In historical terms, he stands prominently in the company of his fellow freebooters: Burr, O'Sullivan, López, Quitman, Crabb, and others. His exploits also link him not only to such robber barons and banana kings as Vanderbilt and Zemurray but, more importantly, to the imperial ambitions and practices of such men as McKinley and Roosevelt. What the filibusters sought in the 1850s—American pocket imperiums in Cuba, Mexico, or Central America—the White House and Congress were able to achieve on a much grander scale in the 1890s. In literary terms, his writings and actions can be read alongside the works and beliefs of such giants as Emerson and Whitman; most importantly, numerous writers and poets have based works upon his life and adventures.

A somewhat liminal figure in American history, he nevertheless helped to inspire the creation of a subgenre of the romance. Harte and Davis, drawing upon the filibuster's memoir and campaigns, pioneered the mercenary romance, and it remains to this day perhaps the favored literary form for sounding the American empire and imperial self. As I set out in the introduction, Walker not only thought he had written a page of U.S. history that would be impossible to forget or erase, but he also believed that his adventures would prove to be a productive theme for novelists. He was right on both counts, and even as he enjoyed a considerable amount of press and notoriety in his lifetime, he has enjoyed a considerable afterlife in American (and Central American) letters.

After these many pages dedicated to the freebooter's adventures and literary resurfacings we might well ask, why, if Walker was one of the most famous Americans of his day, and why, if he has been the subject of so many romances, stories, plays, poems, and films, does he remain largely unknown? More precisely, why does he keep resurfacing in literary and popular culture only to be forgotten again and again? As we have seen, he has been the subject of numerous books, and he refuses to stay in the obscure footnotes of history; if nothing else, he has been persistent in his ghostly way, and he remains,to this day, a prime subject for narratives about the American empire and the imperial self. Why, then, doesn't anyone remember him?

As one possible answer to this curious phenomenon, we can reach back to Fredric Jameson's notion of the *"impensé* or *non-dit"* of history. In his bid to recover "the unity of a single great collective story," the story of "the collective struggle to wrest a realm of Freedom from a realm of Necessity," Jameson offers a telling line on the nature of the political unconscious: "Only Marxism can give us an adequate account of the essential *mystery* of the cultural past, which, like Tiresias drinking the blood, is momentarily returned to life and warmth and allowed once more to speak, and to deliver its long-forgotten message in surroundings utterly alien to it."[1] Walker, like Tiresias, comes back when his countrymen engage in the letting of blood; he returns, unapologetic and without veils, to speak what Jameson calls the intolerable nature of Necessity and exploitation. Walker's resurfacings function as the return of the historical repressed: in each instance, I have argued, contemporary events help call him back to mind, and he briefly reappears to say what most often remains unthinkable and unsayable; he then disappears just as quickly as the forces of containment and repression work to return imperial desires to obscurity. But before we can delineate in more detail what Walker's returns tell us, we must first map out the pattern of forgetting. Nearly everyone who writes about Walker sooner or later offers the same complaint: no one remembers the filibuster.

In his biographical sketch "William Walker, the King of the Filibusters," for example, Richard Harding Davis complains that "it is safe to say that to members of the younger generation the name of William Walker conveys absolutely nothing. To them, as a name, 'William Walker' awakens no pride of race or country." In the forty-six years since his death, Walker—once a celebrity who had rallies and parades held in his honor in San Francisco and New York—had faded from public memory. Davis makes clear why he thinks his readers should remember the filibuster: "And yet had this man with the plain name, the name that to-day means nothing, accomplished what he adventured, he would on this continent have solved the problem of slavery, have established an empire in Mexico and in Central America, and, incidentally, have brought us into war with all of Europe. That is all he would have accomplished."[2] How, he wonders, could Americans forget such a man?

In "Walker in Nicaragua" (1906), a long narrative poem and a rewrite of an earlier poem, "With Walker in Nicaragua" (1871), Joaquin Miller sounds the same lament:

> I sing this man who sought man's good,
> Who fought for peace, unselfish fought,
> Who silent fell and murmured not,
> This man whom no man understood,
> This great man *so well-nigh forgot*,
> This man who led, who faltered not,
> This student, soldier, president,
> Who chose the weaker side and sent
> Such spirit through his fearless few
> As only Khartoum Gordon knew. (emphasis added)[3]

Like Davis, Miller (who falsely claimed to have fought with Walker in Nicaragua) mourns the passing of his hero from popular memory. Not only has the American public forgotten a great man, but it never understood what he was up to in the first place, never gave him the credit he deserved; an archetypal American, Miller contends, he fought for the downtrodden and sought to elevate the civilization of Central America.

Miller also implies, through his reference to General Charles Gordon, that the filibuster needs to be re-remembered and elevated to his proper place in the pantheon of imperial agents. Whereas history recalls Gordon as a heroic defender of the empire, it should remember Walker as a brave soldier who fell in defense of an embryonic American empire. Whereas Gordon fell because William Gladstone failed to provide adequate military support, Miller implies that Walker likewise fell due to a lack of support from Franklin Pierce. Pierce could have stepped in to save the Immortals, but he refused, instead allowing the British to accept Walker's surrender. Miller wants his readers to see Walker as a grand imperial self, as the lone hero on the barricade trying to save the isthmus from its own dark forces, from European interference, and from American timidity. The poem serves as a fine example of imperialist bombast: in a few lines, the poet transforms Walker from a conquistador to a liberator—but a liberator, he makes clear, who would serve American interests.[4]

If journalists and poets early in the twentieth century lament Walker's passing from cultural memory, scholars and writers near the end of the century also wonder about his ever-dwindling renown. In his introduction to Ernesto Cardenal's *With Walker in Nicaragua* (1984), Jonathan Cohen notes, with some puzzlement, Walker's passing from public recollection: "Though lost in American history today, Walker's exploits in Nicaragua were big news in the mid–nineteenth century; in fact, according to the historian Frederic Rosengarten, Jr., 'he was the hottest news personality between the discovery of gold in California and the Civil War.'" In his history of "filibustery," *Destiny and Glory* (1957), Edward S. Wallace puts it this way: "Considering the amount of screaming publicity which he received in his time, William Walker is an astonishingly unknown man today."[5] In *Walker* (1987), the companion text to Alex Cox's movie, American screenwriter Rudy Wurlitzer mocks—rather than mourns—Walker's passing from popular memory: "He has been forgotten in the history books as only a loser can be, and it has been left for the movies to resurrect and identify Walker as an American 'hero'":

> It's interesting that in Latin America Walker is one of the most famous people in their entire history. And in the United States nobody knows who he is. He's never mentioned in American history books. And from 1855 to 1857 he was one of the most famous men in the U.S. Today, he would be on the cover of *Time*. But we completely overlook him because he lost. He was a loser and so his name was stricken from the record.[6]

Although Wurlitzer misrepresents Walker's place in American history—he appears in history books a great deal—he can still make these claims with some justification. The mercenary keeps resurfacing, but only a few notice; he then recedes onto the terrain of specialized readers and scholars. Once more, we must ask: Why does Walker keep resurfacing only to be forgotten?

As a start, we can say that Walker began to fade from public memory almost as soon as his corpse began to cool. In *The World and William Walker* (1963), Albert Z. Carr offers an explanation for why Walker—once one of the most famous men in the country—quickly passed from collective recall: the freebooter sought the wrong sort of empire. His contemporaries sought economic rather than military imperiums. As Carr writes, "Walker's entire career was a romantic challenge to economic man":

> The speed with which Walker's fame evaporated had something of the same phenomenal quality that marked him all his life. The coming of the Civil War, with its new crop of heroes, was no doubt mainly responsible for the country's readiness to forget him, but there may have been also another, more subtle reason—the way of thinking and feeling for which he stood. Men of business had then begun to take possession of the United States; their special outlook and mentality was becoming dominant throughout the North and in parts of the South; and their standards of judgement were more and more regarded as identical with law, morality, and good government. Walker's entire career was a challenge to economic man, his personality wholly antithetic to the great powers then about to reshape the American way of life.[7]

The image of the moody, Byronic wanderer with a painful past does in some measure capture the Tennessean's life,[8] but just as importantly, Carr argues that the filibuster sought the wrong sort of empire according to American capitalists of the 1850s and 1860s. As president of Nicaragua, Walker "nationalized" Cornelius Vanderbilt's Accessory Transit Company, seizing its ships and offices. In retaliation, Vanderbilt helped finance the allied war against the filibusters, and sent his own mercenary, Sylvanus M. Spencer, to recapture his vessels. Vanderbilt wanted the bothersome freebooter out of the way; comparatively quiet, less spectacular imperialists preferred to carry out their interventions under the more polite guises of commerce and international law.

If Walker passed in a moment from collective remembrance, he resurfaces in popular culture only to disappear just as quickly. The reason for this lies, in part, in how the nation's mood for overseas adventures affects literary reception. While some might argue that many of the Walker narratives failed to reach much of an audience because they are not that well written or told—and in some instances, they would be correct—we know that the literary or artistic quality of a work often has little to do with commercial (or perhaps even critical) success. The country's desire for expansionism or invasion—a desire that policy architects in Washington often foster—can sweep a novel to the top of the charts or loft it into the dustbin. For example, the huge success of Davis's *Soldiers of Fortune* or William J. Lederer and Eugene Burdick's *The Ugly American* (1958) can be attributed, respectively, to the pro-expansionist temper gripping the country in the years just before the Spanish-American War and to Cold War anxieties over the United States' role in Asia. These works not only benefited from the climate of the times, they also did their part in nourishing the country's desire for a more truculent foreign policy. Just as importantly, both novels construct the United States as the good, if necessarily stern, neighbor with interests and responsibilities abroad. They say the right things at the right time, and they fit in important ways with the United States' popular conception of itself.

If some works succeed, others—such as Davis's *Captain Macklin* (1902) or Cox's *Walker* (1987)—languish for want of an audience because they say things about Americans and American culture that many people do not want to hear. Davis's critical take on U.S. economic adventurism at the turn of the century and Cox's stinging attack on the Reagan administration did not fit well with the tenor of their eras; they did not say the right things at the right time, at least according to the tastes of many Americans. Furthermore, neither text projects an image of the United States as a friend to the world. Walker simply does not fit the popular image of the good neighbor; many Americans, not surprisingly, do not wish to read books or watch movies that call into question American motives or expose the excesses of American energies.

To explain the relative anonymity of this or that text due to its unpopular themes is another way to approach Jameson's "political unconscious." Walker appears and disappears because he has something to tell us that, as Jameson would have it, would be intolerable to hear. If politics can affect reception, at the little lower layer, to admit the truth of imperialism—to say aloud its human costs and to once more confront Necessity and the dialectic of master and slave—remains a painful, almost unthinkable proposition. Walker keeps returning to popular culture because his narrative continues to resonate within the broader history of U.S. interventionism; historical events (such as the rise of imperial furors, for example, before the Spanish-American War, or after the Korean War, or in advance of renewed U.S. interventions in Central America following defeat in Vietnam) keep calling him back to mind, and whatever a particular author's intentions or ideology, Walker's story—a tale of conquest, colonization, grand visions, rapacity, and defeat—lays bare many of the fantasies and desires for power that run beneath the rhetoric of the good neighbor and American exceptionalism. An imperial self and would-be emperor, he represents, in part, U.S. imperialism at its most unapologetic, its most unmasked, and his story contains within it the history of the oppressed, the history of the Indian Wars, slavery, and the exploitation—and often the destruction—of the less powerful. He tells, in other words, the painful truths of imperialism; an agent of empire, his story makes too plain the nature of the nation. He perpetually fades from public memory because his tale tells what cannot be told; nevertheless, the repressed tries to return to the surface.

Finally, we might ask if Walker has a future in American literature. The answer would seem to be "yes." As I write these last words, President George W. Bush has launched his war against Saddam Hussein. Inspired more, we can deduce, by Reagan-era, neoconservative hawks such as Paul Wolfowitz, Dick Cheney, and Donald Rumsfeld than by realists and coalition-builders such as Colin Powell, the president has taken a dramatic step forward in American foreign policy. In his own corollary to the Monroe Doctrine, he has declared that the United States can, in defense of its interests and security, strike preemptively—and without the support of the United Nations or traditional allies—against any organization or nation. Guided in particular by Wolfowitz and Cheney's original 1992 draft, "Defense Planning Guidance," the Bush White House seems intent upon reshaping the world and on extending, even further, American influence. We might speculate that the American imperial self is alive and well, and we could further wager that, given the imperialist course of the nation in our time, Walker will resurface yet again in literature and film. Ever the ghost in the imperial machine, he will whisper to us about the dreams and desires of the agents of empire.

NOTES

Introduction: The Life, Death, and Literary Resurfacings of William Walker, Filibuster

1. Any mention of Walker brings along with it a term that merits definition: *filibuster*. Although we typically think of a filibuster as an obstructionist tactic in a legislature—a senator stands and speaks without a break in order to block a piece of legislation—the term also refers to a mercenary who raises a private army to invade a foreign country. The word filibuster—or, in Spanish, the more musical-sounding *filibustero*—comes from the Dutch *vrijbuiter*, or freebooter, and first appears in print in English in the sixteenth century. William Garrard, in *The Arte of Warre* (1591), refers to "theeues and filbutors" and "fleebooters" (OED). As the editors of the *Oxford English Dictionary* recount, the term then reappears in English letters in the eighteenth century via the French form, *flibustier*, and refers to pirates or piratical adventurers. In particular, *flibustiers* denoted buccaneers in the seventeenth century who plundered Spanish colonies in the New World. In the nineteenth century, following variant spellings, *filibuster* became the common English form and took hold in the United States between 1850 and 1860 to describe soldiers of fortune such as Walker who sought, in contravention of domestic and international law, to conquer states in Central America and the Spanish West Indies. *Filibuster*, in this context, has many synonyms, and I use them throughout, while acknowledging their specific valences: freebooter, mercenary, soldier of fortune, swashbuckler, adventurer, paladin, freelance fighter, and so on.

2. Richard Harding Davis, *Three Gringos in Venezuela and Central America* (New York: Harper and Brothers, 1896), 146–47.

3. See Christopher P. Wilson, "Plotting the Border: John Reed, Pancho Villa, and *Insurgent Mexico*," in *Cultures of United States Imperialism*, ed. Amy Kaplan and Donald E. Pease (Durham: Duke Univ. Press, 1993), 340–61. See also Charles H. Brown, *The Correspondents' War* (New York: Charles Scribner's Sons, 1967).

4. I borrow this notion of female spectatorship in part from Amy Kaplan's fine essay, "Romancing the Empire: The Embodiment of American Masculinity in the Popular Historical Novel of the 1890s," *American Literary History* 2, no. 4 (1990):

659–90. For a fuller account of Kaplan's arguments, particularly in the context of Davis's works, see chapter 3.

5. For a fuller description of Houston and Greene's views on Walker's sexuality, see chapter 5. There is very little evidence that Walker's contemporaries were "worried" about the freebooter's sexuality. Further, as E. Anthony Rotundo argues in *American Manhood* (New York: Basic Books, 1993), "People of the nineteenth and twentieth centuries have understood same-sex romance in very different ways": for most of the 1800s, "a man who kissed or embraced an intimate male friend in bed did not worry about homosexual impulses because he did not assume that he had them. In the Victorian language of touch, a kiss or an embrace was a pure gesture of deep affection at least as much as it was an act of sexual expression" (83, 84). If Walker was queer by late-twentieth-century standards, his compeers would not readily possess the language to describe him in like terms, and what later readers have taken as evidence of homosexuality would not necessarily have been read that way in his day.

6. Richard Harding Davis, "William Walker, the King of the Filibusters," *Real Soldiers of Fortune* (New York: Charles Scribner's Sons, 1906). As Davis remarks, "Had Walker lived four years longer to exhibit upon the great board of the Civil War his ability as a general, he would, I believe, to-day be ranked as one of America's greatest fighting men" (187).

7. As Robert E. May and Richard Slotkin note, Walker was the subject of plays even while campaigning in Nicaragua. As Slotkin remarks in *The Fatal Environment* (New York: HarperPerennial, 1985), even in his day, "Walker's self-mythologizing was in some ways a success: he was received by many journalistic media, popular melodramatists, and popular historians in just the romantic terms he preferred" (261). While Slotkin does not name any specific melodramas, May cites "Nicaragua, or, Gen. Walker's Victories," a play written by E. F. Distin and performed at Fordy's National Theatre in New York on July 21 and July 22, 1856. See May's "Young American Males and Filibustering in the Age of Manifest Destiny: The United States Army as a Cultural Mirror," *Journal of American History* 78, no. 3 (Dec. 1991): 857–86.

8. My thanks to William B. Eigelsbach and the Special Collections Library at the University of Tennessee for forwarding a copy of this story to me. The story appeared in *Adventure* magazine.

9. I have also found a German novel from 1950: Alfred Neumann, *Der Pakt* (translated from the German as *Look upon This Man* or *Strange Conquest*).

10. William Walker, *The War in Nicaragua* (Mobile, Ala.: S. H. Goetzel, 1860; reprint, Detroit: Blaine Ethridge, 1971), 429.

11. Alejandro Bolaños Geyer, appendix C to *William Walker: The Gray-Eyed Man of Destiny* (Lake Saint Louis, Mo.: Privately printed, 1988), 4:281. The article originally appeared in the newspaper that Walker began once in power in Nicaragua. See *El Nicaragüense*, October 18, 1856, 2, c. 3.

12. Albert Z. Carr, *The World and William Walker* (New York: Harper and Row, 1963), 7, 4.

13. Jane H. Thomas and J. G. Ramsey, *Old Days in Nashville and Historical Sketch of 1854* (Nashville: Charles and Randy Elder, 1980), 78–79. Where late-nineteenth- and twentieth-century readers might take such behavior as a sign of effeminacy—and therefore as potential evidence of Walker's "queerness"—in his day, his dedication to his mother would be evidence of his youthful "refinement" and "sentiment." In other words, his contemporary observers would say he possessed attributes proper to his class and education.

14. James J. Roche, *By-Ways of War* (Boston: Small, Maynard, 1901), 60–61; qtd. in Charles H. Brown, *Agents of Manifest Destiny* (Chapel Hill: Univ. of North Carolina Press, 1980), 177; Carr, *Walker*, 38.

15. Quoted in Brown, *Agents*, 202; *Alta California*, Jan. 31, 1854.

16. Walker may have named his force after the elite soldiers in King Xerxes' army. "The Immortals," the Persian empire's best fighters, defeated the Spartans and their allies at the famous battle of Thermopylae during the third Persian war of 480–479 B.C. Ultimately, of course, the Greeks defeated Xerxes' forces on both sea and land.

17. I have assembled this sketch of Walker's education and career from a number of memoirs, biographies, and histories. Among them: William O. Scroggs, *Filibusters and Financiers* (New York: Russell and Russell, 1916); Achmed Abdullah and T. Compton Pakenham, *Dreamers of Empire* (New York: Frederick A. Stokes, 1929); Lawrence Greene, *The Filibuster* (Indianapolis: Bobbs-Merrill, 1937); Albert Z. Carr, *The World and William Walker* (New York: Harper and Row, 1963); and Charles H. Brown, *Agents of Manifest Destiny* (Chapel Hill: Univ. of North Carolina Press, 1980). Memoirs include: Charles W. Doubleday, *Reminiscences of the "Filibuster" War in Nicaragua* (New York: Putnam, 1886); James Carson Jamison, *With Walker in Nicaragua, or Reminiscences of an Officer of the American Phalanx* (Columbia, Mo.: E. W. Stephens, 1909). Walker's *The War in Nicaragua* (1860) remains one of the best sources on the filibuster's adventures.

18. T. Robinson Warren, *Dust and Foam; or, Three Oceans and Two Continents* (New York: Charles Scribner's Sons, 1859), 212–13; Eduardo Galeano, *Memory of Fire: Faces and Masks*, trans. Cedric Belfrage (New York: Pantheon Books, 1987), 179.

19. Darwin Teilhet, *The Lion's Skin* (New York: William Sloane, 1955), 293–94;

Richard Harding Davis, "William Walker, the King of the Filibusters," *Real Soldiers of Fortune* (New York: Charles Scribner's Sons, 1906), 154; Brown, *Agents*, 322.

20. Gore Vidal, *Burr* (New York: Ballantine, 1973), 1–2. Burr also appears as a character in Harriet Beecher Stowe's *The Minister's Wooing* (1859). Vidal, *Burr*, 398.

21. Brown, *Agents*, 80.

22. As John Sepich (*Notes on Blood Meridian* [Louisville: Bellarmine College Press, 1993]: 24–26) and others have noted, Crabb seems to have been, at least in part, the inspiration for Cormac McCarthy's Captain White in *Blood Meridian* (New York: Vintage, 1985). White meets the same unhappy end, as the kid discovers: "He stood before the jar and they urged his consideration of it and tilted it around so that the head should face him. It was Captain White. Lately at war among the heathen" (70).

23. In addition to the filibusters noted here, a number of other real-life adventurers have continued the American freebooting tradition. In 1908, for example, Sam Zemurray, the American banana king, funded a military expedition from New Orleans to Honduras in order to reinstate Manuel Bonilla as president. Zemurray hired Lee Christmas, an African American soldier of fortune, to conduct the coup. Christmas, as Samuel Crowther recounts in *The Romance and the Rise of the American Tropics* (Garden City, N.Y.: Doubleday, Doran, 1929), fits the profile of *the already lost American abroad* (see chapter 2 for a fuller explanation of this narrative paradigm): "He was a railway man from Louisiana. When he was twenty-eight years old, he fell asleep at the throttle and crashed his train. That ended his career in the States" (166). For a much fuller consideration of Christmas and Zemurray, see Lester D. Langley and Thomas Schoonover's *The Banana Men: American Mercenaries and Entrepreneurs in Central America, 1880–1930* (Lexington: Univ. Press of Kentucky, 1995). In the early 1920s, to take another example, a former American marine, Faustin Wirkus, returned to Haiti to serve as a gendarme and eventually became the king of the island of La Gonave. As George Black puts it in *The Good Neighbor* (New York: Pantheon, 1988), "Wirkus was the first white man many of the islanders had seen, and they crowned him king" (40). Wirkus went to Haiti to escape a lifetime working in the coal district of Pennsylvania.

24. One might wish that the late Kathy Acker—the author of such postpunk, postmodern fictions as *Blood and Guts in High School* (1984), *Empire of the Senseless* (1988), and *Pussy, King of the Pirates* (1996), among others—had had the time and inclination to retell Walker's story.

25. Quentin Anderson, *The Imperial Self* (New York: Alfred A. Knopf, 1971), 13, 46–47, 16.

26. For additional views on Anderson and Emerson and on Anderson's standing in American studies, see Stephen Donadio, Stephen Railton, and Ormond Seavey,

eds., *Emerson and His Legacy: Essays in Honor of Quentin Anderson* (Carbondale: Southern Illinois Univ. Press, 1986); and Donald E. Pease, "The Cultural Office of Quentin Anderson," *South Atlantic Quarterly* 89, no. 3 (summer 1990): 583–622.

27. Anderson, *The Imperial Self*, 44.

28. Myra Jehlen, *American Incarnation* (Cambridge: Harvard Univ. Press, 1986), 77, 78.

29. Jehlen, *American Incarnation*, 78, 77.

30. Herman Melville to Nathaniel Hawthorne, 16 April (?) 1851, in *The Letters of Herman Melville*, ed. Merrell R. Davis and William H. Gilman (New Haven: Yale Univ. Press, 1960), 124; qtd. in Wai-chee Dimock, *Empire for Liberty* (Princeton, N.J.: Princeton Univ. Press, 1989), 7.

31. Dimock, *Empire*, 10, 7.

32. If Dimock, like Jehlen, casts the imperial self as inward and outward looking, her methodology suggests a problematic model of homology rather than mediation. Dimock perhaps attributes too much sameness (without, at any rate, a particularly precise explanation of causality) between the age and the artist, and does not allow the writer any particular distance between him- or herself and the macro economic, political, and military forces of the midcentury. As John Carlos Rowe remarks in response to the work of Dimock and others, "We must develop subtler means of assessing the historical and political functions of literature in its own and for our times. We need more varied standards of political and thus aesthetic judgement if we are to respect the complexity of literature's 'action' in a historical moment, especially when such a moment is defined by crisis and conflict" (79). If we reject the homology as overdetermined and agree with Rowe, we can nevertheless argue that Walker, like Melville, was very much a man of his day even if his life and adventures cannot be reduced to a "miniature version" of his era. We must allow for sundry idiosyncratic impulses and desires and for myriad influences and traces. We must argue that the discourses, ideologies, and macro forces of the day flow heterogeneously and variably through individuals even as they give partial, irregular shape to thought and action. See Rowe's *Literary Culture and U.S. Imperialism* (New York: Oxford Univ. Press, 2000).

33. Judith Butler, *Gender Trouble* (New York: Routledge, 1990), 25.

34. Other models may also apply to Walker. Some scholars—Richard Slotkin among them—have asserted that Walker was mad and suffered from an increasing detachment from reality.

35. In his policy statements while in Mexico and Central America, and in his memoir, *The War in Nicaragua*, the freebooter makes clear his loathing not only of Indians but particularly of mestizos and blacks. He offered, as one of the rationales for his invasion of Sonora, a plan for ending Apache raids along the frontier.

36. Carr, *Walker*, 3.

37. We can find an even more precise description of this phenomenon, albeit at a less presidential level. In *Dispatches* (New York: Vintage, 1977), Michael Herr writes about American soldiers in Vietnam "making war movies in their heads": "I kept thinking about all the kids who got wiped out by seventeen years of war movies before coming to Vietnam to get wiped out for good" (209).

38. In *Civilization and Its Discontents* (New York: Norton, 1930; trans. James Strachey), Sigmund Freud observes

> that men are not gentle creatures who want to be loved, and who at the most can defend themselves if they are attacked; they are, on the contrary, creatures among whose instinctual endowments is to be reckoned a powerful share of aggressiveness. As a result, their neighbour is from them not only a potential helper or sexual object, but also someone who tempts them to satisfy their aggressiveness on him, to exploit his capacity for work without compensation, to use him sexually without his consent, to seize his possessions, to humiliate him, to cause him pain, to torture and to kill him. *Homo homini lupus.* (68–69)

In Walker's case, the denial of sexuality works as a supplement to the instinct of aggression. Although I am not undertaking a psychoanalytic reading of Walker, I find Freud suggestive in this instance.

39. James Hurlstone is the benign young American of Bret Harte's *The Crusade of the Excelsior*, vol. 6 of *The Writings of Bret Harte* (Boston: Houghton Mifflin, 1896); Robert Clay the swashbuckling hero of Richard Harding Davis's *Soldiers of Fortune*; Peter Ormerod the stalwart protagonist of Arthur D. Howden Smith's *A Manifest Destiny* (New York: Brentano's, 1926); Frank Goodwin, the genial provocateur of O. Henry's *Cabbages and Kings* (New York: Penguin, 1904).

40. O. Henry, *Cabbages and Kings*, 4.

Chapter One. "Tossing Creation like a Bauble": Walker and Emerson

1. See Eduardo Galeano, *Memory of Fire: Century of the Wind*, trans. Cedric Belfrage (New York: Pantheon, 1988), 151.

2. See John L. O'Sullivan, "Annexation," *United States Magazine and Democratic Review* 17 (July 1845): 5.

3. As Charles H. Brown recounts in *Agents of Manifest Destiny* (Chapel Hill: Univ. of North Carolina Press, 1980), 95–96, O'Sullivan and others could have taken the phrase from a fellow expansionist, Edwin de Leon. In 1845 Leon gave the commencement speech at South Carolina College, where he asserted that "nations, like men, have their seasons of infancy, manly vigor, and decrepitude." The United States, he claimed, was in the flush of "exulting manhood" (qtd. in Brown 96).

4. See "Emerson to Whitman," July 21, 1855, in Walt Whitman, *Leaves of Grass*, ed. Sculley Bradley and Harold W. Blodgett (New York: W. W. Norton, 1973), 731–32.

5. For a (nearly complete) version of Emerson's "Letter to Martin Van Buren," April 23, 1838, see James Elliot Cabot, *A Memoir of Ralph Waldo Emerson*, appendix D (Boston: Houghton, Mifflin, 1887), 2:699. For an explanation of variations in published forms of the letter, see Ralph L. Rusk, *The Letters of Ralph Waldo Emerson* (New York: Columbia Univ. Press, 1939), 2:126–27.

6. Ralph Waldo Emerson, "On Emancipation in the British West Indies," in *Miscellanies*, vol. 11 of *The Works of Ralph Waldo Emerson*, Standard Library ed. (Boston: Houghton, Mifflin, 1883), 172.

7. Ralph Waldo Emerson, "Ode," in *Selections from Ralph Waldo Emerson*, ed. Stephen E. Whicher (Boston: Houghton Mifflin, 1957), 440, 441.

8. We can see, too, that in such later essays as "Experience" (1844) or "Fate" (1860), the early exuberance and idealism of *Nature* has given way to skepticism and a sense that while we must endure our sorrows and travails, we must also learn from them and move forward. As he writes in "Fate," "So when a man is the victim of his fate, has sciatica in his loins, and cramp in his mind; a club-foot and a club in his wit; a sour face, and a selfish temper; a strut in his gait, and a conceit in his affection; or is ground to powder by the vice of his race; he is to rally on his relation to the Universe, which his ruin benefits" (966–67). Emerson sees the world as a much more vexed, even awful place, and the assuredness in progress and human goodness has been tempered by experience, personal grief, and a more worldly sensibility. See *Ralph Waldo Emerson: Essays and Lectures* (New York: Library of America, 1983).

9. Ralph Waldo Emerson, "The Young American," in *Ralph Waldo Emerson: Essays and Lectures* (New York: Library of America, 1983), 225.

10. John L. O'Sullivan, "The Great Nation of Futurity," *United States Magazine and Democratic Review* 6 (November 1839): 426.

11. The Clayton-Bulwer Treaty, signed between the United States and Britain, was designed to guarantee both governments' interests in a potential shipping canal across Nicaragua. In exchange for this guarantee, both nations agreed to abandon their claims to Nicaragua, Costa Rica, and the Mosquito Coast. At the time Clayton negotiated the treaty with Sir Henry Lytton Bulwer, he was Zachary Taylor's secretary of state.

12. U.S. Congress, *Congressional Globe*, 32nd Cong., 3rd sess., 1853, appendix, 262. Although we can only speculate on how Walker's career would have gone if Stephen A. Douglas, rather than Franklin Pierce, had won the Democratic nomination for president in 1852, he might have fared better with a pro-expansionist in the White House. Nevertheless, Pierce's efforts to contain (via the neutrality laws

and other implements) Walker and his fellow freebooters makes very clear who will control the future course of U.S. imperialism: the government, and not privateers.

13. Ralph Waldo Emerson, *Nature*, in *Essays and Lectures* (New York: Library of America, 1983), 34–35.

14. Eric Cheyfitz, *The Poetics of Imperialism*, expanded ed. (Philadelphia: Univ. of Pennsylvania Press, 1997), 27.

15. Emerson, *Nature*, 7.

16. Emerson, "Young American," 228, 226.

17. Emerson, "Young American," 217, 218.

18. Emerson, *Nature*, 20, 22.

19. O'Sullivan, "Annexation," 5. As Myra Jehlen argues in *American Incarnation* (Cambridge: Harvard Univ. Press, 1986), the identification between the self, the land, and the nation has been a profound one in American culture. "Americans saw themselves as building their civilization out of nature itself," she writes, "as neither the analogue nor the translation of Natural Law, but its direct expression. Fusing the political with the natural, human volition with its object, and hope with destiny, they imagined an all-encompassing universe that in effect healed the lapsarian parting of man and his natural kingdom" (3). Emerson, as Jehlen goes on to explain, drew deeply upon these founding beliefs: "Urging each man to build his own world—not only to imagine it but to realize it, to have its value in goods and cash—he could guarantee success because the world already belonged to, in fact *was*, each man" (16). O'Sullivan and the Young Americans also drew upon this remarkable tradition and once more asserted a manifest right to the land of the continent, and beyond.

20. Bolaños Geyer, *William Walker*, 4:281. The article originally appeared in the newspaper that Walker launched once in power in Nicaragua. See *El Nicaragüense*, October 18, 1856, 2, c. 3.

21. Quoted in Albert Z. Carr, *The World and William Walker* (New York: Harper and Row, 1963), 37. Compare Emerson in *Nature*: "He acts it as life, before he apprehends it as truth" (*Essays and Lectures*, 7).

22. Emerson, *Nature*, 47, 10. Emerson's line about finding a forlorn people and making yourself their king, in the context of imperialism, brings to mind another eloquent imperialist: Conrad's Kurtz. When thinking of Kurtz's report for the "International Society for the Suppression of Savage Customs," Marlow recalls the station head's powerful language: "The peroration was magnificent, though difficult to remember, you know. It gave me the notion of an exotic Immensity ruled by an August Benevolence. It made me tingle with enthusiasm. This was the unbounded power of eloquence—of words—of burning noble words" (Joseph Conrad, *Heart of Darkness*, ed. Ross C. Murfin, 2nd ed. [Boston: Bedford, 1996]: 66).

Ironically, although Marlow and the Russian both note Kurtz's eloquence, we almost never hear him speak, and rarely with anything like verbal majesty.

23. An invention of the editors of *El Nicaragüense* (or perhaps of Walker himself), the epithet was given, as Brown notes, as "the fulfillment of a tradition of the Indians that they would be delivered from Spanish oppression by 'the Gray-eyed Man'" (308). The source of this myth was a Baptist missionary, Frederick Crowe, who asserted in *The Gospel in Central America* (1850) that an American would liberate the exploited and abused Indians of the isthmus. Walker's propagandists seized upon Crowe's phrase and made it their own.

24. Herman Melville, *Moby-Dick, or, The Whale* (New York: Penguin, 1992), 219.

25. Emerson, "Young American," 225.

26. William Walker, *The War in Nicaragua* (1860; reprint, Detroit: Blaine Ethridge, 1971), 25, 34.

27. Walt Whitman, "Annexation," June 6, 1846, in *The Gathering of the Forces*, ed. Cleveland Rodgers and John Black (New York: G. P. Putnam, 1920), 1:242–43; Walt Whitman, "Our Territory on the Pacific," July 7, 1846, in *The Gathering of the Forces*, 1:246–47.

28. Quoted in Howard Zinn, *A People's History of the United States, 1492–Present*, rev. and updated ed. (New York: HarperPerennial, 1995), 152. If Walker's language of "regeneration" drew upon the organic and natural imagery of American romanticism, it also collided with another, even more powerful discourse that emerged in the same decade: evolution. The subtitle to Darwin's *On the Origin of the Species by Means of Natural Selection* (New York: Mentor, 1958)—"Or the Preservation of Favoured Races in the Struggle for Life"—sounds like a filibuster slogan, and as Albert K. Weinberg points out in *Manifest Destiny* (Baltimore: Johns Hopkins Univ. Press, 1935), 190–223, the rhetoric of "natural growth" had long been a part of the pro-expansionist argument. Darwin's theories found a sympathetic audience among those interested in annexing Cuba and other lands to add to the republic, and we can hear echoes of "natural selection" in *The War in Nicaragua:* "That which you ignorantly call 'Filibusterism' is not the offspring of hasty passions or ill-regulated desire; it is the fruit of the sure, unerring instincts which act in accordance with laws as old as creation" (429–30).

29. Weinberg, *Manifest Destiny*, 161. Walker worked for the *New Orleans Crescent* (1848–50), a nominally Whig paper that supported the annexation of Cuba but not war with Spain.

30. Richard Slotkin, *The Fatal Environment* (New York: HarperPerennial, 1985), 243, 248.

31. Richard Slotkin, *Regeneration through Violence* (New York: HarperPerennial, 1973), 5.

32. Walker, *War*, 156, 222.
33. Walker, *War*, 253–54.
34. Carr, *Walker*, 200.
35. Walker, *War*, 261, 259.
36. Walker, *War*, 352, 405.
37. Walker, *War*, 340.
38. Quoted in Brown, *Agents*, 451; Melville, *Moby-Dick*, 183.
39. Walker, *War*, 428, 430.

Chapter Two. "What Is Good for Them*": Harte and the Mercenary Romance*

1. For two recent reappraisals of Harte's career and literary achievement, see Alex Nissen, *Bret Harte: Prince and Pauper* (Jackson: Univ. Press of Mississippi, 2000); and Gary Scharnhorst, *Bret Harte: Opening the American Literary West* (Norman: Univ. of Oklahoma Press, 2000).

2. Bret Harte, *The Letters of Bret Harte*, ed. Geoffrey Bret Harte (Boston: Houghton Mifflin, 1926), 321.

3. *Leslie's* (see note 4, below), for example, offers the usual sort of description of Walker as the unlikely looking swashbuckler:

Perhaps nothing about this man has created more surprise in the North, on his present visit, than his personal appearance. . . . Gen. Walker possesses a delicate person, has a hand small and white enough for a lady, speaks in a low tone of voice, and seems in company timid and oppressed. There is nothing remarkable about his face except his eye, and this organ will arrest the most superficial observer. (June 27, 1857, "Walker's Personal Appearance," 187)

Harper's (see note 4 below) also notes the usual details: "He is effeminate in appearance, and rather spare, and of sallow complexion, but has great powers of endurance" (March 7, 1857, "Nicaragua: What General Walker Is Like," 28).

4. Two of the best sources for collected articles on Walker are *La guerra en Nicaragua/The War in Nicaragua según/as reported by Frank Leslie's Illustrated Newspaper, 1855–1857*, ed. Alejandro Bolaños Geyer et al. (Managua, Nicaragua: Banco de América, 1976); and *La Guerra en Nicaragua/The War in Nicaragua según/as reported by Harper's Weekly: Journal of Civilization, 1857–1860*, ed. Alejandro Bolaños Geyer et al. (Managua, Nicaragua: Banco de América, 1976).

5. By the time Harte wrote his freebooting tales, Walker had all but disappeared from public memory. As Albert Z. Carr argues in *The World and William Walker* (New York: Harper and Row, 1963), Walker's fame evaporated quickly after the Civil War; he was replaced by new heroes, villains, and battles. With the freebooter off the cultural map, Harte would have had to rely on memory, the few contempo-

rary histories of Walker, or the memoirs of freebooters who served in Mexico or Nicaragua. Unfortunately, while Harte was writing *Crusade*, he was suffering through a long illness, and his letters mostly refer to his health and family matters. He makes little mention, not surprisingly, of his sources or inspiration for the romance. In other words, we do not know what sources, if any, he had before him, and all we can say is that he based one of the characters on someone he knew: "The wife of Hurlstone was a study from some of my recollections of Ada ———, in the old California days" (*Letters* 321).

6. Many Americans in the 1840s and 1850s strongly opposed U.S. adventurism in any form and for diverse reasons. During the Mexican-American War, for example, Whig leaders such as Daniel Webster and Thomas Corwin found allies among abolitionists such as Frederick Douglass and William Jay (who feared that the annexation of new lands from Mexico would lead to the creation of more slave states) and intellectuals such as Albert Gallatin and James Russell Lowell (who derided arguments of American "superiority" and "destiny"). Similar coalitions also opposed efforts to annex Cuba and to expand U.S. power in Central America. At the same time, not all supporters of expansionism believed that filibustering was the best way to go. Many (including Franklin Pierce and his administration) believed that the White House and Congress should sanction or conduct American ventures abroad; still others (particularly entrepreneurs such as Cornelius Vanderbilt) held that U.S. economic expansion should take precedence over armed conquest or the annexation of territories. These debates were widely disseminated in newspapers and magazines, and Walker, as the most successful of all filibusters, was the subject of countless articles and editorials.

7. Henry Lawrence Kinney was a Texas land speculator, entrepreneur, and would-be filibuster who, among his many ventures, raised funds to establish an American colony on Nicaragua's Mosquito Coast. In direct competition with Walker, he set sail for the isthmus in 1855. Like his competitor, Kinney faced opposition from the U.S. government, and after struggling in Nicaragua for two years, he returned to Corpus Christi, Texas, a town he had helped to found in the early 1840s. Financially ruined by his failed filibustering mission, he eventually left Texas for Mexico where he died—accounts vary as to the particulars—during a gunfight.

8. *Leslie's*, "Yankee Progress in Central America," Dec. 22, 1855: 2.

9. *Leslie's*, "The Central American Question," Dec. 29, 1855: 9.

10. *Leslie's*, "The Nicaraguan Question—Outbreak of Hostilities in Central America," April 12, 1856: 38.

11. Walker was an early and popular subject for *Harper's*; they included a short article on the freebooter in their inaugural issue of Jan. 3, 1857.

12. *Harper's*, "Walker and Nicaragua," Jan. 31, 1857: 12, 13.

13. *Harper's*, "The End of Walker," Oct. 13, 1860: 141.

14. Bret Harte, "Peter Schroeder," in *The Writings of Bret Harte* (Boston: Houghton Mifflin, 1907), 14:70. In addition to Walker, Harte may also have had Aaron Burr in mind as he wrote "Peter Schroeder." When James Wilkinson and Burr began to plot their action against Mexico, they enlisted the financial support of Harmon Blennerhasset, a wealthy Irish American. My thanks to one of the readers at the University of Georgia Press for suggesting this connection.

15. Harte, "Schroeder," 86; see David Spurr, *The Rhetoric of Empire* (Durham: Duke Univ. Press, 1993), 92–108.

16. Harte, "Schroeder," 87–88.

17. Margaret Duckett, "The 'Crusade' of a Nineteenth-Century Liberal," *Tennessee Studies in Literature* 4 (1959): 114; Gary Scharnhorst, *Bret Harte* (New York: Twayne, 1992), 105.

18. Charles H. Brown, *Agents of Manifest Destiny* (Chapel Hill: Univ. of North Carolina Press, 1980), 467.

19. Duckett, "Crusade," 109.

20. For a much more sustained, direct fictional treatment of Bolívar's life, see Gabriel García Márquez's masterful, comic novel, *The General in His Labyrinth*, trans. Edith Grossman (New York: Alfred A. Knopf, 1990).

21. Bret Harte, *The Crusade of the Excelsior*, vol. 6 of *The Writings of Bret Harte*, (Boston: Houghton Mifflin, 1896), 214. The reference to "Todos Santos" reinforces Perkins's connection to Walker: after the raid on La Paz during his Mexican adventure, the filibuster sailed north and declared Ensenada de Todos Santos the capital of his newly formed "republic."

22. Harte, *Crusade*, 15.

23. For his part, Harte found Perkins about the only interesting character in the romance. In a September 15, 1887, letter to his wife, Nan (formerly Miss Anna Griswold of New York), he confesses that the novel lacks a little interest: "Did you read the 'Crusade of the Excelsior'? I am rather disappointed in it, myself. I had really only one strong character on which to base a long story—the character of the wild filibuster. The wife of Hurlstone was a study from some of my recollections of Ada ———, in the old Californian days. But I fear they were each not sufficiently treated to make the story interesting" (*Letters of Bret Harte* 321).

24. Harte, *Crusade*, 14.

25. Harte, *Crusade*, 60.

26. Harte, *Crusade*, 242.

27. Harte, *Crusade*, 108, 109.

28. Harte, *Crusade*, 159.

29. Harte, *Crusade*, 91.

30. Harte, *Crusade*, 179; Duckett, "Crusade," 112–13.

31. Harte, *Crusade*, 64.

32. Harte, *Crusade*, 245, 245–46; Scharnhorst, *Harte*, 105.

33. I have generated this list of interventions and their purposes, in part, from a Department of the Navy–Naval Historical Center document, "Instances of Use of United States Forces Abroad, 1798–1993." Authored by Ellen C. Collier, a "Specialist in U.S. Foreign Policy," the 1993 report builds upon Secretary of State Dean Rusk's presentation to senators in 1962, "Instances of the Use of United States Armed Forces Abroad 1798–1945." Prepared by the State Department, the original report was created as a means to cite precedents for a potential armed invasion of Cuba. For Collier's complete report, see http://www.history.navy.mil/wars/foabroad.htm.

34. Collier, "Instances," 5.

35. Collier, "Instances," 7.

36. George Black, *The Good Neighbor: How the United States Wrote the History of Central America and the Caribbean* (New York: Pantheon, 1988), 8; Lester D. Langley and Thomas Schoonover, *The Banana Men: American Mercenaries and Entrepreneurs in Central America, 1880–1930* (Lexington: Univ. Press of Kentucky, 1995), 14.

37. Quoted in Walter LaFeber, *Inevitable Revolutions*, expanded ed. (New York: W. W. Norton, 1984), 33; William Appleman Williams, *The Tragedy of American Diplomacy*, new ed. (New York: W. W. Norton, 1972), 45.

38. Gore Vidal, *Dark Green, Bright Red* (New York: Ballantine, 1950), 1, 3.

39. For these reasons, I would distinguish the romances of Harte, Davis, and other rewriters of the Walker narrative from what John McClure, in *Late Imperial Romance* (New York: Verso, 1994), calls the "late imperial romance." In his extraordinary study of the influence of Conrad, Kipling, and Forster on the generation of American writers who "came of age in the fifties, when Anglo-American modernism was the reigning tradition in American literary culture and the American academy" (5), McClure argues that the American practitioners of the late imperial romance—or those works that decry imperialism even as they "tell stories of worlds rich with marvels and monsters, that engineer a re-enchantment of the world" (29)—bemoan the rationalization of the world and set their characters into realms of stubborn enchantment. Harte and Davis, in contrast, worry less about spiritual or magical matters and more about economics and geopolitics. We can see Harte (who wrote before Conrad or Kipling) and Davis (a contemporary of the two English writers) as establishing a different form of romance to explore American imperialism and the imperial self. Instead of the "late imperial romance," we have

the mercenary romance. And, as in the case of Didion, the late imperial and mercenary romances inhabit the same text.

40. Northrop Frye, *Anatomy of Criticism* (Princeton: Princeton Univ. Press, 1957), 186.

41. Amy Kaplan, "'Left Alone with America': The Absence of Empire in the Study of American Culture," in *Cultures of United States Imperialism*, ed. Amy Kaplan and Donald E. Pease (Durham: Duke Univ. Press, 1993), 17.

42. Richard Drinnon, in *Facing West: The Metaphysics of Indian-Hating and Empire-Building* (Norman: Univ. of Oklahoma Press, 1980), a pioneering study on the literatures of American continental expansionism and overseas adventurism, makes the historical and literary connection between the cowboy–and–slave trader and the agent of empire: "All along, the obverse of Indian-hating had been the metaphysics of empire-building—the backwoods 'captain in the vanguard of conquering civilization' merely became the overseas outrider of the same empire" (464). Drinnon shows how Euro-American "hatred" for Indians easily transformed itself into a fluid, strategically articulated racism: "In its more inclusive form, Western racism is another name for native-hating—in North America, of 'niggers,' 'Chinks,' 'Japs,' 'greasers,' 'dagoes,' etc.; in the Philippines, of 'goo-goos' and in Indochina of 'gooks'" (xvi). The romance hero partakes of the metaphysics of Indian-hating and empire-building, and the histories of the Indian Wars and the African slave trade are hardwired into tales of the imperial self abroad.

43. Richard Slotkin, *Regeneration through Violence* (New York: HarperPerennial, 1973), 506, 507.

44. Richard Harding Davis, "William Walker, the King of the Filibusters," in *Real Soldiers of Fortune* (New York: Charles Scribner's Sons, 1906), 148.

Chapter Three. The Spectacular Empire: Davis and Roosevelt

1. As John Seelye, Arthur Lubow, and other scholars have noted, Davis drew inspiration from a number of others writers—including Anthony Hope, Robert Louis Stevenson, and Rudyard Kipling—and modeled his romances in part on their adventure tales. See Seelye, *War Games: Richard Harding Davis and the New Imperialism* (Amherst: Univ. of Massachusetts Press, 2003); and Lubow, *The Reporter Who Would Be King* (New York: Charles Scribner's Sons, 1992).

2. The phrase "Spectacular Empire" perhaps merits brief definition. In the most basic sense, it denotes what many commentators and apologists have asserted for over one hundred years: for a time around the turn of the century, the United States aggressively pursued an overseas empire. In that sense, 1898 stands as the year of the Spectacular Empire: in short order, the United States annexed or seized con-

trol of Hawaii, Samoa, the Philippines, Cuba, Puerto Rico, and the Ladrones. As Robert L. Beisner remarks in *Twelve against Empire: The Anti-Imperialists, 1898–1900* (New York: McGraw Hill, 1968), "In less than a year a strong but largely self-contained America had changed into a far-flung empire already harassed by a colonial rebellion" (x). Few could argue that the United States was not acting as an imperialist nation, and Roosevelt did his part to give the folks at home a good show of imperial ardor and intensity. Riding at the front of his cowboy–and–ivy league force—and always making sure that reporters such as Davis were around—he charged up hills, firing his pistols; he provided a media-ready spectacle of American power. Almost as famously, Commodore George Dewey directed the quick American victory over the Spanish at Manila Bay in the Philippines. In 1898 the United States had its spoils, spectacles, and heroes of empire.

Although the phrase acknowledges this eruption of martial power, more importantly, it suggests that the Spanish-American War must be seen as part of the ongoing processes of American imperialism. As the history of westward expansion and of U.S. economic, political, and military interventions throughout the Americas prior to 1898 makes clear, the war against Spain should not be seen as an aberration but rather as the coming-out celebration of the American empire. At the cotillion, McKinley and Roosevelt presented the already experienced creature for public consideration. As we have seen, U.S. forces—either military or paramilitary—had already intervened in Algeria, Panama, Argentina, Japan, Uruguay, China, and Guatemala, and following the assertion of U.S. colonial rule in Hawaii, Puerto Rico, and the Philippines, the United States resumed its traditionally less spectacular pattern of interventions. In the years leading up to World War I, for example, U.S. forces were deployed in Panama, Honduras, Cuba, the Dominican Republic, Nicaragua, and Haiti. The phrase suggests, therefore, that the empire existed before and after the Spanish-American War, but that it was comparatively unspectacular.

In addition to being so much smoke over the potent combination of military force and economic power, and rather than being an anomaly in American history, we can perhaps better understand the turn-of-the-century spectacle as performing a number of functions for U.S. imperialists and jingoes. For one, it announced the United States' official membership in the imperial club; as Ernest R. May argues in *Imperial Democracy*, new ed. (Chicago: Imprint, 1991), "In the early 1880s diplomats and writers rarely spoke of the United States in the same breath with the six recognized great powers—Britain, France, Germany, Austria-Hungary, Russia, and Italy. By the beginning of the twentieth century, they included it almost invariably" (xi). The spectacle also functioned as a dramatic assertion of the Monroe Doctrine; as Roosevelt wrote in 1896, "If the Monroe Doctrine did not already exist it would be necessary forthwith to create it." Two years before landing in Cuba, Roosevelt was already thinking about a bold move to declare, once and for all, U.S. hegemony in the hemisphere.

3. Cuba had long been the object of filibuster fancies. Even as Walker dreamed of an empire in Mexico or Central American, several other annexationists and filibusters had set their sights on the "Pearl of the Antilles." In 1851, for example, Narciso López, with the support of high-profile Americans such as John L. O'Sullivan, landed a contingent at Bahía Honda, Cuba, only to be captured by the Spanish two weeks later; in 1855 John Quitman, the former governor of Mississippi, likewise attempted to raise a force against the island. Cuba, like Mexico and Nicaragua, had long been an expansionist target, yet the conquest of the island would have to wait for Roosevelt, for the efforts of a latter-day American adventurer. In about half a century, the ambitions of criminal freebooters—they routinely violated American neutrality laws—became the fully sanctioned, if widely contested policies of McKinley and Roosevelt.

4. If Roosevelt, perhaps more than any man of his day, exemplified and championed the young imperial self, he was not without his detractors. William James, in a "Letter on Governor Roosevelt's Oration" (*Boston Evening Transcript*, April 15, 1899), showed his fierce anti-imperialism and mocked the Rough Rider for his youthful excitability. For James, Roosevelt was a case of arrested development, and he charged that Roosevelt maintained an irresponsible and dangerous exuberance for action and danger well beyond that typical of men his age:

> Although in middle life, as the years age, and in a situation of responsibility concrete enough, [Roosevelt] is still mentally in the Sturm und Drang period of early adolescence, treats human affairs, when he makes speeches about them, from the sole point of view of the organic excitement and difficulty they may bring, gushes over war as the ideal condition of human society, for the manly strenuousness which it involves, and treats peace as a condition of blubberlike and swollen ignobility, fit only for huckstering weaklings, dwelling in gray twilight and heedless of the higher life. Not a word of the cause—one foe is as good as another, for aught he tells us; not a word of the conditions of success. (6)

James adopts a savage anti-imperial eloquence and savors the attack; at the same time, he accurately captures some of his former student's view of "human affairs."

5. In "William Walker, the King of the Filibusters" (New York: Charles Scribner's Sons, 1906), Davis at last puts Walker and Roosevelt together, if in an oblique and somewhat tortured manner: "[Walker] now had under him a remarkable force, one of the most effective known to military history. For although six months had not yet passed, the organization he now commanded was as unlike the Phalanx of

the fifty-eight adventurers who were driven back at Rivas, as were Falstaff's followers from the regiment of picked men commanded by Colonel Roosevelt" (172–73).

6. Theodore Roosevelt, "The Strenuous Life," in *The Works of Theodore Roosevelt*, National ed. (New York: Charles Scribner's Sons, 1901), 13:320, 323.

7. Lubow, *Reporter*, 156; Theodore Roosevelt to James Brander Matthews, Dec. 6, 1892, in Elting E. Morison, ed., *The Letters of Theodore Roosevelt* (Cambridge: Harvard Univ. Press, 1951), 298 [qtd. in Lubow, *Reporter*, 167].

8. Theodore Roosevelt to James Brander Matthews, Jan. 30, 1894, in Morison, *Letters of Theodore Roosevelt*, 358 [qtd. in Lubow, *Reporter*, 167].

9. Edward W. Said, *Culture and Imperialism* (New York: Vintage, 1993), xii, 12.

10. Amy Kaplan, "Romancing the Empire: The Embodiment of American Masculinity in the Popular Historical Novel of the 1890s," *American Literary History* 2, no. 4 (winter 1990): 677. For a fuller view of Josiah Strong's views on the American role in world affairs, see his quasi-religious polemic, *Expansion* (New York: Baker and Taylor, 1900).

11. See also Timothy Brennan's "The National Longing for Form" in *Nation and Narration*, ed. Homi K. Bhabha (New York: Routledge, 1990), 44–70. In his analysis of "the *institutional* uses of fiction in nationalist movements" (47), Brennan historicizes the rise of the European colonial powers and argues that "literature participated in the formation of nations through the creation of 'national print media'—the newspaper and the novel" (48). Just as literature plays a role in nation-building, it has its part in empire-building.

12. Christopher P. Wilson, "Plotting the Border: John Reed, Pancho Villa, and *Insurgent Mexico*," in *Cultures of United States Imperialism*, ed. Amy Kaplan and Donald E. Pease (Durham: Duke Univ. Press, 1993), 343.

13. Richard Harding Davis, *Three Gringos in Venezuela and Central America* (New York: Harper and Brothers, 1896), 147.

14. Charles H. Brown, *The Correspondents' War* (New York: Charles Scribner's Sons, 1967), 77. Booth Tarkington rather melodramatically recalls Davis's celebrity status among college men of the 1890s: "His stalwart good looks were as familiar to us as were those of our own football captain; we knew his face as we knew the face of the President of the United States, but we infinitely preferred Davis's" (see "Richard Harding Davis," in *Van Bibber and Others*, vol. 1 of *The Novels and Stories of Richard Harding Davis*, Crossroads ed. [New York: Charles Scribner's Sons, 1916], ix). He goes on, "Of all the great people of every continent, this was the one we most desired to see" (ix). Tarkington evinces an almost homoerotic admiration for the reporter, and Davis clearly had a following among young men. We know, as well, that the readers of his romances tended to be young women and girls. Blessed with a good chin, he appealed to both men and women, and the reproduction of his

image in countless newspapers and magazines added even more glitz to his political pronouncements.

15. For a much fuller treatment of Davis's journalism, see Seelye's excellent study, *War Games*.

16. Davis, *Gringos*, 142–43.

17. Davis, *Gringos*, 146.

18. "Occupation of Mexico," *United States Magazine and Democratic Review* 21 (November 1847): 381.

19. Richard Harding Davis, *Cuba in War Time* (R. H. Russell, 1897), 129.

20. In his own book on the war, *The Rough Riders* (New York: Signet, 1899), Roosevelt offers almost the same argument: "[Both Leonard Wood and I] felt very strongly that such a war would be as righteous as it would be advantageous to the honor and the interests of the nation" (5). Still, Davis was not without sympathy for the plight of the Cubans, and he records their sufferings at length in *Cuba in War Time* (1897).

21. Richard Harding Davis, *The Cuban and Porto Rican Campaigns* (New York: Charles Scribner's Sons, 1898), 360.

22. In fact, Davis modeled Olancho after Cuba and its capital after Havana, having taken a trip to the island during his college years.

23. See Alice Payne Hackett, *Seventy Years of Best Sellers, 1895–1965* (New York: R. R. Bowker, 1967), 93.

24. In a letter to his mother dated June 27, 1901 (*Adventures and Letters of Richard Harding Davis*, ed. Charles Belmont Davis [New York: Charles Scribner's Sons, 1917]), Davis shows his true admiration for her work:

From the day you struck the first blow for labor, in *The Iron Mills* on to the editorials in *The Tribune, The Youth's Companion* and *The Independent*, with all the good the novels, the stories brought to people, you were always year after year making the ways straighter, lifting up people, making them happier and better. No woman ever did better for her time than you and no shrieking suffragette will ever understand the influence you wielded, greater than hundreds of thousands of women's votes. (293)

25. Rebecca Harding Davis, *Life in the Iron Mills and Other Stories*, ed. Tillie Olsen (New York: Feminist Press, 1985), 34.

26. Richard Harding Davis, *Soldiers of Fortune* (New York: Charles Scribner's Sons, 1897), 126.

27. Davis, *Life*, 22, 22–23, 42.

28. Davis, *Soldiers*, 292, 297.

29. Davis, in one passage, seems to take a shot at his mother. After the tour of the

mine, Alice Langham complains of a headache, and pretty clearly has not enjoyed the day or the spectacle of the operation. Clay takes her boredom personally: "He was greatly hurt that she should have cared so little, and indignant at himself for being so unjust. Why should he expect a *woman* to find interest in that hive of noise and sweating energy?" (*Soldiers* 133–34, emphasis added). His mother, a daughter of an upper-middle-class family, demonstrated just such an interest in *Life*. Once more, we cannot say if Davis intended to slight his mother, but one could certainly read the passage that way.

30. Davis, *Life*, 23–24, 24.

31. Davis, *Soldiers*, 8. In perhaps yet another reference to his mother's novella, Richard has Alice Langham study Clay's profile. She thinks of him as "very fine, and the head on his broad shoulders was as well-modelled as the head of an Athenian statue" (*Soldiers* 115). As Cecelia Tichi notes in her critical edition of *Life in the Iron Mills* (Boston: Bedford, 1998), Hugh's statues stand in stark contrast to the classically influenced works preferred by the American middle and upper classes in the latter half of the nineteenth century. As Tichi argues, "The new nation likened itself to the ancient Roman Republic and based its democratic ideals on those of ancient Greece. If the United States were to become a major civilization, then surely in time it, like these ancient civilizations, would need to demonstrate its status through great achievement in art" (294). For Richard, Clay is the new Greek or Roman, the agent of the new empire, and he looks the classical part; Hugh, on the other hand, has no access to classical models or to an artist's education, and he fashions his art from the raw and primitive conditions of his life. Whereas Rebecca deliberately challenges upper-class tastes and conceits, Richard embraces them and their assurances of American greatness.

32. Davis, *Soldiers*, 10–11.

33. Davis, *Soldiers*, 96.

34. Carson, under the command of Brigadier General James Carleton, was charged with subduing the Navajo in the American Southwest. Although Carson had little luck tracking down the elusive Navajo themselves, he set about destroying their homes, goods, and food sources. These tactics caused many Navajo to starve, and most eventually surrendered to Carson. A great many died while being relocated to Bosque Redondo in New Mexico, and a number were seized along the way by the Ute and sold as slaves.

35. Davis, *Soldiers*, 170.

36. Davis, *Soldiers*, 194, 330, 333.

37. Davis, *Soldiers*, 240.

38. Davis, *Soldiers*, 240.

39. Davis, *Soldiers*, 51, 50, 57.

40. Davis, *Soldiers*, 131, 185.

41. Davis, *Soldiers*, 334.

42. Walter LaFeber, *Inevitable Revolutions*, expanded ed. (New York: W. W. Norton, 1983), 69.

43. Kaplan, "Romancing the Empire," 661, 671.

44. Seelye, *War Games*, 8–10.

45. Roosevelt first articulated the "Roosevelt Corollary" to the Monroe Doctrine in a May 20, 1904, letter to Elihu Root. Root read the letter at a Cuban anniversary dinner in New York on the 20th, and the document was then published in the *New York Tribune* on May 21, 1904:

> Brutal wrongdoing, or an impotence which results in a general loosening of the ties of civilized society, may finally require intervention by some civilized nation, and in the Western Hemisphere the United States cannot ignore this duty; but it remains true that our interests, and those of our southern neighbors, are in reality identical. All that we ask is that they shall govern themselves well, and be prosperous and orderly.

For a complete text of the letter, see *The Letters of Theodore Roosevelt*, ed. Elting E. Morison (Cambridge: Harvard Univ. Press, 1951), 801.

46. Theodore Roosevelt, *Theodore Roosevelt: An Autobiography* (New York: Charles Scribner's Sons, 1913), 30. I first came across this passage in Edmund Morris's remarkable biography of Roosevelt's early years, *The Rise of Theodore Roosevelt* (New York: Random Books, 1979), 16. H. W. Brands, *T.R.: The Last Romantic* (New York: Basic, 1997), 28.

47. Theodore Roosevelt, "The Strenuous Life," in *The Works of Theodore Roosevelt*, National ed. (New York: Charles Scribner's Sons, 1901), 13:319, 323. Though one does not usually say such things in academic discourse, I cannot help but hear this speech as if Dennis Hopper were delivering it in the guise of the harlequin-photographer in Francis Ford Coppola's *Apocalypse Now* (1979).

48. Theodore Roosevelt, "The Administration of the Island Possessions," in *The Works of Theodore Roosevelt*, National ed. (New York: Charles Scribner's Sons, 1925), 16:270.

49. Theodore Roosevelt, "The Duties of American Citizenship," in *The Works of Theodore Roosevelt*, National ed. (New York: Charles Scribner's Sons, 1925), 13:281.

50. Judith Butler, *Gender Trouble* (New York: Routledge, 1990), 25, 33.

51. Kristin L. Hoganson, *Fighting for American Manhood* (New Haven: Yale Univ. Press, 1998), 35, 139.

52. Gail Bederman, *Manliness and Civilization* (Chicago: Univ. of Chicago Press,

1995), 171, 170, 183. Here, we have yet another connection between Walker and Roosevelt, but whereas some commentators believe that Walker may have been homosexual, Roosevelt's foes seemed more intent on wounding than labeling him.

53. For more on Roosevelt and masculinity, see E. Anthony Rotundo, *American Manhood* (New York: Basic, 1993); and Kim Townsend, *Manhood at Harvard* (New York: Norton, 1996).

54. Roosevelt knew Emerson from his Harvard days, and as H. W. Brands recounts in *T.R.: The Last Romantic* (New York: Basic, 1997), 35–36, Roosevelt and his family met Emerson while on a "Nile journey": "Theodore introduced the children to the New England sage, who struck Corinne as past his prime." Roosevelt, "Strenuous," 329.

55. As part of his vision of the imperial self, Roosevelt endorses the European notion of *la mission civilisatrice* and the white man's burden, and he replaces the Americanized language of "regeneration" with the Europeanized language of "uplift." In "The Strenuous Life," for example, he asserts that English rule in India and Egypt "has advanced the cause of civilization" (330) and casts the war against Spain as an honorable form of imperialism. As always, the imperial self must do what needs to be done: "So, if we do our duty aright in the Philippines, we will add to that national renown which is the highest and finest part of national life, will greatly benefit the people of the Philippine Islands, and, above all, we will play our part well in the great work of uplifting mankind" (330). He adopts the traditional arguments of colonialism—when Kipling published "The White Man's Burden" in the *Times* of London in 1899, he subtitled it, "The United States and the Philippine Islands"—and makes it clear that imperialism benefits both Filipinos and Americans. Whereas regeneration bespoke the desire to renew and elevate the civilization and political and economic systems of the Mexicans or Central Americans, uplift bespeaks Roosevelt and his fellow jingoes' belief that empire-building not only improves the lot of the other but tempers and makes virtuous the self.

56. Rubén Darío, the famous Nicaraguan poet and opponent of American expansionism, saw many of these same contradictions in Roosevelt. In "A Roosevelt," a poem in *Cantos de vida y esperanza* (Barcelona, Spain: Casa Editorial Maucci, 1902), he dubs Roosevelt *cazador*, the hunter:

> Es con voz de la Biblia, o verso de Walt Whitman,
> Que habría de llegar hasta ti, Cazador!
> Primitivo y moderno, sencillo y complicado,
> con un algo de Washington y cuatro de Nemrod!
> Eres los Estados Unidos,

eres el futuro invasor
de la América ingenua que tiene sangre indígena,
que aún reza a Jesucristo y aún habla en español.

(With the voice of the Bible, and the verse of Walt Whitman,
One could have reached you, Hunter!
Primitive and modern, simple and complex,
One part Washington, and four parts Nimrod!
You are the United States,
You are the future invader
Of ingenuous America that has Indian blood,
And even prays to Jesus, and even speaks in Spanish.)

The poet casts the Rough Rider as the incarnation of imperial America, and he sees in him America's many contradictions: atavistic yet forward thinking, dedicated to democratic ideals but ready to fight, to conquer, to make others see matters his way. Roosevelt, as the invader, as the American imperial self, heralds the future course of U.S.–Latin American relations; just as Simón Bolívar in 1828 knew that the United States was "destined to plague and torment the continent in the name of freedom," Darío realizes that Roosevelt represents a much more invasive form of torment.

57. Theodore Roosevelt, *The Rough Riders* (New York: Signet, 1899), 20.

58. Theodore Roosevelt, "The Expansion of the White Races," in *The Works of Theodore Roosevelt*, National ed. (New York: Charles Scribner's Sons, 1925), 16:259.

59. Obviously, these numbers remain a matter of speculation. For a summary of recent estimates see, for example, Mark C. Carnes and John A. Garraty (with Patrick Williams), *Mapping America's Past* (New York: Henry Holt, 1996), 38–39.

60. Roosevelt, "Expansion," 269, 268, 267.

Chapter Four. Soldiers of Misfortune: Davis and O. Henry

1. Quoted in Gerald Langford, *The Richard Harding Davis Years: A Biography of a Mother and a Son* (New York: Holt, Rinehart, and Winston, 1961), 224.

2. Quoted in Arthur Lubow, *The Reporter Who Would Be King* (New York: Charles Scribner's Sons, 1992), 154.

3. In chapter 3, I dubbed the 1890s the era of the Spectacular Empire. "The Ugly American Empire" is a phrase that could be used to describe the state of the imperium during the Cold War. It begins with stalemate in Korea, finds its fullest expression in Vietnam and Watergate, and culminates in the *contra* war in Nicaragua. I adapt the phrase, of course, from William J. Lederer and Eugene Burdick's pot-

boiler, *The Ugly American* (1958), but whereas Lederer and Burdick portray Homer Atkins, the titular "ugly American," as an able, albeit homely American hero, I use the phrase not to suggest American commonsense and heroism but rather imperial violence and destructiveness. The workings of the empire have become increasingly vicious and "ugly."

4. Michael Herr, *Dispatches* (New York: Vintage, 1977), 46.

5. O. Henry, *Cabbages and Kings* (New York: Penguin, 1993), 119–20.

6. See Lubow, *Reporter*, 228; Richard Harding Davis, *Adventures and Letters of Richard Harding Davis*, ed. Charles Belmont Davis (New York: Charles Scribner's Sons, 1917), 317.

7. Davis, *Letters*, 317. Earlier in 1902, Davis had dramatized *Soldiers of Fortune* for the New York stage. The play was a critical and financial success. After the relative failure of *Captain Macklin*, Davis produced *The Dictator* (1904), his first play not based on one of his earlier stories or novels. The farce, set in "Porto Banos, Republic of San Mañana, Central America," proved very popular. See Richard Harding Davis, *Farces* (New York: Charles Scribner's Sons, 1906).

8. Lubow, *Reporter*, 229.

9. Langford, *RHD Years*, 226. I find curious Langford's use of the phrase, "the familiar stage props." The props are, of course, familiar elements of Davis's fiction, but by 1961 they were also the thoroughly familiar, culturally embedded elements of the narrative of the already lost American abroad. They are familiar to Langford, in other words, not only because of his reading of Davis but also because most people could probably use similar terms to describe Central American countries.

10. Lubow, *Reporter*, 227, 228.

11. John Seelye, *War Games* (Amherst: Univ. of Massachusetts Press, 2003), 225.

12. Richard Harding Davis, *Captain Macklin* (New York: Charles Scribner's Sons, 1902), 46.

13. Davis, *Captain Macklin*, 46, 34.

14. Davis, *Captain Macklin*, 48.

15. Fairfax Downey, *Richard Harding Davis: His Day* (New York: Charles Scribner's Sons, 1933), 201.

16. Since Churchill was never actually a mercenary, Davis invents a broader definition of soldier of fortune: "In the bigger sense he is the kind of man who in any walk of life makes his own fortune, who, when he sees it coming, leaps to meet it, and turns it to his advantage" (77). See Richard Harding Davis, "Winston Spencer Churchill," in *Real Soldiers of Fortune* (New York: Charles Scribner's Sons, 1906).

17. Davis, "Major-General Henry Ronald Douglas MacIver," *Real Soldiers*, 5.

18. Richard Harding Davis, *Three Gringos in Venezuela and Central America* (New York: Harper and Brothers, 1896), 58.

19. Davis, *Captain Macklin*, 225, 199. As Lester D. Langley and Thomas Schoonover explain, in Walker's era, the five Central American republics were Nicaragua, Costa Rica, Honduras, Guatemala, and El Salvador: "In the nineteenth century . . . Panama was a part of Columbia, a South American nation. Belize (before 1981, British Honduras) lies *in* Central America, but its social, cultural, racial, and political character bespeaks a Caribbean nation" (5). See *The Banana Men* (Lexington: Univ. Press of Kentucky, 1995).

20. Davis, *Captain Macklin*, 259, 275.

21. Davis, *Captain Macklin*, 291, 263, 291, 293.

22. Richard Harding Davis, "William Walker, the King of the Filibusters," in *Real Soldiers of Fortune* (New York: Charles Scribner's Sons, 1906), 175, 187.

23. Davis, *Captain Macklin*, 199, 197, 200.

24. Davis, *Captain Macklin*, 325.

25. In his relative thoughtlessness and scorning of women, Macklin recalls what David G. Pugh calls the nineteenth-century "cult of masculinity." Like Pugh's "Jacksonian Man," Macklin would rather fight than think, and he would rather do just about anything than spend time in the company of women. For a fuller explanation of the cult of masculinity—and Roosevelt's late place in the cult—see Pugh's *Sons of Liberty* (Westport, Conn.: Greenwood, 1983).

26. Davis, *Captain Macklin*, 77, 74.

27. Davis, *Captain Macklin*, 76, 92. Walker, as president of Nicaragua, accused Vanderbilt of owing the republic a similar debt. When Walker seized Vanderbilt's assets (as Laguerre seizes Fiske's assets in *Captain Macklin*), the magnate helped finance the successful war against the filibusters.

28. Davis, *Captain Macklin*, 315.

29. Theodore Roosevelt, "The Control of Corporations," in *The Works of Theodore Roosevelt*, National ed. (New York: Charles Scribner's Sons, 1925), 16: 62, 65.

30. Langford, *RHD Years*, 191.

31. Lubow, *Reporter*, 109.

32. Daniel B. Schirmer, *Republic or Empire* (Cambridge, Massachusetts: Schenkman, 1972), 226; qtd. in Howard Zinn, *A People's History of the United States, 1492–Present*, rev. and updated ed. (New York: HarperPerennial, 1995), 308.

33. Seelye, *War Games*, 310–11, 309.

34. Davis, *Macklin*, 257, 267, 272, 321. Though Davis's choice of a French expedition to Southeast Asia was probably more or less randomly selected—he could have chosen from any number of European interventions in any number of places—it does carry, for later readers, a chill: the United States, as we know, be-

came increasingly involved in the war to reassert French colonial control in Vietnam after World War II. Although Davis was no Nostradamus, to be sure, he at least hints that U.S. and European interests around the world would increasingly come to overlap.

35. Stanhope Searles, "O. Henry's 'Cabbages and Kings,'" *Bookman* 20, no. 6 (1905): 561–62.

36. O. Henry, *Cabbages*, 12.

37. See, for example, William Lyon Phelps, *The Advance of the English Novel* (New York: Dodd, Mead, 1916); E. Hudson Long, *O. Henry: The Man and His Work* (Philadelphia: Univ. of Pennsylvania Press, 1949), 112, 85.

38. Eugene Current-Garcia, *O. Henry* (New York: Twayne, 1965), 91; Guy Davenport, introduction to *Cabbages and Kings* (New York: Penguin, 1993), xix.

39. O. Henry, *Cabbages*, 4, 56.

40. Many critics have compared Porter to Harte as masters of local color and the short story. If we do not know definitively which of Harte's books Porter read, we do know that he admired Harte's work well enough to base a play on one of his short stories, "Salomy Jane." (For further details, see Richard O'Connor, *O. Henry: The Legendary Life of William S. Porter* [Garden City, N.Y.: Doubleday, 1970]: 214.) Davis, in turn, respected Porter well enough to serve as a pallbearer at the satirist's funeral.

41. O. Henry, *Cabbages*, 12.

42. Porter, perhaps more than Davis, knew whereof he spoke when he dramatized the condition of the lost American abroad. Although Davis traveled widely throughout the Caribbean basin, Porter fled to Central America (1896–97) after being charged with embezzlement. Like many of the characters in *Cabbages*, Porter found himself among on-the-lam American bank robbers and bank presidents. If we are to believe Al Jennings, an "ex-highwayman" turned memoirist, he and Porter discussed "a suitable investment for my stolen funds" over drinks in a Honduran bar: "Porter suggested a coconut plantation, a campaign for the presidency, an indigo concession" (74). If we cannot trust Jennings's account of his adventures in Central America, he did meet Porter in the isthmus, and the bank robber's remarks capture the substance of much of *Cabbages:* American crooks possess the necessary qualities and cash to run for office in Honduras. For more on Jennings's adventures, see *Through the Shadows with O. Henry* (New York: H. K. Fly, 1921).

43. Walter LaFeber, *Inevitable Revolutions*, expanded ed. (New York: W. W. Norton, 1984), 42.

44. O. Henry, *Cabbages*, 7.

45. O. Henry, *Cabbages*, 21, 204, 213–14. We can perhaps note an ironic echo of

Rudyard Kipling's *Kim* (Rutland, Vt.: Everyman, 1994) in the agent's remarks. Whereas Kim serves the "Great Game" of direct colonial rule, the Vesuvius Company's agents serve the "little game" of American rule by proxy.

46. O. Henry, *Cabbages*, 214.

47. Pablo Neruda, *Five Decades: Poems, 1925–1970*, ed. and trans. Ben Belitt (New York: Grove, 1974), 78–79.

48. O. Henry, *Cabbages*, 120, 122, 125.

49. O. Henry, *Cabbages*, 120–21.

Chapter Five. "The Female of the Species": Teilhet and Cardenal

1. Theodore Roosevelt, "The Strenuous Life," in *The Works of Theodore Roosevelt*, National ed. (New York: Charles Scribner's Sons, 1901), 13:331, 320–21.

2. Edward S. Wallace, *Destiny and Glory* (New York: Coward-McCann, 1957), 6, 257, 251.

3. See, for example, El Centinela Democrata (pseud.), *A los libres* (1859), Nicomedes Zubaga Pocaterra, *Epitafio para un filibustero* (1989), and José Roberto Cea, *La guerra nacional* (1992), among many others.

4. As a poet of *exteriorismo*—or Cardenal's synthesis of modernism's avant-garde techniques with Pablo Neruda's and other poets' visions of a liberated Latin America—he believes that poetry can oppose repressive forces, that it can change the world. In *Poesía nueva de Nicaragua: Selección y prólogo de Ernesto Cardenal* (Buenos Aires: Lohlé, 1974), he writes: "Poetry can serve a function: to construct a country and create a new humanity, change society, make the future of Nicaragua as part of the future great country that is Latin America" (qtd. in Marc Zimmerman, "Introduction: Ernesto Cardenal after the Revolution," in *Flights of Victory/Vuelos de victoria*, by Ernesto Cardenal, ed. and trans. Zimmerman [Willimantic, Conn.: Curbstone, 1988]), x.

5. Jonathan Cohen, "Introduction: From Nicaragua with Love," in *With Walker in Nicaragua and Other Early Poems, 1949–1954*, ed. and trans. Jonathan Cohen (Middletown, Connecticut: Wesleyan Univ. Press, 1984), 11.

6. Charles H. Brown, *Agents of Manifest Destiny* (Chapel Hill: Univ. of North Carolina Press, 1980), 174.

7. The letter, signed "A. Hemmingson," is part of the C. I. Fayssoux Collection of Walker papers at Tulane University. The letter, sent to Fayssoux—one of the Immortals—expresses concern over Walker's safety after his arrest in Honduras in 1860. The woman—Hermann B. Deutsch (see the Fayssoux Collection holdings) speculates that her handwriting is that of a schoolteacher—also expresses her support for filibustering and her belief in Walker's abilities:

How unwise it was of him to venture into an undertaking with so small a force, that was perilous in the extreme! Were General Walker the commander and leader of a disciplined army of 2000 men, he might sweep Central America and from Mexico to the Panama, and beyond, even, of every Spaniard and Briton among them and never pause in his career of triumph.... In his death the Central American cause (you see I am as great a filibuster as either of you) would receive an irreparable injury.

Historians have not established the identity of "A. Hemmingson."

8. Most of Teilhet's novels—often written in collaboration with his wife, Hildegarde—are out of print, but many can be found in used bookstores. Among his many titles include works of mystery, science fiction, and adventure. See, for example, *The Crimson Hair Murders* (New York: Doubleday, 1935), *Something Wonderful to Happen* (New York: Bantam, 1948), *Russian Flag over Hawaii: The Mission of Jeffrey Toland* (New York: William Sloane, 1951), and *The Big Runaround* (New York: Coward-McCann, 1964).

9. Darwin Teilhet, *The Lion's Skin* (New York: William Sloane, 1955), 48, 52.

10. Teilhet, *Lion's*, 10, 10–11.

11. *The Lion's Skin* expresses the same fears, but before exploring the idea of American defeat, Teilhet must first contain the notion that American adventurism in Central America signals the defeat of American ideals. Sanderson, the already lost American abroad, wants to do some good in the world, and he translates his father's abolitionist beliefs into what he sees as a benevolent form of imperialism. He believes that Africans should be free; he holds ideals of liberation. At the same time, he wants to quell any doubts he has about the American presence in Nicaragua, but his conscience, once he falls in love with Tarra, begins to tweak him:

> There was something else dragging and bothering me, though. I was enlisted under Walker. I wished, as he wished, to see Nicaragua a territory of the United States. I was Mr. Manning's and Tarra's guest. Soon Tarra would be my wife. What to do? Never tell her until we were married, when it was too late for her to object, that I was a brigand and filibuster in her country for what might seem to her a dishonorable purpose? You go so far obeying orders and keeping your mouth shut and then, as I learned, you discover all at once you have a conscience; you wonder where that came from and it kicks up, and the more you are in love the more your conscience wrestles you. (134–35)

Sanderson recognizes that he may be a "brigand" from the Nicaraguan perspective, and he senses that he may be acting dishonorably in his wish for American dominance over the isthmus. He believes in freedom, but realizes at some level that filibustering may well not be about securing the isthmians' freedom. Still, after Manning (an Englishman, in fact, and not a Nicaraguan) explains that Nicaraguans want to be part of the United States, Sanderson represses any qualms he may have in favor of his imperialist desires. Once Teilhet quiets his hero's doubts, he worries more and more over American *self-defeat* in its imperialist venture. We can see this best in Sanderson's failed efforts to secure masculine dominance over Walker.

12. In fact, with a little tweaking, the description of Roosevelt's "ideal citizen" could sound like the description of the archetypal romance hero. As Janice Radway remarks in *Reading the Romance* (Chapel Hill: Univ. of North Carolina Press, 1991), in a romance, the hero must be a man's man (and a woman's man): "The hero of the romantic fantasy is always characterized by spectacular masculinity. Indeed, it is insufficient for the author to remark in passing that the romantic hero has a muscular physique. The reader must be told, instead, that every aspect of his being, whether his body, his face, or his general demeanor, is informed by the purity of his maleness" (128).

13. Teilhet, *Lion's*, 293–94.

14. Teilhet, *Lion's*, 51.

15. Teilhet, *Lion's*, 145.

16. Teilhet, *Lion's*, 62, 145.

17. Teilhet, *Lion's*, 214.

18. William Walker, *The War in Nicaragua* (1860; reprint, Detroit: Blaine Ethridge, 1971), 53.

19. Laurence Greene, *The Filibuster: The Career of William Walker* (Indianapolis: Bobbs-Merrill, 1937), 21–22.

20. Robert Houston, foreword to *The War in Nicaragua*, by William Walker (1860; reprint, Tucson: Univ. of Arizona Press, 1985), 3, 3–4.

21. Teilhet, *Lion's*, 344,

22. Stephen J. Whitfield, *The Culture of the Cold War* (Baltimore: Johns Hopkins Univ. Press, 1991), 43–44; Teilhet, *Lion's*, 298.

23. Joseph McCarthy, *Major Speeches and Debates* (Washington, D.C.: Government Printing Office, 1953), 357.

24. Teilhet, *Lion's*, 285, 302.

25. Teilhet, *Lion's*, 341.

26. As Pring-Mill explains in "The Redemption of Reality Through Documentary Poetry," in Ernesto Cardenal, *Zero Hour and Other Documentary Poems*, selected and ed. Donald D. Walsh, trans. Paul Borgeson et al. (New York: New Directions, 1980), "The label 'documentary poems' is mine not his, but Cardenal seemed pleased with it when I coined it in 1972 in order to highlight the features which distinguished 'Zero Hour'" (x). The fact-based "documentary style" fuses, Pring-Mill argues, a "clear-cut sociopolitical commitment" with such cinematic and photographic devices as "filmic editing," "montage," and "crosscutting" to cre-

ate a unique—and visually compelling—poetic form (ix). Like "Zero Hour," Cardenal's Walker poems also present historical events and personages in highly visual, highly cinematic ways; the poet offers his poems almost as documentary films.

27. Ernesto Cardenal, "Con Walker en Nicaragua," in *With Walker in Nicaragua and Other Early Poems, 1949–1954*, ed. and trans. Jonathan Cohen (Middletown, Connecticut: Wesleyan Univ. Press, 1984), 44–45, 46–47.

28. For a fuller consideration of "negation," see David Spurr, *The Rhetoric of Empire* (Durham: Duke Univ. Press, 1993), 92–108; Spurr, *Rhetoric*, 107.

29. Walker, *War*, 340. As Richard Slotkin points out in *The Fatal Environment* (New York: HarperPerennial, 1985), Henningsen's banner was not without its historical allusions: "As he left, Walker's local commander planted a sign on the ruins, that echoed Scipio's epitaph for Carthage (and Díaz del Castillo's for Tenochtitlán)—'Here stood Granada'" (250).

30. Cardenal, "Con Walker," 56–57.

31. Spurr, *Rhetoric*, 107. In this context, a more thoroughgoing materialist critique of the Nietzschean line of Western thought would certainly be in order. I do not have the space here, but it would be possible to respond to—and thereby dissect—the trope of negation.

32. Cardenal, "Con Walker," 70–71.

33. Cardenal, "Con Walker," 54–55.

34. Like Cardenal, McCarthy offers dark representations of the American imperial self and explores the origins of violence. For a view of McCarthy's treatment of imperialism, see my "'That immense and bloodslaked waste': Negation in *Blood Meridian*," *Southwestern American Literature* 25, no. 1 (fall 1999): 35–42. Needless to say, perhaps, McCarthy and Cardenal hold rather different views of the world and politics. Cardenal cares deeply about political events and human dignity; McCarthy seems more interested in pursuing a despairing existential vision than in changing the world.

35. Ernesto Cardenal, "Los Filibusteros," in *With Walker*, 72–73.

36. Cardenal, "Con Walker," 42–43, 44–45.

Chapter Six. Walker, with a Vengeance: Cox and Didion

1. In Robert Stone's *A Flag for Sunrise* (New York: Vintage, 1981), Walker has a cameo: when Holliwell, a former CIA agent in Vietnam, stops at the border of Tecan, an imaginary Central American republic based upon Nicaragua, he sees a picture of Walker's "last defeat" on a wall (149). If Walker appears explicitly only for an instant, the three main characters—Holliwell, Justin, and Pablo—are all already lost Americans abroad, and the novel can be read as a mercenary romance.

Stone follows in the tradition of Harte and Davis. In McCarthy's *Blood Meridian*, the kid joins a filibuster army and then a band of scalp-hunters. Like Stone's characters, he, too, is an already lost American abroad, and, once more, the novel can be read as a (darkly existential) mercenary romance.

2. Alex Cox and Rudy Wurlitzer, "A Conversation with Alex Cox and Rudy Wurlitzer," in *Walker*, ed. Rudy Wurlitzer (New York: Harper and Row, 1987), 23, 52.

3. J. Hoberman, "Vietnam, the Remake," in *Remaking History*, ed. Barbara Kruger and Phil Mariani (Seattle: Bay Press, 1989), 189.

4. Rudy Wurlitzer with Ed Harris and Alex Cox, introduction to *Walker*, ed. Rudy Wurlitzer (New York: Harper and Row, 1987), 11.

5. Leonard Maltin, in his capsule review of *Walker*, rates the film a "bomb": "[Marlee] Matlin's follow-up to her Oscar is actually an inglorious cameo; the sorry screenplay is by Rudy Wurlitzer. A self-indulgent mess" (1384). See *Leonard Maltin's 2001 Movie and Video Guide* (New York: New American Library, 2000).

6. Joan Didion, *A Book of Common Prayer* (New York: Washington Square Press: 1977), 6, 4, 276, 280.

7. Didion, *Book*, 10.

8. Lester D. Langley and Thomas Schoonover, *The Banana Men* (Lexington: Univ. Press of Kentucky, 1995), 27.

9. Didion, *Book*, 12, 279.

10. Didion, *Book*, 14.

11. Didion, *Book*, 22.

12. Didion, *Book*, 11, 6.

13. Joan Didion, *Salvador* (New York: Washington Square Press, 1983), 87–88.

14. Didion, *Book*, 13; Eduardo Galeano, *Memory of Fire: Century of the Wind*, trans. Cedric Belfrage (New York: Pantheon, 1988), 212.

15. John McClure, *Late Imperial Romance* (London: Verso, 1994), 4, 8.

16. Robert Stone, "We Are Not Excused," in *Paths of Resistance: The Art and Craft of the Political Novel*, ed. William Zinsser (Boston: Houghton Mifflin, 1989), 32–33.

17. Didion, *Book*, 146, 3.

18. Lynne T. Hanley, "To El Salvador," *Massachusetts Review* 24, no. 1 (spring 1983): 18.

19. The Tupamaros, an organization of students and workers, are infamously known in the United States for the kidnapping and execution of Dan Mitrione, an American advisor to the Uruguayan police. Mitrione, the Tupamaros charged, was instructing security forces in counterinsurgency and torture techniques. Richard Nixon, then in the White House, refused to negotiate or lobby for the release of political prisoners. For a cinematic treatment of this event, see Constantin Costa-

Gavras's *State of Siege* (1972). Costa-Gavras has also made *Missing* (1982), another thriller about an American abducted during a Latin American revolution.

20. Didion, *Book*, 247.
21. Didion, *Book*, 80, 120.
22. Didion, *Book*, 80, 81, 199.
23. Didion, *Book*, 149, 152–53.
24. Didion, *Book*, 56, 55–56, 57.
25. Didion, *Book*, 260, 83, 83–84.
26. Didion, *Book*, 57–58, 198.
27. Didion, *Book*, 228–29.

Conclusion: William Walker, Redux?

1. Fredric Jameson, *The Political Unconscious* (Ithaca, N.Y.: Cornell Univ. Press, 1981), 49, 19.

2. Richard Harding Davis, "William Walker, the King of the Filibusters," in *Real Soldiers of Fortune* (New York: Charles Scribner's Sons, 1906), 147.

3. Joaquin Miller, "With Walker in Nicaragua," in *Joaquin Miller's Poems* (San Francisco: Whitaker and Ray, 1909), 2:3.

4. In a long endnote to the poem, Miller casts Walker as an agent of the Monroe Doctrine and argues that the mercenary went to Nicaragua with "one colossal idea": to build a transcontinental canal. Miller employs Walker's story as a means to comment on the politics of his own era, and he complains that "we allowed France to embark in the costly venture [of building the Panama Canal] and we could not now refuse a like courtesy to any other nation, even if we would" (59). He sums up his imperialist argument with a flourish: "A great canal must and will be built across Nicaragua. And we this great republic, with its millions and billions, must build it. We have more than a right. We have a Duty!" (60). The poet suggests that the United States missed a perfect opportunity to secure American interests in the region when it allowed Walker to fall. For Miller, Walker was doubly betrayed: first by Pierce, and then by the American public who forgot about his grand efforts on their behalf; now it remains for the poet's contemporaries to go back and do the job correctly and to resurrect the freebooter's fame.

5. Jonathan Cohen, "Introduction: From Nicaragua with Love," in *With Walker in Nicaragua and other Early Poems, 1949–1954*, by Ernesto Cardenal, ed. and trans. Jonathan Cohen (Middletown, Connecticut: Wesleyan Univ. Press, 1984), 8; Edward S. Wallace, *Destiny and Glory* (New York: Coward-McCann, 1957), 142.

6. Rudy Wurlitzer, with Ed Harris and William Walker, introduction to *Walker*, ed. Rudy Wurlitzer (New York: Harper & Row, 1987), 3; Alex Cox and Rudy Wurl-

itzer, "An Interview with Alex Cox and Rudy Wurlitzer," in *Walker*, ed. Wurlitzer, 24.

7. Albert Z. Carr, *The World and William Walker* (New York: Harper and Row, 1963), 272, 272–73.

8. Other students of Walker have also seen the freebooter in Byronic terms. In *The Nation Thief* (New York: Pantheon, 1984), a novel about Walker's conquest of Nicaragua, Robert Houston opens the narrative with a prologue, dated "Trujillo, Honduras: September, 1860," in which Walker, soon to be executed, thinks back about his life and career: "I have done something few other men have been given to do: I created myself. I am William Walker. I created William Walker in Central America, and it is that single, overwhelming event which must concern me." Walker, in this act of self-creation, links himself to the poet: "He is as of last May thirty-six years old, the age at which Lord Byron died." He sees himself, Houston asserts, as a great, moody adventurer and exile.

INDEX

Accessory Transit Company, 196
Africans: enslavement of, 76, 97, 115; Roosevelt's attitudes toward, 116–17; Teilhet's attitudes toward, 225 (n. 11); Walker's attitude toward, 47
Ah Sin (Harte), 53
Allen, James Lane, 91
Allen, Merritt Parmelee, 144
American imperialism. *See* imperialism, U.S.
Anderson, Quentin, 16–17, 30
Armas, Carlos Castillo, 162

Bederman, Gail, 111–12
Beisner, Robert L., 213 (n. 2)
benevolent imperialism, 24, 59–72, 93, 152–54. *See also* imperialism, U.S.
Black, George, 71, 202 (n. 23)
Blaine, James G., 71
Blennerhasset, Harmon, 210 (n. 14)
Blood Meridian (McCarthy), 73, 171, 202 (n. 22)
Bolívar, Simón, 63, 220 (n. 56)
Bonilla, Manuel, 202 (n. 23)
Book of Common Prayer, A (Didion): imperialism in, 171, 177–82; and the imperial self, 184–90; as mercenary romance, 182–84
Bowles, Paul, 73
Brands, H. W., 105, 219 (n. 54)
Brennan, Timothy, 215 (n. 11)

Brown, Charles H., 10, 62, 86–87, 148–49, 204 (n. 3)
Burdick, Eugene, 196, 220–21 (n. 3)
Burr, Aaron, 10–11, 191, 210 (n. 14)
Bush, George W., 197–98
Butler, Judith, 19–20, 109, 157

Cabbages and Kings (Porter), 120, 134–41
Cabot, John Moors, 27
Cabot, Thomas, 27
Captain Macklin (Davis): and the imperial self, 15, 98, 142–43; as mercenary romance, 53, 118–21; reception of, 121–22, 196–97; and U.S. imperialism, 122–34
Caputo, Philip, 73
Cardenal, Ernesto, 144, 147, 148, 161–69; "Con Walker en Nicaragua," 161–66; "Los filibusteros," 168–69; *With Walker in Nicaragua and Other Early Poems, 1949–1954*, 161
Carías, Tiburcio, 140
Carr, Albert Z., 6–7, 21, 47, 104, 195–96
Carvajal, José, 12
Castellón, Francisco, 8
Caudra, Pablo Antonio, 156
Cazneau, William Leslie, 146
Central Intelligence Agency (CIA), 27
Chamorro, Fruto, 8

231

Cheney, Dick, 198
Cheyfitz, Eric, 33–34
Choir Invisible, The (Allen), 91
Christmas, Lee, 202 (n. 23)
Churchill, Winston, 2
Clayton, John M., 32
Clayton-Bulwer Treaty, 205 (n. 11)
Cohen, Jonathan, 147, 194
Cold War, 150, 157–58, 161–62, 169–70, 220 (n. 3)
Collier, Ellen C., 69, 211 (n. 33)
"Colonial Survival, A" (Roosevelt), 83
Conrad, Joseph, 183; *Heart of Darkness*, 206 (n. 22)
"Control of Corporations, The" (Roosevelt), 129–30
"Con Walker en Nicaragua" (Cardenal), 161–66
Cooper, James Fenimore, 76–77
Corral, Ponciano, 166
Cox, Alex, 13, 171, 172–77
Crabb, Henry A., 12, 191
Crittenden, William L., 12
Crocker, Timothy, 155
Crowther, Samuel, 202 (n. 23)
Crusade of the Excelsior, The (Harte), 52, 54, 62–72
Cuba, as expansionist target, 89–90, 214 (n. 3)
Cuba in War Time (Davis), 87, 89–90
Cuban and Porto Rican Campaigns, The (Davis), 87, 90
Current-Garcia, Eugene, 136
Cuyamel Fruit Company, 138

Darío, Rubén, 219–20 (n. 56)
Dark Green, Bright Red (Vidal), 73
Davenport, Guy, 136
Davis, Rebecca Harding, 2, 91–95, 130–31, 132

Davis, Richard Beale, 34
Davis, Richard Harding: and the imperial self, 15, 23, 142–43; literary life of, 61, 75, 83–87; and Roosevelt, 80–83; and U.S. imperialism, 87–103, 118–21; and Walker, 1–3, 9–10, 78, 193. Works: *Cuba in War Time*, 87, 89–90; *The Cuban and Porto Rican Campaigns*, 87, 90; *The Dictator*, 221 (n. 7); *Life in the Iron Mills*, 91–95, 130; *Margret Howth*, 130; *Real Soldiers of Fortune*, 2, 98, 124; *Three Gringos in Venezuela and Central America*, 1, 85–86, 87–88; "William Walker, the King of the Filibusters," 3, 78, 98, 126, 193, 214–15 (n. 5); *A Year from a Reporter's Notebook*, 87. See also *Captain Macklin*; *Soldiers of Fortune*
"Defense Planning Guidance" (Wolfowitz and Cheney), 198
DeLillo, Don, 183
Democrats of León, 8
Destiny and Glory (Wallace), 145–46, 194
Dewey, Commodore George, 213 (n. 2)
Dictator, The (Davis), 221 (n. 7)
Didion, Joan: and imperialism, 177–82; and the imperial self, 171, 184–90; and mercenary romance, 182–83. Works: *A Book of Common Prayer*, 171, 177–90; *Salvador*, 181–82
Dimock, Wai-chee, 18–19
Distin, E. F., 200 (n. 7)
Dog Soldiers (R. Stone), 73
domesticity, 84
Douglas, Stephen A., 28, 32
Downey, Fairfax, 124
Drinnon, Richard, 97, 212 (n. 42)
Duckett, Margaret, 61–62, 63, 68

Dulles, John Foster, 27
"Duties of American Citizenship, The" (Roosevelt), 108

economic imperialism, U.S.: Davis's treatment of, 129–31; Didion's treatment of, 179; examples of, 69–72, 101; Porter's treatment of, 120, 135, 137–41
El Hilo Azul, 147
El Salvador, U.S. imperialism in, 181
Emerson, Ralph Waldo: eloquence of, 37, 39–40; and the imperial self, 16–18, 23, 32–36, 41, 43; and U.S. expansion, 30–32; and Walker, 28–29. Works: "Fate," 205 (n. 8); *Nature*, 33–34, 39–40, 41; "Ode," 30–31; "The Young American," 28, 34–35, 43
expansion, U.S.: agents of, 27–28; Harte's treatment of, 53–54, 63–64; historical examples of, 69–72, 101, 212–13 (n. 2); and the imperial self, 21, 44–45. *See also* imperialism, U.S.
"Expansion of the White Races, The" (Roosevelt), 115

"Fate" (Emerson), 205 (n. 8)
femininity, 148
Figueres, José, 161–62
filibuster. *See* filibustering
Filibuster, The (Greene), 155–56
filibustering: Cardenal's treatment of, 168; Davis's treatment of, 2, 127; definition of, 199 (n. 1); Harte's treatment of, 61, 63, 65; and mercenary romance, 72–78; Porter's treatment of, 120–21, 135, 140; textual attitudes toward, 56; and women, 146

"filibusteros, Los" (Cardenal), 168–69
Filson, John, 76
Flag for Sunrise, A (R. Stone), 13, 73, 171
Frank Leslie's Illustrated Newspaper, 55, 56–57
freebooting. *See* filibustering
French, Parker H., 57
Freud, Sigmund, 204 (n. 38)
Frye, Northrop, 75

Galeano, Eduardo, 9, 27, 182
gender. *See* femininity; homosexuality; masculinity
Gerrard, William, 199 (n. 1)
Gibson, Charles Dana, 80, 86
Gibson girl, 86
Gifford, Barry, 73
Gordon, Charles, 194
Greene, Laurence, 155–56
Griscom, Lloyd, 85–86
Guerard, Albert J., 171
Guzmán, Jacobo Arbenz, 27

Hanley, Lynn T., 185
Harper's Weekly, 58–59
Harte, Bret: influences on, 56–59; literary life of, 52–55, 75; treatment of Walker by, 59–72, 78–79. Works: *Ah Sin*, 53; *The Crusade of the Excelsior*, 52, 54, 62–72; *The Luck of Roaring Camp and Other Sketches*, 52; "Peter Schroeder," 54, 60–61; "Salomy Jane," 223 (n. 40)
Heart of Darkness (Conrad), 206 (n. 22)
Henningsen, George F., 164
Herr, Michael, 204 (n. 37)
Hilo Azul, El, 147
Hoberman, J., 175
Hoganson, Kristin, 110–11

homosexuality, 146, 148, 154–58, 163
Horn of Africa (Caputo), 73
Hotel in the Jungle, The (Guerard), 171
House Un-American Activities Committee (HUAC), 157
Houston, Robert, 156; *The Nation Thief*, 171, 230 (n. 8)
Howells, William Dean, 132

Immortals, the, 8, 46
imperial eloquence, 29, 35–37, 39–40, 64, 99, 107, 144–45
imperialism, U.S.: Cox's treatment of, 175, 177; Davis's treatment of, 1–2, 80–103, 122–34; Didion's treatment of, 177–78, 180, 181, 185; Harte's treatment of, 59–72; historical events of, 212–14 (n. 2); and homosexuality, 158; ideology of, 44–45, 53, 76; literary explorations of, 4–5, 12–14, 72–78, 83–85, 119, 183; Porter's treatment of, 136–41; Teilhet's treatment of, 152–54, 153, 160–61; and Walker, 57, 195–96. *See also* economic imperialism, U.S.; expansion, U.S.; filibustering
imperial self: Cardenal's treatment of, 163–68; Cox's treatment of, 172–75; Davis's conception of, 99–100; Davis's treatment of, 80–103, 119, 122–34, 142–43; definition of, 16–24; description of, 29, 31, 36; Didion's treatment of, 177, 181, 184–89; discourse of, 32, 37; Emerson's theory of, 32–36; Harte's treatment of, 54, 60–62, 64–69, 71; and mercenary romance, 72–78, 160; Porter's treatment of, 136–37; Roosevelt's conception of, 114;

Roosevelt's theory of, 106–14, 144–45; Teilhet's treatment of, 146, 149, 152, 159; and Walker, 14–15, 37–42, 44–51, 58, 104, 197
Indian Wars, 76, 97, 115
"Instances of Use of United States Forces Abroad, 1798–1993" (Collier), 211 (n. 33)

James, William, 132, 214 (n. 4)
Jameson, Fredric, 192, 197
Jeffs, Charles, 124
Jehlen, Myra, 17–18, 30, 206 (n. 19)

Kaplan, Amy, 76, 84–85, 102
Keith, Minor, 70
Kennedy, John F., 21
Kim (Kipling), 223–24 (n. 45)
Kinney, Henry L., 56, 146
Kipling, Rudyard, 223–24 (n. 45)

LaFeber, Walter, 101, 137–38
Langford, Gerald, 121, 130
Langley, Lester D., 71, 179, 222 (n. 19)
Lederer, William J., 196, 220–21 (n. 3)
Lee, Alice Hathaway, 105
Legitimists of Granada, 8
Leon, Edwin de, 28, 204 (n. 3)
Life in the Iron Mills (Davis), 91–95, 130
Lion's Skin, The (Teilhet): and homosexuality, 158–59; imperialism in, 160–61; summary of, 150–52; treatment of Walker in, 9, 146, 152–55
literary forms, cultural work of, 84–85. *See also* mercenary romance
Lodge, Henry Cabot, 27
Long, E. Hudson, 135–36
López, Narciso, 12, 191, 214 (n. 3)

Lubow, Arthur, 83, 121, 130–31
Luck of Roaring Camp and Other Sketches, The (Harte), 52

MacArthur, Arthur, 131
MacIver, Henry Ronald Douglas, 124
Maltin, Leonard, 228 (n. 5)
Manifest Destiny: in Didion, 179; and the imperial self, 21; Melville's interest in, 19; Walker as representative of, 12–13
Manifest Destiny, A (Smith), 144
Marcy, William L., 3, 48
Margret Howth (Davis), 130
Martin, Helen Galt, 7, 105, 166–67
Martínez, Maximiliano Hernández, 140
masculinity: cult of, 222 (n. 25); Davis's conception of, 1–3, 85–87, 88, 95–96, 142; Didion's conception of, 177, 184, 185; Roosevelt's conception of, 82, 107–13, 144–45; Teilhet's conception of, 146–47, 148, 149–50, 154, 160; of Walker, 148–49
May, Ernest R., 213 (n. 2)
May, Robert E., 200 (n. 7)
McCarthy, Cormac, 73, 171, 202 (n. 22)
McCarthy, Joseph, 157, 158
McClure, John, 183, 211 (n. 39)
McGiffin, Philo Norton, 2
McKinley, William, 213 (n. 2)
McManus, Jane, 145–46
Melville, Herman, 18–19, 20
mercenary. *See* filibustering
mercenary romance: Cox's use of, 176–77; Davis's use of, 97, 118; description of, 53, 72–78, 120, 159–60; Didion's use of, 182–83, 189–90; gender in, 146–47; imperialism in, 56, 192. *See also specific novels*
Michalski, Picado, 162
military, and U.S. imperialism, 69–70, 131–32, 213 (n. 2)
Miller, Joaquin: "Walker in Nicaragua," 144, 193–94; "With Walker in Nicaragua," 55, 193
Monroe Doctrine, 103, 213–14 (n. 2)

nationalism, 53, 76
Nation Thief, The (Houston), 171, 230 (n. 8)
Native Americans, 76, 97, 115–16
Nature (Emerson), 33–34, 39–40, 41
Neruda, Pablo, 139–40
New Orleans Crescent, 6, 28, 172
"Nicaragua, or, Gen. Walker's Victories" (Distin), 200 (n. 7)
Nicaragüense, El, 5
Nixon, Richard, 228 (n. 19)
North, Oliver, 174–75
Norvell, Mary, 6

"Ode" (Emerson), 30–31
O. Henry. *See* Porter, William Sydney
Olsen, Tillie, 91
O'Sullivan, John L., 12, 27–28, 32, 37, 173

Pacific Mail Steamship Company, 71
performativity: by Davis, 85–87; of gender, 82, 157; for the imperial self, 19–20; by Roosevelt, 109–12
Perry, Matthew Calbraith, 69–70
"Peter Schroeder" (Harte), 54, 60–61
Pierce, Franklin, 3, 28, 57, 70, 194
Platoon (O. Stone), 73

"political unconscious," 197
Polk, James, 28
Porter, William Sydney: *Cabbages and Kings*, 120, 134–41; imperialism in, 140–41; and the imperial self, 24, 136–39; and mercenary romance, 120–21, 134–36
Port Tropique (Gifford), 73
Pring-Mill, Robert, 161, 226–27 (n. 26)
Pugh, David G., 222 (n. 25)
Pynchon, Thomas, 183

Quitman, John A., 12, 191, 214 (n. 3)
Quo Vadis (Sienkiewicz), 91

racism: in Davis, 88–90, 97–98, 125–26; in Harte, 64–65; and the imperial self, 20–21, 75–76; in Porter, 140–41; in Roosevelt, 73, 114–17; in Walker, 47
Radway, Janice, 226 (n. 12)
Reagan, Ronald, 22, 174–75
Real Soldiers of Fortune (Davis), 2, 98, 124. *See also* "William Walker, the King of the Filibusters"
Roche, James J., 6–7
romance, literary, 21–22. *See also* mercenary romance
"Roosevelt, A" (Darío), 219–20 (n. 56)
Roosevelt, Martha Bulloch, 105
Roosevelt, Theodore: and Davis, 2, 80, 83; and imperialism, 129–30; and the imperial self, 23–24, 81, 106–14, 144–45; literary tastes of, 21, 104–5; racism of, 73, 114–17; and Walker, 78–79, 81–82, 103–6, 191. Works: "A Colonial Survival," 83; "The Control of Corporations," 129–30; "The Duties of American Citizenship," 108; "The Expansion of the White Races," 115; *The Rough Riders*, 115, 216 (n. 20); "The Strenuous Life," 82, 106–7, 144–45; *Theodore Roosevelt: An Autobiography*, 105
"Roosevelt Corollary, The," to the Monroe Doctrine, 103, 218 (n. 45)
Rotundo, E. Anthony, 200 (n. 5)
Rough Riders, The (Roosevelt), 115, 216 (n. 20)
Rowe, John Carlos, 203 (n. 32)

Said, Edward, 84–85
"Salomy Jane" (Harte), 223 (n. 40)
Salvador (Didion), 181–82
Salvador (O. Stone), 73
Sanders, George, 28
San Francisco Herald, 6
Scharnhorst, Gary, 62, 69
Schirmer, Daniel B., 131
Schoonover, Thomas, 71, 179, 222 (n. 19)
Searles, Stanhope, 134
Seelye, John, 102, 103, 122, 132
sexuality. *See* homosexuality
Shakespeare, William, 33–34
Sienkiewicz, Henryk, 91
slavery, 47, 76, 97, 115
Slotkin, Richard, 45, 76–77, 200 (n. 7), 227 (n. 29)
Smith, Arthur D. Howden, 144
Smith, John, 14
Soldiers of Fortune (Davis): and the imperial self, 2, 15, 90–91, 96–103; and *Life in the Iron Mills*, 91–95; literary form of, 53, 221 (n. 7); reception of, 80, 196

Somerset, H. Somers, 85–86
Somoza, Tacho, 139–40
Spencer, Sylvanus M., 196
Spurr, David, 60, 163–64, 165
Standard Fruit Company, 138
Stone, Oliver, 73
Stone, Robert, 183; *Dog Soldiers*, 73; *A Flag for Sunrise*, 13, 73, 171; "We Are Not Excused," 184
"Strenuous Life, The" (Roosevelt), 82, 106–7, 144–45

Taft, William Howard, 104
Tarkington, Booth, 215 (n. 14)
Teilhet, Darwin: and the imperial self, 144, 170; and sexuality, 146, 148, 149–50, 156–57, 158; on Walker, 3, 9. See also *The Lion's Skin*
Tempest, The (Shakespeare), 33, 34
Theodore Roosevelt: An Autobiography (Roosevelt), 105
Three Gringos in Venezuela and Central America (Davis), 1, 85–86, 87–88
Tichi, Cecelia, 217 (n. 31)
Tropical Trading Company, 70
True Declaration of the Estate of the Colonie in Virginia, A, 34
Trujillo, Rafael, 139
Tupamaros, 186
Twain, Mark, 132

Ubico, Jorge, 140
Ugly American, The (Lederer and Burdick), 196, 220–21 (n. 3)
"United Fruit Co., The" (Neruda), 139–40
United Fruit Company, 27, 71, 138–40, 162

United States Magazine and Democratic Review, 88–89, 173
Up above the World (Bowles), 73
U.S. imperialism. *See* imperialism, U.S.
Utrecho, José Cornel, 147

Vanderbilt, Cornelius, 8, 14, 69, 196, 222 (n. 27)
Vidal, Gore, 11–12; *Dark Green, Bright Red*, 73
Vietnam War, 15–16, 175–76, 186

Walker (Cox), 13, 171, 172–77, 196–97
Walker (Wurlitzer), 194–95
Walker, James, 6
Walker, Mary Norvell, 6
Walker, William: biographical details of, 6–10, 20–22, 104; figures similar to, 10–12, 81–82, 103–6, 219 (n. 52); and the imperial self, 18, 37–42; imperial theory of, 28–29, 42–50, 125; literary resurfacings of, 4–5, 12–16, 147, 192–98; literary treatment of, by Cardenal, 163–67, 169;—, by Cox, 172–77;—, by Davis, 1–3, 98–103, 124;—, by Didion, 179, 183–84;—, by Harte, 54, 59–72, 78–79;—, by Porter, 120–21;—, by Teilhet, 152–55, 158–59; media treatment of, 56–59; sexuality of, 148–49, 155–56; *The War in Nicaragua*, 14, 42–50, 98, 125, 155, 164
"Walker in Nicaragua" (Miller), 144, 193–94
Wallace, Edward S., 145–46, 194
War in Nicaragua, The (Walker), 14, 42–50, 98, 125, 155, 164

Warren, T. Robinson, 8–9
"We Are Not Excused" (R. Stone), 184
Weinberg, Albert K., 44, 207 (n. 28)
Whitfield, Stephen J., 157–58
Whitman, Walt, 28, 44
Wilkinson, James, 10, 210 (n. 14)
Williams, William Appleman, 72
William Walker, Filibuster (Allen), 144
"William Walker, Filibuster" (Young), 144
"William Walker, the King of the Filibusters" (Davis), 3, 78, 98, 126, 193, 214–15 (n. 5)
Wilson, Christopher P., 85
Wirkus, Faustin, 202 (n. 23)
"With Walker in Nicaragua" (Miller), 55, 193

With Walker in Nicaragua and Other Early Poems, 1949–1954 (Cardenal), 161
Wolfowitz, Paul, 198
women, 2, 145, 146, 177, 189–90
Wurlitzer, Rudy, 173; *Walker*, 194–95

Year from a Reporter's Notebook, A (Davis), 87
Young, Edgar, 144
young American. *See* imperial self
"Young American, The" (Emerson), 28, 34–35, 43
Young American movement, 28, 29, 31–32, 36–37

Zemurray, Sam, 162, 191, 202 (n. 23)